# ACCENTS ON SHAKESPEARE

## General Editor: TERENCE HAWKES

P

*Presentist Shakespeares* is the first extended study
tice of 'presentism', a critical movement that takes account of the
never-ending dialogue between past and present, seeking out salient
aspects of the present as a trigger for its investigations and arguing that an
intrusive, shaping awareness of ourselves deserves not condemnation but
our closest attention.

In this bold and consistently thought-provoking collection of presentist
readings, the contributors:

- argue that the ironies generated by our involvement in time are a
  fruitful, necessary and unavoidable aspect of any text's being, and that
  presentism allows us to engage with them more fully and productively
- demonstrate how these ironies can function as agents of change,
  flowing unstoppably back into the events of the past, colouring how
  we perceive them and modifying our sense of what they signify
- show that a critic's inability to step beyond time and specifically the
  present does not, as has been argued elsewhere, 'contaminate' readings of Shakespeare's plays, but rather points to shades of implication
  suddenly available here and now within the wide range of plays
  examined
- suggest that presentism might not merely challenge or expand our
  sense of what Shakespeare's plays are able to tell us, but may in fact
  offer the only effective purchase on these texts that is available to us.

Contributors include Terence Hawkes, Catherine Belsey, Michael
Bristol, Linda Charnes, John Drakakis, Ewan Fernie, Evelyn Gajowski,
Hugh Grady and Kiernan Ryan.

**Hugh Grady** is Professor of English at Arcadia University, Pennsylvania.

**Terence Hawkes** is Emeritus Professor at Cardiff University.

# ACCENTS ON SHAKESPEARE
## General Editor: TERENCE HAWKES

It is more than twenty years since the New Accents series helped to establish 'theory' as a fundamental and continuing feature of the study of literature at the undergraduate level. Since then, the need for short, powerful 'cutting edge' accounts of and comments on new developments has increased sharply. In the case of Shakespeare, books with this sort of focus have not been readily available. **Accents on Shakespeare** aims to supply them.

**Accents on Shakespeare** volumes will either 'apply' theory, or broaden and adapt it in order to connect with concrete teaching concerns. In the process, they will also reflect and engage with the major developments in Shakespeare studies of the last ten years.

The series will lead as well as follow. In pursuit of this goal it will be a two-tiered series. In addition to affordable, 'adoptable' titles aimed at modular undergraduate courses, it will include a number of research-based books. Spirited and committed, these second-tier volumes advocate radical change rather than stolidly reinforcing the status quo.

## IN THE SAME SERIES

# Presentist Shakespeares

Edited by

**HUGH GRADY**

and

**TERENCE HAWKES**

Routledge
Taylor & Francis Group

LONDON AND NEW YORK

First published 2007
by Routledge
2 Park Square, Milton Park,
Abingdon, Oxon OX14 4RN

Simultaneously published in
the USA and Canada
by Routledge
270 Madison Ave,
New York, NY 10016

Routledge is an imprint of the
Taylor & Francis Group,
an informa business

© 2007 Hugh Grady and Terence Hawkes
for selection and editorial matter; the
contributors, their contributions

Typeset in Baskerville MT by
Taylor & Francis Books
Printed and bound in Great Britain
by Antony Rowe Ltd,
Chippenham, Wiltshire

British Library Cataloguing in
Publication Data
A catalogue record for this book is available
from the British Library

Library of Congress Cataloging in
Publication Data
A catalog record for this book has been
requested

ISBN10: 0–415–38528–8 (hbk)
ISBN10: 0–415–38529–6 (pbk)
ISBN10: 0–203–96587–6 (ebk)

ISBN13: 978–0–415–38528–2 (hbk)
ISBN13: 978–0–415–38529–9 (pbk)
ISBN13: 978–0–203–96587–0 (ebk)

To Sue
To Ann

# Contents

# Contributors

**Catherine Belsey** is Research Professor of English at the University of Wales, Swansea. Her books include *Critical Practice* (1980, 2002), *The Subject of Tragedy* (1985), *Shakespeare and the Loss of Eden* (1999) and *Culture and the Real* (2005). *Why Shakespeare?* will be published in 2007.

**Michael Bristol** is Greenshields Professor of English at McGill University, Montreal. His books include *Carnival and Theatre: Plebeian Culture and the Structure of Authority in Renaissance England* (1985), *Shakespeare's America, America's Shakespeare* (1990) and *Big Time Shakespeare* (1996). He is currently researching Shakespeare and contemporary popular culture; questions of moral agency in Renaissance drama.

**Linda Charnes** is Associate Professor of English and West European Studies at Indiana University, Bloomington. She is the author of *Notorious Identity: Materializing the Subject in Shakespeare* (Harvard, 1993), and *Hamlet's Heirs: Shakespeare and the Politics of a New Millennium* (Routledge, 2006).

**John Drakakis** is Professor of English Studies at the University of Stirling, Scotland. He is the editor of *Alternative Shakespeare* (1985, 2002) of *Shakespearean Tragedy* (1992) and of the Palgrave New Casebook of *Antony and Cleopatra*. He has written many articles on Shakespeare, Renaissance drama and critical theory, and is currently completing the new Arden edition of *The Merchant of Venice*.

**Ewan Fernie** is Senior Lecturer in Shakespeare and Renaissance Literature at Royal Holloway, University of London. He is the author of *Shame in Shakespeare* (Routledge, 2002), editor of *Spiritual Shakespeares* (Routledge, 2005) and co-ordinating editor of *Reconceiving the Renaissance* (Oxford University Press, 2005). He edits the 'Shakespeare Now!' series of 'minigraphs' (Continuum) with Simon Palfrey, with whom he is also writing a book which begins the day after *Macbeth*.

**Evelyn Gajowski** is an Associate Professor of English at the University of Nevada, Las Vegas. She has published two books, *Re-Visions of Shakespeare: Essays in Honor of Robert Ornstein* (2004) and *The Art of Loving: Female Subjectivity and Male Discursive Traditions in Shakespeare's Tragedies* (1992), as well as several articles on Shakespeare. Her current book-length projects include a collection of essays on Shakespeare, presentism, and gender and an edition of Mary Wroth's pastoral tragicomedy, *Love's Victory*.

**Hugh Grady** is Professor of English at Arcadia University in Glenside, Pennsylvania and a specialist in Shakespeare and contemporary critical theory. He is the author of *The Modernist Shakespeare: Critical Texts in a Material World* (1991), *Shakespeare's Universal Wolf: Studies in Early Modern Reification* (1996), and *Shakespeare, Machiavelli and Montaigne: Power and Subjectivity from* Richard II *to* Hamlet (2002). He has edited *Shakespeare and Modernity* (Routledge 2000) for the *Accents on Shakespeare* series, and is currently working on a monograph investigating the connections of Shakespeare's plays with aesthetic theory.

**Terence Hawkes** is Emeritus Professor of English at Cardiff University. He is the author of *Metaphor* (Methuen, 1972), *Structuralism and Semiotics* (Routledge, 1977, 2003), *Shakespeare and the Reason* (Routledge 1964, 2005), *Shakespeare's Talking Animals* (Arnold, 1973), *That Shakespeherian Rag* (Methuen, 1986, Routledge, 2005), *Meaning By Shakespeare* (Routledge, 1992), *Shakespeare's King Lear* (Northcote House/British Council, 1995) and *Shakespeare In The Present* (Routledge, 2002).

**Kiernan Ryan** is Professor of English at Royal Holloway, University of London and a Fellow of New Hall, University of Cambridge. His most recent books include *Shakespeare* (3rd edition, 2002), *King Lear: Contemporary Critical Essays* (1993), *New Historicism and Cultural Materialism: A Reader* (1996), *Shakespeare: The Last Plays* (1999) and *Shakespeare: Texts and Contexts* (2000). He wrote the Introduction for the new Penguin edition of *King Lear* (2005), and is currently completing a study of Shakespearean comedy.

# General editor's preface

In our time, the field of literary studies has rarely been a settled, tranquil place. Indeed, for over two decades, the clash of opposed theories, prejudices and points of view has made it more of a battlefield. Echoing across its most beleaguered terrain, the student's weary complaint 'Why can't I just pick up Shakespeare's plays and read them?' seems to demand a sympathetic response.

Nevertheless, we know that modern spectacles will always impose their own particular characteristics on the vision of those who unthinkingly don them. This must mean, at the very least, that an apparently simple confrontation with, or pious contemplation of, the text of a four-hundred-year-old play can scarcely supply the grounding for an adequate response to its complex demands. For this reason, a transfer of emphasis from 'text' towards 'context' has increasingly been the concern of critics and scholars since the Second World War: a tendency that has perhaps reached its climax in more recent movements such as 'New Historicism', 'Cultural Materialism' or 'Presentism'.

A consideration of the conditions – social, political, or economic – within which the play came to exist, from which its derives, and to which it speaks will certainly make legitimate demands on the attention of any well-prepared student nowadays. Of course, the serious pursuit of those interests will also inevitably start to undermine ancient and inherited prejudices, such as the supposed distinction between 'foreground' and 'background' in literary studies. And even the slightest awareness of the pressures of gender or of race, or the most cursory glance at the role played by that strange creature 'Shakespeare' in our cultural politics, will reinforce a similar turn towards questions that sometimes appear scandalously 'non-literary'. It seems clear that very different and unsettling notions of the ways in which literature might be addressed can hardly be avoided. The worrying truth is that nobody can just pick up Shakespeare's plays and read them. Perhaps – even more worrying – they never could.

The aim of *Accents on Shakespeare* is to encourage students and teachers to explore the implications of this situation by means of an engagement with the major developments in Shakespeare studies over recent years. It will offer a continuing and challenging reflection on those ideas through a series of multi- and single-author books which will also supply the basis for adapting or augmenting them in the light of changing concerns.

*Accents on Shakespeare* also intends to lead as well as follow. In pursuit of this goal, the series will operate on more than one level. In addition to titles aimed at modular undergraduate courses, it will include a number of books embodying polemical, strongly argued cases aimed at expanding the horizons of a specific aspect of the subject and at challenging the preconceptions on which it is based. These volumes will not be learned 'monographs' in any traditional sense. They will, it is hoped, offer a platform for the work of the liveliest younger scholars and teachers at their most outspoken and provocative. Committed and contentious, they will be reporting from the forefront of current critical activity and will have something new to say. The fact that each book in the series promises a Shakespeare inflected in terms of a specific urgency should ensure that, in the present as in the recent past, the accent will be on change.

Terence Hawkes

# Introduction
## Presenting presentism

## Hugh Grady and Terence Hawkes

### Past and present

What is 'presentism'? It's easier to begin with what it's not.

At the moment, a number of siren songs drift invitingly across the field of Shakespeare Studies. The commanding cadences of New Historicism, now institutionalised in teaching, in new editions of Shakespeare's plays and in a plethora of study guides, still ring strongly out. But alternative strains are also discernible. In the last few years the opening chords of a new formalism, a new aestheticism, a new economic criticism, and most prominently, what has been called a 'new new historicism' or a 'new materialism' have been sounded.[1]

Rooted in new historicism and cultural materialism, this latter project proposes a radical focus on material objects, their production, their use in daily life, and the array of cultural meanings and practices in which they are involved. But despite its commitment to the material world, crucial theoretical matters concerning criticism and culture remain largely undiscussed.

Of course, if the alternative is to deal with the plays in blissful ignorance of their historical context, to impose on them, as many teachers seem unthinkingly to do, some kind of absurd contemporaneity with ourselves, usually justified by windy rhetoric about the Bard's 'universality', then perhaps historical specificity of some sort is desirable. The new materialism's apparently simple focus on objects, for example, seems a case in point. Yet inevitably it tends to remain fixed and strangely fixated on objects as such in a practice that threatens to replicate rather than critique what Marx called the fetishism of commodities. Maybe a resolute insistence on the concrete, on objects and their material production and use in daily life, carries with it its own anti-traditional, anti-idealistic values. But if this materialism is 'new', it is so precisely because of its indifference to any engagement with the politics and way of life of our own day on which an older materialism insisted.

The greatest problem remains the more general one. It occurs when – horror of horrors – contact with the actualities and particular contingencies of the past is felt to have been contaminated by the critic's own 'situatedness' in the present. In a nightmare situation we confront the Bard's most sinister enemy. Its name – one to harrow us with fear and wonder – is 'presentism'.[2]

## Just the facts

The principal talisman charged with warding off this spectre is often referred to as 'the facts'. The facts will save us. The facts about specific historical conditions that have determined the reading and writing of literature, the facts about the market place, the facts about the material circumstances in which plays were performed, books and playscripts actually produced, distributed, sold and received. Retrieved and analysed, these facts will lay bare, it's claimed, not so much the author's unique meaning, concealed within the text, but the true nature of the context from which – and to which – the work speaks and by which it is effectively shaped. They will show that the text itself speaks of 'the corporate activities that have brought it into being'.[3]

All well and good. If the aim of historical scholarship were simply to establish 'how it really was' – in the words of Leopold von Ranke, *wie es eigentlich gewesen* – then the present might reasonably be thought of as an intervening, distracting fog that an effective literary criticism ought rigorously to blow away. The facts cannot help but save us. However, as this volume will argue, the present's relation to the past is a much subtler matter than that.

All restorations of the past that are undertaken in the name of 'historicism' face at least one major problem. Reaching resolutely backwards, they can't afford to examine the position in the present from which that manoeuvre is undertaken. As a result, they discount the nature of the choosing and the omission, the selections and suppressions which determine it. Genuinely to capture, or repeat the past, is fundamentally impossible for a variety of reasons. So although restoration may aim to be the thief of time, it usually turns out to be a notoriously unsuccessful one.

The truth is that none of us can step beyond time. The present can't be drained out of our experience. As a result, the critic's own 'situatedness' does not – cannot – *contaminate* the past. In effect, it constitutes the only means by which it's possible to see and perhaps comprehend it. And since we can only see the past through the eyes of the present, few serious historians would deny that the one has a major influence on their account of the other. Of course we should read Shakespeare historically. But given that what we term history develops out of a never-ending dialogue between past and present, how can we decide whose historical circumstances will have priority in the process, Shakespeare's, or our own?

Facts, after all, do not speak for themselves. Nor do texts. This doesn't mean that facts or texts don't exist. It does mean that all of them are capable of genuinely contradictory meanings, none of which has any independent, 'given', undeniable, or self-evident status. Indeed, they don't speak at all unless and until they are inserted into and perceived as part of specific discourses which impose on them their own shaping requirements and agendas. We choose the facts. We choose the texts. We do the inserting. We do the perceiving. We order the priorities which govern everything. Facts and texts, that is to say, don't simply speak, don't merely mean. *We* speak, *we* mean, *by* them.

And we do so in the present. All history, as Benedetto Croce puts it, is contemporary history and we need urgently to recognise the permanence of the present's role in all our dealings with the past. We cannot make contact with a past unshaped by our own concerns. We must accept, in short, that there can be 'no historicism without a latent presentism' to use a slogan coined by Hugh Grady (2005: 115). On the other hand, taking one's present situation fully into account seems bound to complicate and foreground that dialectical relationship. If the present is such a universal and inescapable factor, it necessarily dissolves the possibility of any engagement with a past not altogether, always, and already shaped and determined by it. By the same token, all our experience of the 'present' is shaped and determined by the past and so to some degree only realisable in and on its terms. The truth is that we can't ever step off that roundabout.

## New kid

But whatever the dilemmas it brings, the same roundabout nevertheless requires that the present be ranked, not as an obstacle to be avoided, or a prison to be escaped from. Quite the reverse: it's a factor actively to be sought out, grasped and perhaps, as a result, understood. If an intrusive, shaping awareness of ourselves, alive and active in our own world, defines us, then it deserves our closest attention. Paying the present that degree of respect might more profitably be judged to be, not a 'mistake', egregious and insouciant, blandly imposing a tritely modern perspective on whatever texts confront it, but rather the basis of a critical stance whose engagement with the text is of a particular character. A Shakespeare criticism which takes that on board will aim scrupulously to seek out salient aspects of the present as a crucial trigger for its investigations. Reversing, to some degree, the stratagems of new historicism, it will deliberately begin with the material present and allow that to set its interrogative agenda. It will not only yearn to speak with the dead. It will aim, in the end, to talk to the living.

Such a criticism's engagement with the text will take place precisely in terms of those dimensions of the present that most ringingly chime – perhaps as ends to its beginnings – with the events of the past. Deliberately employing crucial aspects of the present as a trigger for its investigations, its centre of gravity will accordingly be 'now', rather than 'then'. Perhaps this simply makes overt what covertly happens anyway. In principle, it involves the radical act of putting one's cards on the table. In practice, it calls for a heightened degree of critical self-awareness and for a committed engagement with the developments in critical and cultural theory that have taken place since the 1980s.

Criticism has in recent years largely ignored the aesthetic quality of Shakespearean and other poems, plays, and essays of the early modern period, treating them instead as documents not fundamentally dissimilar from religious tracts, acts of parliament, royal or Privy Council decrees, and the like. While this perspective has suggested new modes of access to the plays, it has also proven to be singularly reductive. In particular it has obscured how the works function for us in the present. For even though the immediate social context of the plays has disappeared, they evidently continue to speak to us with urgency and insight. One of a number of directions a presentist criticism will take will be to focus on this phenomenon and thus attempt to come to terms with a play's paradoxical presentness. The old aesthetics of Kant and the New Critics are unable to offer much help in this, but the arguments of figures like Jacques Derrida (especially his late work) and Emmanuel Levinas, as well as the writings of older theorists such as Martin Heidegger, Theodor Adorno, and Walter Benjamin, suggest new approaches. All of them have important things to say about how the art-work continues to produce meanings in historical eras different from that in which it was created and to which it was initially directed.

Of course, several modes of critical practice already in existence, such as feminist criticism, post-colonialist criticism, and performance studies, can be said to be presentist in principle if not in name. In the end, each of them makes possible a fuller engagement with the ironies generated by our inescapable involvement in time. These are frequently not *merely* ironic, if that implies a sterile, haphazard coincidence. Instead, they function for us as agents of radical change, flowing unstoppably back into the events of the past, colouring how we perceive them, modifying our sense of what they signify. In respect of Shakespeare, they also point, as irony must, to layers and shades of implication suddenly available here and now within the *plays*, subtly challenging, changing and adding to our sense of what they are able to tell us.

For we can never, finally, evade the present. And if it's always and only the present that makes the past speak, it speaks always and only to – and about – ourselves. It follows that the first duty of a credible presentist criticism must be to acknowledge that the questions we ask of any literary text will inevitably be shaped by our own concerns, even when these include what we call 'the past'. The irony which that situation generates constitutes a fruitful, necessary and inescapable aspect of any text's being. Perhaps it's the basis of the only effective purchase on Shakespeare that we're able to make.

The call for a more 'presentist' critical practice implicit in this anthology should thus be understood as a call for an understanding of and engagement with a particularly interesting and demanding juncture in modern and Shakespeare studies. It has already been called the 'new kid on the Shakespeare block' in the *Times Literary Supplement* (Moore 15 August 2003). We believe that presentist criticism is very much an open-ended and on-going project. Its boundaries remain to be defined. It is our hope that the new essays of this collection will reflect, make use of, develop and even rejoice in this indeterminacy.

## Notes

1 See Bruster 2003: 191–205, and Harris 2000, for two critical accounts of the 'new materialism.'
2 See Kastan 1999: 17. For a more detailed account and critique of presentism see Robin Headlam Wells 2000.
3 See Kastan op. cit., p. 38.

# 1

# Band of Brothers

Terence Hawkes

## Water

His name was George W. Childs.[1] He was an American: from Philadelphia, Pennsylvania. He was rich: a self-made millionaire, a newspaper proprietor and (if that's not an oxymoron) a philanthropist. And on 17 October 1887, in the Jubilee year of the reign of Queen Victoria, he was responsible for a curious ceremony which took place in England, in Stratford-upon-Avon. It marked the formal opening of a facility which Mr Childs had recently donated to the town: a large, ornate drinking fountain. He had allowed himself to be persuaded that the provision of pure water for the people of Stratford, their horses, their sheep and their cattle would serve, not only as a 'useful gift to both man and beast', but also as a fitting monument to the genius of their fellow-citizen, William Shakespeare (Davis 1890: 5).

The fountain's still there, at the junction of Wood St. and the Rother Market Place. An impressive piece of Victorian Gothic, nearly 18 feet high, its slight oddity is reinforced by the two quotations from the Bard's works which it prominently displays. First, from *Timon of Athens*, Apemantus's tribute to 'Honest water, which ne'er left man i' the mire.' Second, from *Henry VIII*, Archbishop Cranmer's pious forecast of the blissful way of life awaiting Shakespeare's countrymen in the coming reign of Queen Elizabeth:

> In her days every man shall eat in safety
> Under his own vine what he plants, and sing

The merry songs of peace to all his neighbours.
God shall be truly known, and those about her
From her shall read the perfect ways of honour,
And by those claim their greatness, not by blood.

(5. 4. 33–38)

In context, of course, the lines from *Timon* function less as a tribute to
water's healthful properties than as part of Apemantus's scornful
dismissal of Timon's lavish banquet for his friends. Worse, to some
embarrassment, modern scholarship has overtaken them. They were
almost certainly written, not by Shakespeare, but by Middleton.[2] And
the lines from *Henry VIII* make no mention of water at all.

## Blood

In fact, they refer to another liquid altogether. But there's no real
mystery here. It must have quickly become clear that the fountain's
cascades were always destined to engage with issues richer and more
complex than water. Presented to the people of Stratford by a transatlantic benefactor, there's an obvious sense in which they also involved
blood.

The speeches marking the opening ceremony make no bones about
that. Time and again they stress a central, arresting notion: that the
two cultures of the United States and the United Kingdom exemplify
a genuine blood brotherhood: that in their collective veins flow the
same corpuscles, and that these guarantee and reinforce a unity of
race, way of life and general outlook that amounts to a common inher-
itance.[3] In a letter read out at the ceremony, the American writer James
Russell Lowell spoke of the fountain as a symbol of 'the kindred blood
of two great nations, joint heirs of the same noble language', and as
a different chronicler announced, the gift added 'another link –
however slight – to that chain of brotherhood between Englishmen
and Americans' (Davis 1890: iv and 36). Mr Childs was, after all, a
prominent citizen of the city of brotherly love, and such a clear proposal
of a blood bond – in a context featuring water – contained the obvious
implication that the former substance was thicker than the latter.

Fittingly, the opening ceremony was performed by the famous
Shakespearean actor Sir Henry Irving. Ringing with impassioned
declarations of 'kinship' and 'common heritage', his speech stressed
that the fountain symbolised the fundamental racial unity of the
United States and the United Kingdom, and that he rejoiced '. . . in
the happy inspiration which prompted a gift that so worthily represents

the common homage of two great peoples to the most famous man of their common race'. The fact of genetic identity, of 'common race', meant, he added, that, in Stratford above all other places, American citizens 'cease to be aliens' (Davis 1890: 44–48 passim).

Sir Henry then duly turned the water on, sampled it and pronounced it 'clear, palatable and good', at which the Snitterfield Brass Band struck up with 'God Save The Queen' followed by 'Hail Columbia'. The US Ambassador next proposed a toast which, in the process of referring to 'kinsmen who have so much in common', stressed how appropriate it was that both the 'straightforward Saxon race' and Stratford itself, should be recipients of a gift from an American (Davis 1890: 54–57). He was followed by the proprietor of *The Times* who spoke of Stratford's appeal to the hearts of 'most educated Americans' and confirmed its capacity to 'make them feel that they were of one kindred and one race with ourselves' (Davis 1890: 63).[4] The national and international press concurred. The next day, an editorial in the *London Standard* referred directly to England as the United States' 'parent country', and the editorial page of the *Daily Telegraph* carried an article stating that 'We might, indeed, almost call Stratford-upon-Avon the joint capital of the British England and of the American England'. It was left to *The New York Herald* to signal the final triumph of hope over expectation, with its prediction that, from now on, 'The names of William Shakespeare and George William Childs will be indissolubly united' (Davis 1890: 82, 101–2, 125).

In short, the essence of the fountain lies in its proclamation and reinforcement of the notion that the United States and Great Britain are historically, genetically, culturally and racially forever bonded. In a sublime paradox, its waters declare that we are blood brothers. And as if to underline the sanguinary dimension of the ceremony, prominent amongst the luminaries present was Sir Henry Irving's long-serving secretary: Bram Stoker.[5]

## Money

There's little doubt that the author of *Dracula* (1897) would have concurred with most of the sentiments expressed on that day. As Irving's general factotum, Bram Stoker may even have had a hand in writing his master's speech (Murray 2004: 93, 148). Just two years before, in 1885, he had offered a large audience at the London Institute what he termed 'A Glimpse of America' which projected a future alliance between that country and Britain 'based on ties of culture and blood'. The old country would be rejuvenated, he claimed, by new compatible transfusions from the United States. For America was 'a nation, not merely like ourselves, but ourselves – the same in blood, religion, and social ideas, with an almost identical common law' (Stoker 1886: 11) and as a result 'We are bound to each other by the instinct of a common race, which makes brotherhood and the love of brothers a natural law' (Stoker 1886: 30).[6]

It's well known that *Dracula* readily lends itself to a number of schematic interpretations.[7] The Count himself is a crudely-drawn symbol, easily potent enough to fuel an allegory of its author's relationship with the ever-demanding Irving. Certainly, Stoker seems to have been almost in thrall to, if not dependent on the actor, to have sacrificed his civil service career to him, to have gained energy and vitality from the connection, and to have seriously declined when Irving died.[8] Nonetheless, Stoker's broad interest in Shakespeare was also clear. Allusions to the plays occur throughout his early work, and *Dracula* itself makes mention of *Hamlet*, *The Merchant of Venice*, *Twelfth Night* and *King Lear*. It also seems likely that the novel is set in 1887, the year in which the Stratford fountain was opened (Murray 2004: 179–80).[9]

*Dracula* also generates an extraordinary range of metaphors of almost Shakespearean scope which seem pointedly to equate blood with money (Ellman 1996: xx–xxi).[10] The Count's castle contains heaps of buried gold, and these become readily interchangeable with the blood for which the vampire lusts. Lunged at with a knife, the Count doesn't bleed. Instead, his coat tears open 'making a wide gap whence a bundle of banknotes and a stream of gold fell out'.

## Marx

None of this would have surprised money's most formidable analyst and, together with Bram Stoker, perhaps the nineteenth century's twin genius as a spinner of tales of Gothic horror, Karl Marx (1818–83). Dracula, who can assume virtually any shape he pleases, wolf, bat, cloud of dust, shares exactly the capacity for transgressive shape-shifting and reincarnation in the form of any commodity that Marx noticed in money: 'Just as every qualitative difference between commodities is extinguished in money, so money, on its side, like the radical leveller that it is, does away with all distinctions' (Marx 1967: 132–33). It 'exchanges . . . any quality for any other, even for its opposite'. Indeed his indictment of capitalism persistently makes the replacement of ties of blood by those of money a central theme. Capital, Marx writes, 'is dead labour which, vampire-like, lives only by sucking living labour, and lives the more, the more labour it sucks'.[11]

Of all Shakespeare's plays, Marx's favourite was *Timon of Athens*. The play's stark focus on money had an obvious appeal. Ludicrously generous to his friends, Timon is wholly rejected by them once his own finances collapse. In turn, he exiles himself from Athens and subjects its citizens and their way of life to some scorching invective. Marx was always impressed with Timon's famous diatribes on the nature and enormous power of money. In his 1844 *Political Economy and Philosophy* (Marx 1964) he cites key passages from the play, such as Timon's denunciation of 'Yellow, glittering, precious gold':

> . . . Thus much of this will make
> Black, white; foul, fair; wrong, right;
> Base, noble; old, young; coward, valiant.
> . . . This yellow slave
> Will knit and break religions, bless th'accursed,
> Make the hoar leprosy adored, place thieves,
> And give them title, knee, and approbation . . .
>
> (4.3.26–45)

His analysis is incisive:

> Shakespeare excellently depicts the real nature of money . . .
> (1) It is the visible divinity – the transformation of all human
> and natural properties into their contraries, the universal
> confounding and overturning of things; it makes brothers of
> impossibilities. (2) It is the common whore, the common
> pimp of people and nations . . .
>
> (Marx 1964: 167–68)[12]

Marx's telling comment 'is not money the bond of all bonds?' reaches to capitalism's heart as well as to the centre of *Timon*.[13]

Nevertheless, he would no doubt have been amongst the first to observe that the two plays cited on the Stratford fountain make uneasy companions. If *Henry VIII* famously looks forward to the golden era of Elizabethan settlement, *Timon of Athens* offers a spectacular and seriously different point of view. The play's initial account of Athens may suggest a closely integrated society based on mutual obligation, generosity and support. But it sets up this vision only drastically to undermine it through its depiction of the brutal power of money. In Athens, there's no singing of the merry songs of peace to all one's neighbours, there's no eating in safety whatever one plants under one's own vine. Quite the reverse: in fact, eating gradually takes on a new, disturbing aspect in the play, one which both reinforces and significantly darkens the blood-money relationship. It's the cynic Apemantus who, at the same banquet in Act One where he praises 'honest water', also hints that the figure of Judas, the very symbol of blood-money, stalks such feasts;

> The fellow that sits next to him, now parts bread with him, pledges the breath of him in a divided draught, is the read-iest man to kill him. 'T has been proved . . .
>
> (1. 2. 45–48)[14]

– and he goes on to develop this image in horrific terms,

> O you gods! What a number of men eats Timon, and he sees 'em not! It grieves me to see so many dip their meat in one man's blood.
>
> (1. 2. 38–40)

The nightmare spectacle of human beings eating each other becomes closely woven into the play's texture. Timon's light-hearted comment to Alcibiades that he'd rather be 'at a breakfast of enemies than a dinner of friends' provokes the almost off-hand response 'So they were bleeding new, my lord. There's no meat like 'em.' Pared to its essential features, the play's focus on blood and money highlights a savage, reductive relationship between the two, hinted at by Marx, explicit in Stoker's *Dracula*. In it, the heart's blood, the essence of humanity, tragi-cally dwindles to become a mere commodity, negotiable or edible. 'Five thousand drops' of it, we're told, will match Timon's debt of five thou-sand crowns. And when a thief observes 'We cannot live on grass, on berries, water', Timon advises 'You must eat men' (14, 422–25).[15]

## Brothers

Less than sixty years after the opening of the George W. Childs foun-tain in Stratford, a rather larger issue came to require the attention of the commingled corpuscles of Britain and the United States: it was called World War II. By then, it was clear that the idea of 'blood brotherhood' had lost something of its potency. Indeed, for the British, resuscitation of the concept had become a matter of considerable urgency and efforts to promote it were by no means limited to regular diplomacy.[16] To give just one example: in 1920 a small press bureau, funded by the British government, had been established in New York as an 'experimental branch of the Foreign Office News department'.

Dedicated to the relatively mundane business of enhancing the image of the British Empire in the United States by means of lectures and exhibitions, it was called the British Library of Information.[17] However, the advent of the war against Germany, and the growing isolationism of large sections of American public opinion, forced a huge escalation of the Library's role. Its major aim became the persuasion of Americans at large that the British armed struggle was worthy of support.

Perhaps surprisingly, this proved to be a considerable task. By 1940, ideas of 'kindred blood' had certainly atrophied and notions of 'common race' seemed barely tenable. In fact, a distinct anti-British chill could be detected in some quarters of President Roosevelt's administration.[18] One senior State Department official even became anxious to have both the British and the German Libraries of Information closed down, describing them as 'foreign propaganda offices' whose activities might encourage the United States to become embroiled in a European war. US Secretary of State Cordell Hull was finally persuaded to draft a bill 'to make unlawful the distribution or publication of matter of a political nature by agents of foreign governments in this country'.[19]

No doubt that word 'foreign' came as something of a shock. Of course, later events at Pearl Harbor, in December 1941, changed everything.[20] Yet, as the war dragged on, the question of 'blood brotherhood' continued to prove a complex business. The British found themselves more and more dependent on the Americans, particularly when it came to the mounting of an effective invasion of northern France in 1944, and it began to dawn on them that the game might finally be up. When an American general, Eisenhower, was made Supreme Commander of Allied forces and given charge of the D-Day operation, it signalled a descisive shift in the balance of power. A massive and soul-gelding realignment of the transatlantic brotherhood became unavoidable.[21] In the face of it, Prime Minister Harold Macmillan's later attempt at a new formulation of the relationship, 'These Americans represent the new Roman Empire and we Britons, like the Greeks of old, must teach them how to make it go' sounded like whistling in the dark. And as *Timon of Athens* suggests, the 'Greeks of old' were not necessarily a good example.[22]

## Modern Dress

One of the many figures involved with the British propaganda effort in the United States was a Scottish academic called Allardyce Nicoll (1894–1976). Educated at Glasgow University, he had been appointed lecturer in English at King's College, University of London in 1920.[23] In September 1924, aged thirty, Nicoll moved to the chair of English at

East London College (later Queen Mary and Westfield), in the University of London, where he remained until 1933. In that year he crossed the Atlantic, to become professor of the history of drama and chair of the drama department at Yale University.[24]

One or two curious sightings of Nicoll survive from those years. The playwright Max Wilk, speaking of the delights of the cinema in New Haven in 1940, says:

> One could go to a different double feature practically every night. We weren't playing hooky; we were studying. What more proof of that than to encounter, in the line waiting to get into the Poli to see the new Alfred Hitchcock, that erudite Britisher, the dean of the Drama School himself, Allardyce Nicoll? If he were such a film fan, didn't that make the movies our homework?[25]

If erudite Britishness seems here to underwrite the dissolution of the boundaries between 'work' and play, studying and 'playing hooky', it's perhaps an indication of how well Nicoll was blending in: the same blurring of boundaries and distinctions was part and parcel of the 'ambiguity'-focused Anglo-American enterprise called 'New Criticism', just then establishing firm roots at Yale. Committed to the perception and analysis of duplicitous or contrary meanings in any and all texts in the spirit of William Empson's *Seven Types of Ambiguity*, this was of course not only a feature of the intellectual atmosphere of the Yale English department. In the world beyond it, boundary-blurring and shape-shifting was rife. As Wilk puts it, while he and his companions were safe in New Haven, 'In Europe, Hitler was advancing on the Maginot Line, and was destroying Jews, gypsies, and Communists.' Presumably the Hitchcock film that Nicoll had lined up to see was *Rebecca* (1940), starring Laurence Olivier and Joan Fontaine – itself a shape-shifting, boundary-blurring, double-dealing tale of compelling power.

In an account of undergraduate productions at the Yale Dramatic Society in 1940, Wilk mentions his involvement in what, in the circumstances, seems a surprising choice of a Shakespeare play: *Timon of Athens*. It took place in modern dress, with modern scenery, energetic dance routines and 'original songs'. The text was cut and occasionally re-arranged.[26] Nicoll's involvement in the production was close enough for him to have contributed a note especially written for the programme. It focused on the issue of *Timon*'s continuing relevance and, predictably, on its capacity for blurring boundaries, particularly those between past and present, saying that although the Bard's lines 'sing and sear and inspire now as they did over three centuries past', to clothe their speakers in contemporary dress helps to highlight the 'eternal verity of his imaginative vision'. After all, he continues, since 'Humanity's essential problems were the same in 1600 as they are in 1940 . . . *Timon* addresses our own age as directly as any'.[27]

Of course, at this time Yale was notoriously beginning to address 'our own age' in a particularly interesting, if rather less than direct, manner. The university had begun to establish itself as a crucial seedbed and recruitment agency for the major American organisation concerned with intelligence operations, or espionage, initially known as the OSS and later the CIA. Nicoll would have known Norman Holmes Pearson, a member of the Yale English Department, who during the War was to head the office of X-2 (counterintelligence) in London, and who made it his business to enlist a number of Yale graduates to the cause.[28] Needless to say, the ambiguity-obsessed, boundary-blurring, duplicitous concerns of New Criticism provided an appropriate context, even methodology, for that sort of work.

And Nicoll himself was not without a war-time role. Certainly, from 1942–45, he seems to have become attached, on some sort of secondment, to the British Embassy in Washington DC.[29] The precise nature of his official work there has a certain air of mystery about it, but before moving full-time to the Embassy there's no doubt that Nicoll was also involved in part-time activity at the British Library of Information in New York.[30] No less a figure than Isaiah Berlin offers another sighting in August 1940, when he refers to a meeting there with Sir Angus Fletcher, the director, and a 'Professor Nicoll of Yale . . . who seems also to belong to the Brit. Library [of Information] & pressed me to visit him in New Haven. They both hinted that great issues were at stake, that reorganisation (i.e. chaos) was occurring in the Brit. Library . . .'. Berlin evidently puts this 'chaos' down to the inefficiency of those in charge, and in a later reference, dated 4 April 1945 from the British Embassy, he refers loftily to 'Nicoll', now employed there full time, as if to a rather lowly employee. On the other hand, another expatriate British academic, David Daiches, reports Nicoll as handling the fairly exalted matters of 'educational and cultural affairs'.[31] To this day, for what it's worth, the British Foreign & Commonwealth Office reports no record of Nicoll's having served at the Embassy.[32]

## Brum

In 1945, as the war approached its end, Nicoll wrote to the President of Yale (strangely enough, on British Embassy note-paper), to say that he had accepted an invitation to take up the Chair and Headship of the Department of English at the University of Birmingham.[33] Once there, he lost no time in involving himself in two related projects that finally return us to Stratford: a continuing sequence of 'International Shakespeare Conferences' to be held there and, within a few years, the foundation in Stratford of Birmingham University's Shakespeare Institute.

The first International Shakespeare Conference took place in Stratford in 1946. Its beginnings were slightly low-key. Meetings were held at Mason Croft, the novelist Mari Corelli's old house in Church Street, then the British Council Centre. The impetus generated by the event's success would lead directly to the founding of the Shakespeare Institute in the same location in 1951.[34] The Conference's theme was announced bluntly as 'The Study of Shakespeare' and it attracted a total of 27 delegates. Main speakers included Henri Fluchère (France) and Robert de Smet (Belgium). There were no American partici-pants.[35] The *Stratford-upon-Avon Herald* made it quite clear that the focus of the event was Europe and the impact of the recent war: 'Striking comments on the value of Shakespeare . . . to the people of the occu-pied countries on the Continent were made' it announced, and major British scholars were in attendance to back this up.[36]

Reconciliation was in the air. There were newspaper reports of 'renewed contact' between closed minds. With its command of cliché at full throttle, the *Times Educational Supplement* began to limn the Bard as a kind of bearded English nanny benignly bent on the maintenance of world peace, his birth-place a sort of thatched-cottage United Nations. It looked forward to Stratford's becoming 'not merely one of the nation's shrines, but a truly international centre of Shakespearean study, a hearth to which not only lovers of Shakespeare, but all those who seek to know England, truth and beauty may come from all the four corners of the earth' (31 August 1946). A new *Pax Shakespeareana* was in prospect.

The paper was nevertheless honest enough to report that the confer-ence 'did not include representatives from the United States, and the whole of Europe' – that is, from those areas in the West and East whose hostility would become the basis of the Cold War destined to last most of the next 50 years. But at the second Conference, held on 16–23 August 1947, this situation had changed radically. The confer-ence theme was 'The Problem Plays and the Romances' and American speakers were there in force. The attendance rose to 30 and delegates included such American academic 'stars' as Hardin Craig, Alfred Harbage, and James G. McManaway.

In his welcoming speech, Lt. Colonel Fordham Flower accordingly used the occasion to remind his audience that 'Stratford . . . would ever be grateful to America for the help it gave in the building and endowing of the Memorial Theatre' (*Birmingham Post*, 18 August 1947). Setting aside the Cold War's off-stage rumblings, he advised the delegates that 'one thing is abiding and constant and that is the beauty and truth of Shakespeare's poetry' (*Stratford-upon-Avon Herald*, 22 August 1947). It was a sentiment difficult to dispute. Indeed, speaking at the Garden Party held to mark the centenary of the purchase of the Birthplace for the nation, the eminent scholar John Dover Wilson confirmed that 'Shakespeare is the eternal preservative of the value, the dignity, of human nature' (*Stratford-upon-Avon Herald*, 22 August 1947). The conjunction of Shakespeare and human nature is a confection always hard to resist, and the pronouncement that the one eternally preserves the other inevitably cues, as Harold Bloom has discovered, tumultuous, even grateful, applause. The conference's endorsement of the principle can thus be no surprise. Probably the model of the academic gatherings that now form such a feature of academic life, the Stratford International Shakespeare Conference can be said to mark the first stirrings of a cultural juggernaut.

## Timons

And, perhaps suprisingly, *Timon of Athens* played its part. As part of the 1946–47 season, Sir Barry Jackson, famous director of the Birmingham Repertory Theatre, and a friend of Allardyce Nicoll, decided to stage a modern-dress production of the play as 'an experiment' in Birmingham. It's hard to judge the extent to which this production echoed the one in which Nicoll had been involved at Yale in 1940, but his view that '*Timon* addresses our own age as directly as any' can be detected throughout. Some of the play's action was cut or re-arranged, and speeches of minor characters were amalgamated. The central personalities became modern cigarette-smoking businessmen, or Senators with umbrellas and brief-cases. Apemantus was portrayed as a rather 'weedy' personage addicted to crossword puzzles. The soldiers carried rifles and ammunition belts, some of the women appeared as modern prostitutes or as blowsy ATS girls. The second half of the play took place beside a bomb crater dominated by an enormous field gun. An atmosphere of war-torn desolation, bankruptcy and decay prevailed and a powerful impact was created by blackouts during which a telephone rang insistently, suggesting creditors besieging the house.[37] Jackson had decided to produce the play, and in modern dress, he said, because, adapting Nicoll's Yale judgement, 'it has a good deal in common with contemporary Birmingham' (Trewin 1963: 142).

It's easy to see why. War certainly pervades *Timon*. Alcibiades' assault on Athens is sparked by his unsuccessful plea on behalf of a soldier. Conscripted men's resentment would have found plenty of echoes in his comment to the Senators 'My wounds ache at you' (3. 5. 97). Large areas of Birmingham did feature bomb-craters. Worse, the winter of 1946–47 proved astonishingly inclement – massive snow-falls, unprecedented frost, and a wholesale fuel crisis almost brought about social collapse. Acceptable housing was in short supply, and though nobody starved, food was harshly rationed. For many who looked for the fruits of victory, life turned out to be wretchedly unpleasant, shamingly drab. Britain teetered alarmingly on the edge of financial ruin, and its situation might well be symbolized by blackouts and the unanswered ringing of a telephone.[38]

But *Timon*'s central themes of betrayal, self-interest, and greed, its presentation of the human condition at its most basic, were also more broadly compelling, and you can feel these tugging at any purely local moorings. Beyond the English Midlands, the British Empire was finally crumbling. In August, 1947, India became independent, and the subcontinent was partitioned to create the new nation of Pakistan. British troops would soon begin withdrawing from Palestine, pending the establishment of the new state of Israel.[39]

As a feature of the 1947 Shakespeare Conference, Allardyce Nicoll persuaded Jackson to put on a single performance of his Birmingham production of *Timon* in Stratford, especially for Conference members, on the evening of Sunday 17 August.[40] The director's account of the event is graphic: 'We took the production to Stratford one Sunday night and played it in the Assembly Hall at the back of the theatre for the annual conference of Shakespearean scholars. No scenery, just a rostrum between the two staircases, a telephone, modern dress, and some records by Ravel. The impact was astounding.'[41]

What astounded most was perhaps the way in which, in one critic's words, this emphatically 'shook the play free of period' (Kemp 1948: 135). It might have been nearer the truth to suggest that it transferred it from one period to another and in the process began the extension of its significance. J. C. Trewin notes that 'The hall was the Conference Hall, converted from the burnt-out shell of the first Shakespeare Memorial Theatre' (Trewin 1963: 142) – something which no doubt added to the atmosphere of general decay and, in this context, expands this performance's frame of reference spectacularly. In effect, it moves the play decisively beyond 'contemporary Birmingham'. Played before that specific audience of high-powered academic Shakespeareans engaged in the construction of a brave new role for a possibly 'burnt-out' subject, this production of *Timon of Athens* clearly had something 'astounding' to say to Shakespeare studies at large.

At first sight, the play seems a most unsuitable vehicle for such a mission. Of all Shakespeare's works it must be the one least likely to sponsor the integration of a broken world under the benign aegis of democracy, liberal humanism and, dread word, capitalism. Indeed, as Karl Marx points out, *Timon* seems to attack capitalism's first princi-ples.[42] Yet anybody who doubts the power of particularly 'situated' or 'presentist' readings to shape a work to specific purposes will find here a clear example of that process in action. After all, in 1887, *Timon of Athens* had readily enough supplied an epigraph for a triumphalist cere-mony – the opening of George W. Childs's fountain – celebrating the expansion of a transatlantic – and undoubtedly capitalist – English-speaking culture. Sixty years on, in 1947, the same play seemed no less ready to speak to a world in ruins. If the *Timon* of 1887 supports a somewhat self-satisfied monument commemorating unity and consan-guinity with the United States, in 1947 the same play can speak of desolation and decay, whist helping to establish a different monument in the form of a Shakespeare Institute, rooted in the wartime American, and Yale-tinged, experience of its founder. Both structures, fountain and Institute, comemmorate an Anglo-American alliance, based on blood, whose emblem is *Timon of Athens*. But if Barry Jackson's production of the play offers a pessimistic response to post-war England, there's no doubt that it also acted, on this occasion, as the springboard for a much more robust and optimistic academic enterprise whose goals lay in quite the opposite direction.

## Above politics

For, as one war ended, another had decisively begun: an epic interna-tional *Kulturkampf* between East and West. And *Timon of Athens* was in the thick of it. In Britain the new Labour government looked to many to be a disturbingly radical, even revolutionary force aiming at socialism if not communism. Significantly, Karl Marx's view of the play had re-surfaced in this context in 1947, cannily reinforced by Kenneth Muir's article *'Timon of Athens* and the Cash Nexus' (1947).

Muir's case is clear enough. Shakespeare, he says, 'was one of the spiritual godparents of the Communist Manifesto', and *Timon* depicts a bleak amoral world in which money is 'the new basis of ... an authority without responsibility, a power animated entirely by self-interest' (Muir 1947: 69–75). This was fighting talk. But heavyweight opposition was to hand. With the Cold War well under way, the infamous US House of Representatives Unamerican Activities Committee (HUAC) was already in session. Hollywood had come under close scrutiny, and the politics implicit in drama and artistic activity in general would not be exempted from its inquisitions. By October 1947, the Committee were questioning Bertolt Brecht.[43]

In that sort of atmosphere, where intelligence, counter-intelligence and methods of covert infiltration were already fuelling a conflict in which hearts and minds were at stake, we can see Shakespeare inevitably taking on a new and specific role for a British–American alliance. It involved, crucially, the removal of overt political issues from the equation. If the Bard's works could somehow be presented as rising 'above politics', that act – itself wholly political – would release a vast new area for manoeuvre.[44] It would indemnify whole swathes of cultural activity, whole areas of the canon, against the charge that they function merely as vulgar political propaganda. And it would help to counter Soviet claims that the Anglo-American way of life depended on a simple-minded, gum-chewing populace capable of little other than crass Hollywood melodrama, sentimental musicals, and the productions of Walt Disney.[45] To this extent, the year 1946–47 could be said – just sixty years after the opening of the George W. Childs fountain – to mark the birth of a new creature.

You know him well. Enter William Shakespeare, International Superstar: an undeniably 'modern dress', shape-shifting, boundary-blurring Bard who, anchored strategically in his home town, nonetheless readily breaks those bonds, to float vacuously up and away as a force for a nebulous and undefined freedom: his stock-in-trade the dispensation of gaudy pop-star favours; peace, tolerance and love, to be pinned promiscuously to the chests of the self-applauding. This Shakespeare somehow comes to be equated, less with a firmly grounded Englishness, than with a cloudy, portable, one-size-fits-all, transatlantic Goodness. As a result of it, he's able to soar hygienically above the messy differences in which individual concrete cultures deal, to dispense wisdom and understanding to a vaguely conceived but always grateful 'humanity'.[46] He stands, in short, as a serene ahistorical, apolitical wonder, 'timeless', 'universal', 'transcendent', even God-like. His essence is heralded in a book called simply – what else – *Shakespeare*:

> . . . of late we have been becoming more and more aware of "The Shakespeare Wonder" . . . It is true that there are other

authors, Homer and Dante for example, who have passed
beyond the frontiers of place and time . . . but not one of
these other poets can claim such allegiance as Shakespeare
does . . . he has also penetrated into the farthest reaches of
the globe. The East celebrates his glories hardly less than the
West. Beyond religion and politics he has moved serene.
Amid the clash of modern ideologies his works are secure.
Moscow and Warsaw join with his own London in paying
tribute to his genius . . . only he is the true magician, god-like
in his empery . . .

It's no surprise to discover that the author of these words is Allardyce
Nicoll, fomerly head of the Drama Department at Yale, now head of
the Shakespeare Institute at Stratford. His book *Shakespeare* was
published in 1952, in the year of the Institute's founding, and it
concludes by quoting the very lines that adorn George W. Childs's
fountain, situated less than 200 yards from the Institute's grounds:

In her days every man shall eat in safety
Under his own vine what he plants, and sing
The merry songs of peace to all his neighbours.
God shall be truly known, and those about her
From her shall read the perfect ways of honour,
And by those claim their greatness, not by blood.

Nicoll's comment is revealing:

No more fitting lines could have closed Shakespeare's career
. . . "Thou speakest wonders" King Henry says to Cranmer,
but now the wonder, although it exists in the world of
nostalgic memory, has become the real.
(Nicoll 1952: 1–2 and 177)

How right he is. The growth of this bloated 'wonder' called
Shakespeare has, over the last 50 years, indeed become 'the real': a
central feature of our way of life. In fact from 2006, we'll experience
the ultimately inflated Bard finally and freely drifting above Stratford
in all his gaseous glory. From April on, the Royal Shakespeare
Company plans to present what it calls 'The Complete Works', a
year-long Festival featuring all 37 of Shakespeare's plays. A plethora of
multi-cultural companies will perform them to multi-national audiences
in their thousands. Embracing 'film, new writing, and contemporary

music', the event will demonstrate 'the truly global reach of the greatest writer in the English language'. The Festival publicity gives the chilling details:

> Visiting companies from South and North America, Russia, the Middle East, Asia, Africa and across Europe will explore Shakespeare's continuing influence on cultures around the world . . . Yukio Ninagawa brings his Japanese *Titus Andronicus* to the RST, Anglo-Kuwaiti director Sulayman Al-Bassam directs a Pan-Arab version of *Richard III* focusing on Saddam Hussein's early days as a secular Arab hero before he murdered his way through the Ba'ath party. Tim Supple directs *A Midsummer Night's Dream* with a company of performers from across India and Sri Lanka. Roy Williams . . . has written a response to *Much Ado About Nothing* set against the backdrop of the Iraq War . . .

This is modern-dress boundary-blurring with a vengeance. Indeed, it's a prospect that's recently inspired the director of London's Globe Theatre to speak – with apparent seriousness – of a forthcoming 'Shakespearetastic' year in which this non-specific, virtually non-terrestrial figure, will dominate the cultural horizon, 'floating around in a hot-air balloon, waving benignly at everyone . . .' More than capable of an 'easy leap of national and cultural boundaries', he continues, the Bard's 'spirit of inclusion, his love for everything, is our last best hope' (Dromgoole, 13 July 2005). Needless to say, *Timon*'s involvement is assured, its probing of the blood-money-cannibalism nexus suitably blunted. A theatre company consisting of homeless people called 'The Cardboard Citizens' will stage the play, not just in modern dress, but 'as a management-training course in a local hotel'. We'd be forgiven for thinking that the Bard had finally turned into Bob Geldof.

But perhaps, in effect, he's become an even more sinister figure. 'Above politics', certainly, this Shakespeare now speaks with trans-fixing power, to any and all ways of life. Not dead, so much as – well – Undead, he effortlessly blurs and transgresses all boundaries. Shape-shifting at will, his 'love for everything' signals a voracious and insatiable appetite: he sucks the life-blood from any and all cultures, Russian, African, Indian, for these transfusions guarantee his 'truly global reach'.

With this dubious creature at its head, and perhaps with the applauding spirit of Bram Stoker at its rear, the 'band of brothers' can march confidently, indefatigably on. As it does so, maybe it's just possible to detect, coming either from the Shakespeare Institute, or from George W. Childs's fountain, a disconcerting Transylvanian chuckle. It might be better not to drink the water.

## Notes

1   See Davis 1890: iv. This account is also published as part of Childs 1890. George William Childs (1829–94) was born in Philadelphia as the unacknowledged child of a father 'belonging to a prominent family'. His was a classic rags to riches story. The early years remain 'hidden in mystery', but when he entered the book-selling business he quickly prospered, later joining the publishers J. B. Lippincott. In 1864 he bought the failing Philadelphia newspaper *The Public Ledger* and turned it into a great success and himself into a person of some considerable influence. He married Emma Bouvier Peterson, daughter of his former business partner, Robert E. Peterson. He made a point of meeting and entertaining the famous, such as Generals Grant and Sherman and the writers Hawthorne and Longfellow. General Grant became a particular friend. Dickens and Thackeray were his guests when they visited the United States, and his wife's 'album' contains comments from an array of other distinguished visitors to his Philadelphia home, including Oscar Wilde, Walt Whitman, Matthew Arnold, and Henry Irving. He amassed a very large collection of manuscripts. In addition to the fountain in Stratford, he also endowed the Herbert and Cowper windows in Westminster Abbey, the Milton Window in St. Margaret's church, Westminster, and the Bishops Andrewes and Ken reredos in St. Thomas's Church, Winchester. He gave money to Bryn Mawr college, helped found what became Drexel University, and sat as President of the Board of Visitors on the governing body of West Point. He wrote *Recollections of General Grant* (1885), and an autobiography, *Recollections of George W. Childs* (1890) in which he claimed his success was owing to 'industry, temperance and frugality'. He died on 3 February 1894 and his remains lie in a mausoleum in Laurel Hill Cemetery, Philadelphia. See Johnson and Malone 1930 IV: 70–71.
2   See Jowett 2004: 136–53.
3   See Davis 1890: 5.
4   He went further, quoting a poem from 'a remarkable book, by an American' which presents Shakespeare as redeeming the crime of George III and re-uniting the child with the parent-state:

> Our Roman-hearted fathers broke
> Thy parent empire's galling yoke;
> But thou, harmonious master of the mind
> Around their sons a gentler claim shall bind!
> Once more in thee shall Albion's sceptre wave
> And what her Monarch lost her Monarch-bard shall save.
>
> (Davis 1890: 66)

5   See Stoker 1906: II: 126–28. Interestingly, Stoker gives the date of the fountain opening, in passing, as 'June' (his major concern is an anecdote concerning a monkey at the house of Mr C. E. Flower). Cf. Murray 2004: 127, 131. His presence at the ceremony in October is independently confirmed, however. See Davis 1890.

6  William Hughes confirms that 'such encodings punctuate Stoker's writings'. See Hughes 2000: 139.

7  See Ellman 1996: xxviii.

8  See Murray 2004: 177

9  Indeed, in preparing the novel, it appears he took particular note of the suggestion that St. George's Day (popularly, of course, Shakespeare's birthday) could be identified with the Witches Sabbath. See Murray 2004: 171.

10  See also Moretti 1983: 91.

11  From *Capital*, see Ellman 1996: xxi. Together with the rest of his family, Marx, like Stoker, was a fervent admirer of Shakespeare and of the interpretations given to the tragedies by Irving. He listed the Bard with Aeschylus and Goethe, as one of his three favourite poets (McLellan 1973: 457). In fact, his daughter Jenny, aided by her sister Eleanor, published a series of articles in the *Frankfurter Zeitung* defending the actor, and Eleanor was a keen member of Furnivall's New Shakspere Society as well as a friend of actors like Ernest Radford and Dolly Maitland. Both daughters were members of the 'Dogberry Club', a Shakespeare reading society which often met at Marx's house. See McLellan 1973: 418.

12  See Brockbank 1989: 10–11.

13  See McLellan 1973: 113. See also Jowett 2004: 53–56.

14  Kermode 2000: 237 records other allusions to the Last Supper in this play.

15  No wonder that, at the end of Act 3, his banquet for his enemies should confront them with a radically reduced menu of stones and water. After it, he abandons the city, to enter, not some utopian 'wood near Athens', but its dystopian reverse: a wilderness which he roams like an animal, ravenous and naked.

16  See Cull 1995: 3.

17  See Cull 1995: 10. In 1935, the BLI recruited the young Alastair Cooke, who had just arrived in New York to work for NBC and the London *Times*. The Library no doubt felt that the fact that Cooke, who had studied as a postgraduate at Yale, could perhaps help link some of that institution's anglophilia to the Library's cause.

18  See Stevenson 1978: 289, 305, 385.

19  See Cull 1995: 95–96.

20  The implications of this for the British proved, and continue to prove, complex. The post-war notion that the UK had somehow to choose between allegiance to America or Europe unjustly polarizes a complex issue. The concept of a necessary, once and future 'unity' in Europe, which Britain, duly divested of Empire, was destined to join, is to a large extent an American fantasy. It depends on a particular reading of history and derives from a transatlantic notion of Europe as, somehow, originally a single location, disastrously fragmented, over the centuries, by human perversity, to be redeemed by and in the New World. (T. S. Eliot offers at large the sense that redemption from this corrupted waste land may – must – become available via the restitution of religion.) For the British to choose to 'join Europe' was in that sense less to opt against an American commitment, than to fulfil an American New Critical and CIA-inspired dream. Its imagined 'Europe' was the most American of all the futures on offer.

21  The case is persuasively put by Christopher Hitchens (1990).

22  I am aware of the 'Greeks'/'Merrygreeks' connection made by T. J. B. Spencer (1962).

23  It's said that he had been a conscientious objector during the First World War and had been imprisoned as a result See Edwards 1991: 1.

24  There is material about Nicoll in the Yale Presidential files of Presidents Angell and Seymour, and I am referred to this by the kindness of Michael Holzman. The Angell materials pertain to Nicoll's hiring by Yale in the period October to December 1932. Nicoll was then at the University of London, with what he terms life-time tenure. The correspondence in 1932 is between Nicoll and Baker, his predecessor at Yale, and Meeks, the Dean. Nicoll was offered a salary of $8,000 dollars to be chairman of the Drama Department at Yale. He 1) wanted more money; 2) wanted to know about tenure; 3) wanted to know about pensions; 4) wanted moving expenses; 5) wanted help with immigration. He received 1) $8,500; 2) tenure to age 65 or 66; 3) pension at a cost of $400 p.a. matched by the college; 4) $1,000 moving expenses; 5) information that he could have either a special professorial visa or come in under the normal British quota.

25  Writing about his memories of Yale, in the *Yale Alumni Magazine* (this has appeared on the world wide web: http://www.yalealumnimagazine.com/issues/97_03/wilk.html). Presumably the film was *Rebecca* (1940), directed by Hitchcock and starring Laurence Olivier and Joan Fontaine.

26  See *The Yale Freshman Weekly*, Vol. 111, no. 14, 18 January 1940, p. 1. See also Butler 1966.

27  Oddly enough, this modern dress production was shadowed, in the same year (in February and March) and on the same continent by a production of the play by the Shakespeare Society of Toronto, featuring as main participant and director the critic G. Wilson Knight. Knight's commitment to *Timon*'s ultimate import – a wholesale stripping away of the trappings of human culture symbolised by actual on-stage nakedness – was reflected in the production's costuming, or lack of it. It was almost as if the European war generated two versions of what Knight unambiguously calls 'that great play, *Timon of Athens*', umbilically linked by the conflict, and responding to it in terms of costume: one 'modern dress' version, stressing its evident engagement with the issues prominent in the modern world, and one 'un-dress' version, stressing its transcendent, far-reaching engagement with fundamental and universal human matters. A programme of Knight's production, signed 'with compliments' by him exists in the *Timon of Athens* file of the Yale Dramatic Society (Yale Archives, Folder no. 28). See Knight 1940: 26.

28  See the information afforded by Michael Holzman, to which I am extremely grateful. One of Pearson's most influential recruits was James Jesus Angleton, a student who got to know writers such as Ezra Pound, William Empson, and T. S. Eliot in person. He became fascinated by the 'wilderness of mirrors' generated by the close analysis of texts and the taste for ambiguity characteristic of the so-called 'New Criticism'. Angleton went on to head the counter-intelligence division of the CIA in Washington, and was later almost to wreck the entire operation as a result of his developing paranoia.

29  As Michael Holzman indicates, the Seymour files begin with a leave of absence request on 18 August 1942. No reason was given. The request is granted by President Seymour on 20 August 1942, at half pay through June 1943. There are references to conversations on the topic. There is an exchange on 10 July 1944, concerning a visit by Kenneth Lindsay, M.P. on 17 July. Lindsay was formerly Parliamentary Under-secretary for Education. Nicoll's letter is on British Embassy (Room 222) paper.

30 This was before he joined the BLI set-up in 1942, when it was operating under the authority of the British Embassy. See Cull 1995: 131 and 159. It's also possible that he may have worked in some capacity for the British Political Warfare Mission (an organisation devoted to broadcasting programmes to enemy or occupied countries during the war).

31 See Hardy 2004: 341 and 543. David Daiches was a British academic who found himself working during these years both at the British Information Services and later as a Second Secretary at the Embassy (where he was involved with the Information Office). He took over the field of 'educational and cultural affairs' from Nicoll at the Embassy, in 1945 (Daiches 1971: 132).

32 In response to a personal inquiry made in 2004.

33 He gives two reasons: 1) He has found he has no time to write or do research, given his administrative duties as department chair; 2) His departure will help resolve the controversy about whether the department is to give more 'practical instruction' in the theatre.

34 The foundation of the Institute, which is part of the University of Birmingham, was aided by funds from Scribbans-Kemp the bakers, and industrialist H. Oliver-King. The Institute received a $100,000 grant from the Ford Foundation in 1964, described as follows: 'In the cultural field, the Foundation made grants to . . . the Shakespeare Institute of the University of Birmingham for strengthening of its research and advanced training.' This would have been part of that foundation's international cultural policy which, according to Holzman, was closely co-ordinated with US governmental agencies, such as the Congress for Cultural Freedom and other bodies.

35 These details are taken from the archives of the International Shakespeare Conferences held at the Shakespeare Institute Library in Stratford. I am grateful to the Institute's Librarian, Mr Jim Shaw, for kindly making them available to me. I am also grateful to Professor Philip Edwards and Professor Stanley Wells for their reminiscences of the Institute's early days.

36 They included E. M. W. Tillyard, J. Dover Wilson, Peter Alexander, C. J. Sisson, F. P. Wilson, M. C. Bradbrook, H. S. Bennett, Joan Bennett, G. Wilson Knight, F. S. Boas, B. Ifor Evans, and George Rylands. See *Stratford-upon-Avon Herald*, 23 August 1946.

37 See the account of the production in Trewin 1963: 139–42. See also Kemp 1948: 134 ff.; *Stratford-upon-Avon Herald*, 22 August 1947, and Oliver 1959.

38 As if to underline the play's appropriateness, within twelve months, just a few hundred miles to the north, at the Leeds University Union Theatre, G. Wilson Knight directed his 'undress' production of *Timon*, based on his 1940 Toronto version – again with himself in the title role. See above, no. 27.

39 Timon's regretful 'To Lacedaemon did my land extend' (2.2.157) would have struck an appropriate chord.

40 The 1946–47 season also marked the first of Barry Jackson's three seasons as director of the Shakespeare Memorial Theatre at Stratford.

41 See Trewin 1963: 142. See also Marshall 1957: 175.

42 See Jowett 2004: 53.

43 He was questioned on 30 October 1947. His inquisitor was called Mr Stripling.

44 As Stanley Wells puts it, 'As Britain tried to pull itself together at the end of the Second World War in 1945, stressing cultural rather than militaristic values . . . Shakespeare was considered in some quarters to be above politics and therefore as a potent healing force in the international arena. A seminal event was

the organizing in 1947 of a small international conference on Shakespeare in Stratford upon Avon by the British Council . . . This led to the founding there in 1951 of the Shakespeare Institute' (Wells 2002: 370).

45  See Saunders 1999: 19–21.
46  Of many recent instances, the film *Shakespeare in Love* (1998) perhaps most obviously trades on such presuppositions, lovingly reinforcing on their behalf a number of sentimental modern prejudices: that writers write most powerfully about what they personally 'feel', or that art's primary concern is to express the 'personality' of the artist.

2

# Historicizing new historicism

## Catherine Belsey

## The influence of new historicism

Few works of literary criticism can have exerted a greater influence on their own discipline than Stephen Greenblatt's *Renaissance Self-Fashioning.* Published in 1980, the book was immediately admired, taken up, imitated, and explained, to the point where, within a very short time, it seemed that every American English department needed its resident early modern new historicist, and every Renaissance studies doctoral candidate's research paper began with a historical anecdote. Although other names were associated with this approach, new historicism was in effect Greenblatt's creation, and it swept the board, first in the United States, and then, rather more tentatively, in much of the rest of the world.

A generation later it seems pertinent to ask why, or to locate from the perspective of the present, in the spirit of cultural history, not simply adulation or critique, the moment of new historicism itself. First, then, *Renaissance Self-Fashioning* was an exceptionally good book. Elegantly written, confident, authoritative, it represented the best kind of scholarship. And it told a persuasive story. Though each of the chapters is capable of standing alone, in combination they sustain a narrative concerning the mounting isolation of a perceptible 'self' in relation to authority in the early modern period. While More and Tyndale were able to pit the respective authorities of the Church and the Bible against the despotic charades of the Tudor state, Wyatt was cast more obviously on his own inner resources when that same state abandoned him. Prompted by circumstances, he fashioned a textual self to cope. In the next generation Spenser and Marlowe represent antithetical options. Spenser pays a high price in repression for his loyalty to the state he does not question; Marlowe creates fantasy rebels who progressively lose their individuality and eventually serve only to confirm the omnipresence of the orthodoxy they repudiate. Shakespeare alone recognizes the degree to which power reduces self-making to improvisation. All this is recounted with eloquence and wit, and the book had the effect of reintroducing history and politics into an academy that was beginning to tire of the timeless formalisms of New Criticism.

On the other hand, there have been good books before, without whole institutions turning themselves upside down to take account of them. What was it that proved so special about this one? There were, of course, distinguished historicists already working on the early modern period, among them Stephen Orgel, while other figures rapidly came to be associated with the new movement, including Louis Montrose, Joel Fineman, Don E. Wayne and Jonathan Goldberg. But the credit for establishing the concerns and modelling the outlines of new historicism must go to Greenblatt himself, who invented the name in 1982 (Greenblatt 1990: 146). That credit, or at least the responsibility, was one that Greenblatt himself was disarmingly prepared to accept. In September 1986 he told his Australian audience,

> I have heard – in the last year or so – quite a lot of talk about the 'new historicism' . . . there are articles about it, attacks on it, references to it in dissertations: the whole thing makes me quite giddy with amazement. In any case, as part of this peculiar phenomenon I have been asked to say something of a theoretical kind about the work I'm doing. So I shall try if not to define the new historicism, at least to situate it as a practice – a practice rather than a doctrine, since as far as I can tell (and I should be the one to know) it's no doctrine at all.
>
> (1990: 146)

He should indeed be the one to know. And as he indicates, new historicism was institutionalized extraordinarily fast, academically speaking. As early as 1986 an issue of *English Literary Renaissance* devoted to historicism included Louis Montrose's authoritative account of the movement's main concerns, as well as Jean Howard's searching critique of the practice (a sure sign of success). At the end of that year the

Modern Language Association meeting included a special session devoted to new historicism, while J. Hillis Miller complained in his Presidential Address to the MLA that 'in the past few years' literary study had shifted its attention away from language 'toward history, culture, society, politics, institutions' (1987: 283).

At this stage Greenblatt had published only one book-length work that could be described as new historicist. Several of the chapters had already appeared in journals, and a number of articles followed. In 1983 he became a founding editor of *Representations*. But *Shakespearean Negotiations* did not appear until 1988, *Learning to Curse* in 1990. It is primarily to *Renaissance Self-Fashioning* that we should look, therefore, if we are to account for an influence that in retrospect seems little short of astonishing.

The early accounts stressed the influence of poststructuralism on the composition of the book. Certainly, Michel Foucault, Jacques Lacan and Louis Althusser appeared in the footnotes, though in extremely attenuated form. Later, Greenblatt was to mention Foucault's visits to Berkeley in the 1970s (1990: 3, 146), and by the end of the 1980s it had become an established 'fact' that his model of self-fashioning was derived directly from poststructuralism in general and Foucault in particular (Graff 1989: 169; Fox-Genovese 1989; Lentricchia 1989). Since then, this view has been widely reiterated.[1] While it is true that Montrose made excellent use of Althusser, and Fineman appropriated Lacan with great subtlety, my own view is that poststructuralism played virtually no part in the composition of *Renaissance Self-Fashioning*. There is no obvious resemblance between the Althusserian interpellation of the subject and Greenblatt's self that fashions itself for an authority and in opposition to an alien force; the psychoanalysis that informs his book is Freudian, not Lacanian; and the model of power it assumes owes very little to Foucault. On the contrary, the roots of *Renaissance Self-Fashioning* are to be found in American culture, and this fact played a major part in its extraordinary institutional success.

## Resistance

Since Foucault is the main theorist in the narrative that has grown up about the book, I shall single out his position for special attention. But first, any discussion of Greenblatt's work ought to include a tribute to one of its defining features, the inclusion of a substantial excerpt from another text, drawn from a different field of knowledge, non-fictional, contingent, an allusion to the 'real' (Fineman 1989; Greenblatt 1990: 5; 1997). What was at that time a stylish violation of expectations represented one way of marking the newness of Greenblatt's new historicism (Lentricchia 1989: 234). Apparently excentric to the main topic of the essay, the extract enlists attention, as well as constituting a starting-point for analysis of the treatment of power by the main work in question.

Here, then, is my own contribution to what has now become an established practice. In 1944, in preparation for the Normandy Landings in June of that year, the troops of the British Expeditionary Force were issued with a booklet telling them how to engage with the French civilian population. Called simply *France*, the anonymous pamphlet showed the Arc de Triomphe on the front cover, and French road signs on the back. Inside, the text was broken up by drawings of typical French scenes, including members of the French underground clustered round a radio. Evidently, the British Political Warfare Executive was anxious to remind the troops that, despite the collaboration of the Vichy Government, the French people remained their allies. Unprotected by the Channel, the booklet explains, France had been invaded by Germany along its north-east frontier in 1870 and 1914, as well as in 1940, and, despite the current triumph of the occupying forces, Britain and France were on the same side against Hitler's armies. The assumption, naturally, is that the allied invasion will succeed and the British troops will be welcome. But, the booklet warns,

> the French, after the German occupation, are, generally speaking, in no position to entertain you lavishly, though families may get up from the cellar in your special honour a long-hidden bottle. If so, remember that it may be the last they have. A good many people are likely in any case to lack the energy or the mood to do much 'celebrating', however great their joy and relief at being freed. When anyone has been living for a long time suffering from privation or in a concentration camp, and is suddenly let out, it takes him time to recuperate. And France had developed under the German occupation much of the physical depression of a huge sickroom, and much of the mental stress of a huge concentration camp.
>
>     Lack of food, lack of medicines, lack of soap and towels have spread disease in France to an extent previously unheard of. A recent French estimate suggests that as many as one in twelve of the population may be suffering from tuberculosis. Cases of syphilis were most frequent in the neighbourhood of German military centres and may be as

many as one in eight of the population. As for the spirit of
the concentration-camp, two-thirds of France . . . has been
ruled directly by the German army and the Gestapo since
June, 1940. The rest of France was indirectly controlled by a
quisling Government at Vichy until November, 1942, when
the Germans occupied this portion too. The Vichy
Government was then allowed to carry on as a local administration. The Germans and their Vichy henchmen introduced
all the blessings of the 'New Order'. Getting on for a million
Frenchmen (apart from the 1 ¼ million prisoners of war)
have been deported to Germany. Another 150,000 have been
in actual prisons or concentration camps in France. **Each
year at least 5,000 Frenchmen have been shot for
active resistance – one every two hours.** This includes
anything from derailing a German troop-train to helping
British soldiers or airmen escape.

(Bold type original; *France* 1944: 5–6)

Moreover,

Frenchmen who have risked everything in these resistance
groups feel that they have done all that lay in their power to
redeem the disgrace of their country's collapse in 1940 by
fighting on as our active allies. So, before reminding a
Frenchman that France let us down in 1940, remind yourself
that you may be speaking to one of the thousands of soldiers
without uniform who have been fighting the same fight as
you against the same enemy, but with far fewer advantages.

(26)[2]

Born in 1926, Michel Foucault would have been 18 at the time of the
Normandy Landings. He would have been intensely aware of the
extent of French collaboration with a force that presented itself as
beneficent, but also of the work of those unofficial warriors 'without
uniform' who resisted the occupation that brought them into being.[3]
The isolated French individuals and groups who obstructed German
operations, while smuggling Jews and prisoners of war out of France,
can have had little hope that they would succeed in defeating their
oppressors. Moreover, they lived in constant awareness that they faced
the penalty of summary execution. When Foucault invokes the word
'resistance' for his post-war French readers, it therefore carries a degree
of pessimism, certainly, but at the same time intensely heroic overtones

that were evidently inaudible to the discontented post-Watergate intellectuals of Ronald Reagan's America who so readily coupled Greenblatt's understanding of power with Foucault's.

In Foucault's own version of cultural history, power and resistance are an inseparable couple, each the defining difference of the other, and the heroes of the stories he tells are criminals, sexual misfits and reluctant parricides, all of them soldiers without uniforms, who have no hope of making any serious headway against the order that produces them as its other. Power creates resistance not for the sake of extending its own regime, but as the difference that defines orthodoxy. Here is Foucault's account of the way power and resistance belong together, as well as a question that follows from their necessary conjunction:

> Where there is power, there is resistance, and yet, or rather consequently, this resistance is never in a position of exteriority in relation to power. Should it be said that one is always 'inside' power, there is no escaping it, there is no absolute outside where it is concerned, because one is subject to the law in any case? Or that, history being the ruse of reason, power is the ruse of history, always emerging the winner?
>
> (Foucault 1979: 95)

Should we say that power always prevails over resistance?, Foucault asks. This is pretty much what Greenblatt does say in his early, most influential works. 'Invisible Bullets' was first published in 1981, and again in two separate anthologies in 1985, before, in defiance of all academic convention, Greenblatt included it in his own book, *Shakespearean Negotiations* in 1988.[4] This essay brought down on his seemingly unsuspecting head the combined wrath of the entire academic Left by his now notorious affirmation that subversion merely serves to strengthen the power that contains it. This is not the place to reopen those debates of the 1980s about whether subversion or containment is the motor of history. I mention that essay only to draw attention to the gap I perceive between Greenblatt's work at this time and Foucault's, with a view to calling into question the common perception of a poststructuralist influence on the new historicism that established itself in the first years of the 1980s.

'Invisible Bullets' was not out of line with the general trajectory of Greenblatt's previous analysis of power. Already in *Renaissance Self-Fashioning* he had presented a succession of figures who shaped themselves in relation to the prevailing authority: More, executed only when outward compliance with the secular regime came into direct conflict with the requirements of the more profound jurisdiction of the Church; Tyndale, obedient to the Bible, but preaching submission to the secular powers, while himself prudently moving elsewhere when things got too hot; Wyatt, thrown back on the construction of a discursive image of self-sufficiency when the authority he had served no longer sheltered him; Spenser, the colonial administrator in the service of the state, ruthlessly repressing the barbarism he was drawn to; and Shakespeare, exploring the effects of power without committing himself either way. The exception that proves the rule in the book is Marlowe, whose protagonists consistently fashion themselves in defiance of authority. But, true to type, they do not thereby escape the social system's shaping power. On the contrary,

> the attempts to challenge this system – Tamburlaine's world conquests, Barabas's Machiavellianism, Edward's homosexuality, and Faustus's skepticism – are subjected to relentless probing and exposed as unwitting tributes to that social construction of identity against which they struggle.
>
> (Greenblatt 1980: 209)

There is in Greenblatt's 1980 analysis no rebellion that is not complicit with the power that produced it, and no chance of a revolt that is not subject to co-option or worse. The best Marlowe can do is create a space of fiction that flouts what society endorses, while it attributes to fantasy-figures a 'haunting sense of unsatisfied longing' (221). In Greenblatt's account, we can long all we like, but history will emerge, as Foucault's puts it, 'the winner'.

Here, however, by contrast, is Foucault's answer to his own question.

> To suppose that power always prevails would be to misunderstand the strictly relational character of power relationships. Their existence depends on a multiplicity of points of resistance: these play the role of adversary, target, support, or handle in power relations. These points of resistance are present everywhere in the power network. . . . There is a plurality of resistances, each of them a special case: resistances that are possible, necessary, improbable; others that are spontaneous, savage, solitary, concerted, rampant, or violent; still others that are quick to compromise, interested, or sacrificial; by definition, they can only exist in the strategic field of power relations. But this does not mean that they are only a reaction or rebound, forming with respect to the basic

domination an underside that is in the end passive, doomed
to perpetual defeat.

(Foucault 1979: 95–96)

Resistances as Foucault defines them are untidy, unpredictable: they
are plural, heterogeneous, sometimes co-opted, sometimes not, not
necessarily sympathetic, not always effective. There is no romantic
idealization of resistances here, and no promise that history will permit
them to triumph. But nor is there any concession to the view that they
are 'doomed to perpetual defeat'.

## The anecdote

The extract I have quoted as a tribute to Greenblatt's style is not an
anecdote but an attempt to explain to soldiers the effects of the power
relations they are there to change. And I have brought it to bear not on
a work of fiction but on another explanation, Foucault's own effort to
clarify for cultural historians the way his work changes their sense of
the task in hand. Ironically, the new historicist excerpt proper, the anecdote, is one instance of a direct Foucauldian influence.[5] *Discipline and
Punish* opens with a narrative so violent that scarcely anyone who has
read it can forget the overall impression of the unbearable pain admin-
istered by the state. The story begins, 'On 2 March 1757 Damiens the
regicide was condemned "to make the *amende honorable* before the main
door of the Church of Paris"' (Foucault 1977: 3). *Discipline and Punish*
first appeared in French in 1975, and in English two years later. It
seems likely that it was among the texts Foucault's teaching brought to
Greenblatt's attention when he visited Berkeley 'regularly' in the late
1970s and early 1980s (Greenblatt 1990: 3). Greenblatt's own anecdotes, often violent themselves, follow a similar formula: 'In 1531 a
lawyer named James Bainham, son of a Gloucestershire knight, was
accused of heresy, arrested, and taken from the Middle Temple. . . . '
(Greenblatt 1980: 74); 'On 26 June 1586 a small fleet, financed by the
Earl of Cumberland, set out from Gravesend for the South Seas' (193).
In the second case there follows the contemporary record of a neat and
well-kept town burnt to the ground by English merchants in Sierra
Leone. The first instance forms a prelude to a discussion of Tyndale;
the second is offered 'as a convenient bridge from the world of
Edmund Spenser to the world of Christopher Marlowe' (193–94).

Convenient or not, this bridge is placed at a remarkably oblique
angle to the shores it promises to connect. Guyon violently destroys the
Bower of Bliss; Tamburlaine's conquests find their analogue in the

acquisitiveness of English merchants. The pleasure of Greenblatt's anecdotes lies in the ingenuity with which he coaxes these apparently tangential materials to reveal aspects of works so familiar in another light that we had virtually stopped seeing them. Anyone who attended American conferences in the 1980s will recall the rather less successful efforts of one graduate student after another to wrench a story from its moorings in order to bring it into line with a canonical text.

How different in this respect is the case of Damiens the regicide. Here the story is not tangential to the theme of *Discipline and Punish*. On the contrary, it announces this theme directly and explicitly. In the *ancien régime* state power puts on display the contest between the sovereign and his assassin. Nor, despite an almost infinitely superior power, does the state have it all its own way. The executioner had difficulty with his appointed task of tearing away the regicide's flesh; the quartering proved too much for the horses and the executioner was obliged to cut the joints of the prisoner. All the while, the condemned man took a considerable interest in the proceedings, forgiving his tormentors and asking for their prayers. Even after the horses had pulled away his legs and arms, he did not die, and the trunk was thrown on the fire still alive. This corporeal and spectacular struggle between the sovereign and his opponent gives way, in due course, to the concealed discipline of the penitentiary and the panopticon, but we deceive ourselves, Foucault is eager to make clear, if we suppose that the latter is more liberal, or more humane. Moreover, it does not always succeed. Instead, it recruits delinquents and launches criminal careers (Foucault 1977: 300–1). In short, prison doesn't work, either.

The opening anecdote of *Discipline and Punish* demonstrates, in other words, the nature of the power-resistance couple that drives Foucault's work in the 1970s. In *Renaissance Self-Fashioning*, by contrast, the power is all one-way: Greenblatt characterizes public executions as cautionary spectacles (1980: 201). By the time he reaches *Shakespearean Negotiations*, on the other hand, he does seem to have internalized Foucault's point (1988b: 136–37), and his account of the Chinese goldsmith in *Learning to Curse* bears the marks of Foucault's Damiens (1990: 11–15). Caliban, too, might just qualify as a resistance worker, though a rather ineffectual one. But by then Greenblatt was ready to acknowledge doubts about the 'structural unity and stability' he had portrayed earlier, and to register that 'recent' critical and theoretical work treated texts as sites of 'contestation' (1988b: 2–3).[6] He did not need Foucault to tell him this: by now he could have heard it more or less anywhere in the English-speaking world. Moreover, as the second essay in *Shakespearean Negotiations*, 'Invisible Bullets' tended to eclipse these concessions to the conflict theory of history made in the introduction to that book.

In 1980 it would be possible to point to incidental overlaps between Greenblatt and Foucault, perhaps, but Foucault's legacy to *Renaissance Self-Fashioning* is above all a manner, a mode of address. Foucault's style, elegiac, ironic, lyrical, is only deceptively transparent, it seems, since so many of his readers have missed the point. But it is exceptionally eloquent, fluent and arresting by turns. Greenblatt brought a new elegance to early modern studies. And the word 'power' resonates through his pages as it does through Foucault's. The difference between them, and it is a crucial difference, resides in the meaning each attributes to this remarkably plural term. What is distinctive and surprising in Foucault's version is its instability: power is always threatened, perpetually precarious. In Greenblatt's version, power *works*: irresistible, pervasive, it incites self-fashioning and takes advantage of attempts at subversion to intensify repression.

## Functionalism

How should we account for the fact that the resistance in Foucault's work remained imperceptible to the generation of American intellectuals, including Greenblatt himself, who so evidently believed that new historicism was rooted in poststructuralism in general and in Foucault in particular? As one explanation, while the Normandy Landings were indubitably part of American history – the Supreme Commander Allied Forces was Dwight D. Eisenhower – French collaboration-and-resistance were not. For 1970s America the word 'resistance' carried few of the connotations it had in post-war France. In the wake of the Vietnam War, American pessimism entailed no heroic underground dedicated to oppositional acts of violence, either solitary or concerted, necessary or improbable, savage or sacrificial. For the generation concerned, radical action had meant something very different, centred on public protest and the refusal of military action. Foucault's Pierre Rivière, for example, who had slaughtered his mother, his sister and his brother, must have looked to them more like a mass murderer than a hero.

More substantially, perhaps, America has never shown much enthusiasm for the European assumption that history is made in and by conflict. Whether driven by the contest between capital and labour, or law and desire, or, indeed, power and resistance, change, in the European view, tends to be brought about by struggle. Foucault, for all his originality, is in line with the rest of Europe in this respect. But in post-war American intellectual life, from Talcott Parsons to Francis Fukuyama, functionalism has proved more attractive.

The influence of functionalism on Greenblatt has not gone entirely unnoticed (Stallybrass 1991: 216–17; Harris 1999), but my purpose in invoking it again here is to try to account for the extraordinary impact of *Renaissance Self-Fashioning*. Talcott Parsons was almost certainly the most brilliant social theorist of the 1940s and 1950s. In his analysis the main project of all social systems was their own survival. This did not rule out change, as some of his critics argued. On the contrary, the evolution of societies was best understood by analogy with Darwinian natural selection. All societies, Parsons maintains, encounter obstacles to success, and when they do so, they must adapt or die. Challenges are usually absorbed, therefore, with the effect of strengthening the system itself. For example, social development necessarily produces ever more differentiated forms of expertise, law for stability, writing for long-distance communication, money to facilitate the exchange of resources, politics to secure consent. Successful societies adapt to the social divisions this increasing specialization creates by a corresponding increase in uniformity of norms and values. Ultimately, every feature of a successful society is necessary to it: whatever survives in a social system does so because it functions to maintain the system itself. And Parsons singled out the United States as especially adaptive. In consequence of a characteristic ability to absorb challenges, American society had evolved further than Europe (Parsons 1977: 182–214). Not surprisingly, this confirmation of its own exceptionalism went down well at the time in America itself.

The difference between Parsonian functionalism and French post-structuralism can be seen in a brief comparison between two accounts of education. In 1959 Parsons examined 'The School Class as a Social System: Some of Its Functions in American Society'. He found American schools especially well adapted to their function, which was socialization, or 'the development in individuals of the commitments and capacities which are essential prerequisites of their future role–performance' (Parsons 1964: 130). These commitments were cultural and social, the internalization of shared norms and the willing acceptance of hierarchy, while the capacities were economic, different abilities leading to different occupational levels. Parsons finds little in the classroom to challenge the smooth functioning of the education system: it works well to ensure a satisfactory outcome. Of course, there are always a few pupils on whose nature nurture can never stick. Parsons acknowledges a degree of boundary-testing, but 'only a minority of adolescents comes to be confirmed in a truly unacceptable pattern of living' (152). (We can guess what will become of them.)

At a glance some of this may seem to resemble Louis Althusser's account of education as the central cultural determinant. In what has been perhaps his most influential essay, 'Ideology and Ideological State Apparatuses', Althusser too observes how the school system drills children in the prevailing virtues, ejecting a proportion of them into the production process at intervals to sell their labour-power according to their capabilities. The crucial difference between Parsons and Althusser here is not a matter of evaluation: functionalists may celebrate what they find or they may deplore it, as long as they naturalize it. (Dominick LaCapra ascribes what he wittily calls a 'gallows functionalism' to new historicism (1989: 191–92).) Instead, the critical distinction concerns conflict. Parsons sees education as key in maintaining American society; Althusser identifies the ideological state apparatuses as involved in perpetual struggle to retain bourgeois control of the forces of production against the interests of the working class. And he adds, 'I ask the pardon of those teachers who, in dreadful conditions, attempt to turn the few weapons they can find in the history and learning they "teach" against the ideology, the system and the practices in which they are trapped. They are a kind of hero' (Althusser 1977: 148). In the Althusserian model, the exceptions are not the misfit pupils, but the handful of teachers who fight the system. For all the differences between Althusser's Marxism and Foucault's anti-Marxism, we can glimpse at this moment in Althusser's essay the same resistance warriors, solitary or in small groups, doing their hopeless best against overwhelming odds. These odds, he continues, include the majority of teachers, who collude, or we might say collaborate, with education's own image of itself as beneficent.

The complacent integrationism of Parsons's structural functionalism could not survive the advent of feminism and the Civil Rights movement. In the 1960s and 1970s much of his social analysis was discredited as conservative. And yet functionalism itself by no means lost its hermeneutic value. The tenacity of its explanatory power is evident today in the circularities of evolutionary psychology, where whatever *is* is held to be natural and inevitable. The existing social traits of Western societies have been selected, it is argued, because they fulfil a function: they *must* have survival value, or they would not have survived (Belsey 2006). Whatever the scientific merits of evolutionary psychology, it sells well on airport bookstalls. If the functionalists *are* right, functionalism itself as a way of understanding the world is evidently highly adaptive.

# Clifford Geertz

Stephen Greenblatt does not appear to have much to say about Talcott Parsons. Surely this argues against the influence of functionalism on his work? Not necessarily, in my view. Forms of explanation that penetrate deep into the intellectual life of a culture can resurface without conscious borrowing. A pervasive functionalism would account for the way the protagonists of *Renaissance Self-Fashioning* cannot choose but shape themselves in relation to authority, however this authority is defined; functionalism would explain why even Marlowe's rebellion is absorbed to confirm the orthodoxy it challenges. That a measure of functionalism was taken for granted in the American culture of the period would also help to make sense of the immediate recognition accorded to Greenblatt's book.

But there is in addition a direct link between Parsonian sociology and new historicism. Greenblatt has been very forthcoming about the influence of the anthropologist, Clifford Geertz. It was Geertz on Balinese cockfighting he was reading in the anecdote that contributes to the conclusion of *Renaissance Self-Fashioning* (Greenblatt 1980: 255). And if Geertz ends the book, in a sense he begins it too, as the primary authority for historicism itself. *The Interpretation of Cultures*, first published in 1973, ends with the essay on cockfighting, and includes a discussion of 'The Impact of the Concept of Culture on the Concept of Man' (1993: 33–54). Anthropologists are convinced, Geertz affirms, that there is no such thing as human nature. No single unchanging figure is to be found beneath the alterations of costume history imposes. On the contrary, we are always 'performing' (36). An English major himself, Geertz quotes Shakespeare, Johnson and Racine; he writes with assurance and charm in a manner accessible to non-specialists; and he proclaims with the confidence of fieldwork behind him that specific cultures always interact with biology in shaping human beings. For a generation eager to escape the increasingly untenable proposition that literature provided access to human nature, 'a timeless, cultureless, universal human essence' (Greenblatt 1980: 4), *The Interpretation of Cultures* offered an engaging alternative to the heavy-duty, impenetrable anti-humanism of poststructuralist theory.

'I have attempted', Greenblatt explains, 'to practice a more cultural or anthropological criticism', and he lists a number of specialists in the field, with Geertz first among them (1980: 4). Moreover, it is Geertz who is invoked to authorize the continuity Greenblatt perceives between literature and social life, since human beings are themselves 'cultural artifacts' (1980: 3). As if this were not enough, Geertz also, and in the same essay, adumbrates Greenblatt's own account of self-fashioning. Culture and biology interact to make us what we are, Geertz proposes, by means of positive feedback. Certain cultural practices confer selective advantage on biological features, so that,

> By submitting himself to governance by symbolically mediated programs for producing artifacts, organizing social life, or expressing emotions, man determined, if unwittingly, the culminating stages of his own biological destiny. Quite literally, though quite inadvertently, he created himself.
>
> (Geertz 1993: 48)

Geertz's 'man', as he creates himself by submitting to the cultural conventions for generating cultural products, belonging to his own society, and defining how it feels to do so, namelessly anticipates More, Tyndale, Wyatt, Marlowe, Spenser and Shakespeare. Greenblatt makes no secret of this. Indeed, he quotes from Geertz with approval his remarkably authoritarian account of culture itself, as '"a set of control mechanisms – plans, recipes, rules, instructions . . . – for the governing of behavior"'. 'Self-fashioning', Greenblatt continues, 'is in effect the Renaissance version of these control mechanisms . . . ' (1980: 3).

'The Impact of Culture' evidently exerted a profound influence. Greenblatt was to quote it again in *Learning to Curse*, adding in a footnote, 'I am indebted throughout to this suggestive essay' (1990: 26, 38; see also 1997). Geertz had learnt his anthropology in the early 1950s at the Harvard Department of Social Relations, founded, and chaired at this time, by none other than Talcott Parsons. Geertz took from Parsons his account of culture as a system of signs and meanings, and the distinction Parsons makes between culture and the social system (Geertz 1993: 144–45). On the other hand, he criticizes functionalism for the emphasis it places on synchronicity and stability, which produces 'a somewhat overconservative view' (143). But what he offers in its place turns out to be 'a more dynamic form of functionalist theory' (169). And the brilliant account of Balinese cockfighting Greenblatt wanted to read on the plane demonstrates how this more dynamic functionalism works. It does not seek an adaptive explanation of every social practice, but it does not take any account of resistance either. True, the police break up a cockfight made illegal by the 'elite', but within the male peasant culture that sustains the practice nonetheless, there is simply no space in Geertz's 'thick description' of the meaning of the event for a dissident Balinese who doesn't approve of cockfighting, thinks it's a waste of time, or would rather do something different. How could there be such a person, when attending cockfights represents, 'for the Balinese, a kind of sentimental education. What he learns there is what his culture's ethos and his private sensibility (or, anyway, certain aspects of them) look like when spelled out externally in a collective text' (449)? As an art form in its own right (shades of Hemingway on the bullfight?), the cockfight is no less than constitutive for Balinese men, since 'art forms generate and regenerate the very subjectivity they pretend only to display' (451).

## An American tale

The primary antecedents of *Renaissance Self-Fashioning* are American, then, and the outline of their ideas was already familiar in the United States. There was no need to domesticate and explain theoretical foreign imports. Greenblatt could even have found 'signifiers' in the cockfighting essay, though these are not French signifiers, since they 'point to' 'referents' (447).[7] *Renaissance Self-Fashioning* addresses an American public, and draws on ideas that public might be expected to recognize, even if they might not all have been able to place them.

As soon as this becomes apparent, certain aspects of the analysis come into focus in a way that might begin to explain its remarkable appeal to the American academy. America, or more precisely, the New World, also features prominently in the text. While they confined themselves to canonical literature, English Renaissance studies had traditionally been predominantly – well – English, with special concessions for Ireland, Scotland and Wales. But once the new cultural poetics was licensed to attend to any part of the archive, travellers' tales and merchants' records brought other areas of the world into view. Sierra Leone finds its way into Greenblatt's chapter on Marlowe by analogy with the ruthless conquests of Tamburlaine; Guyon's target in the Bower of Bliss is intelligible as the seductive beauty of the New World itself, '"All that now America men call"' (Greenblatt 1980: 180). And if this last connection seems, on the face of it, something of a stretch,[8] that imaginative leap is nothing compared with the narrative that illustrates Iago's improvisation in terms of Spanish behaviour in the Bahamas. From then on, there would be no difficulty in relocating Prospero's island from the Mediterranean to the Caribbean, or in understanding Shakespeare's history plays in the light of Thomas Harriot's record of Virginia. The new historicism of Stephen Greenblatt was about the New World in a way that the old historicism of C. S. Lewis and E. M. W. Tillyard was not.

Moreover, the old world does not come across at all well in *Renaissance Self-Fashioning*. Disease-ridden, fraudulent, ruthless, driven, repressed, the Europeans grimly enslave the native populations, destroying the local culture to reaffirm their own. Greenblatt threw his considerable weight behind the emerging postcolonial critique of these oppressors. Acting exactly like an exorbitant superego, they justify the pogroms and holocausts they impose on the native Americans by reference to their own dark fantasies of cannibalism and sexual perversity. And all the while, no doubt to avoid the racial implications of calling them 'white', they are identified as 'the Europeans'. Of the range of available non-racist synonyms – travellers, explorers, colonizers, imperialists – Greenblatt opts for 'the Europeans' again and again (see, for example, 1980: 180–84, 226–27). By contrast, the American landscape resembles paradise: unsuspicious, wholesome, sweet-smelling, it harbours a population characterized by 'generosity and wantonness' (181), who represent nothing but life and pleasure. Henry James could hardly have portrayed more persuasively the encounter between American innocence and European corruption. Like the selves it describes (9), Greenblatt's book is fashioned in opposition to an alien force that must be negated.

Some of the representatives of this old world are English, of course. And the old historicism that comes under attack most explicitly is that of the British critics of the previous generation. In his later accounts of Greenblatt's trajectory, it comes to seem that New Criticism was the real target of new historicism (1988b: 3; 1990: 3; Gallagher and Greenblatt 2000: 2) – and, indeed, for the academy at large this was almost certainly true. By 1980 New Criticism had been brought to bear on every text that could be made to speak in its name, and some that could not. It was probably the half-rhyme with New Criticism that made 'new historicism' stick as a label, when Greenblatt's own preferred 'cultural poetics' did not. But while *Renaissance Self-Fashioning* includes a close reading of Wyatt's 'Whoso list to hunt' that was a credit to W. K. Wimsatt's teaching (145–50), it explicitly takes issue with Lewis over Tyndale, Wyatt and the Bower of Bliss (112, 136, 138, 170–71) and with Tillyard's reading of Wyatt, as well as his presentation of Shakespeare as 'an unwavering, unquestioning apologist for Tudor ideology' (131, 254). These disputes are all the more striking in a work which devotes very little energy to disagreement. It is one of the pleasures of *Renaissance Self-Fashioning* that the book is altogether too mild-mannered and too immersed in the story it has to tell to waste time combing the MLA Bibliography for errors to correct.

Tillyard's hierarchic Elizabethan world picture, like Lewis's endorsements of the Anglican Church, were well and truly due for revision, of course. But these authorities were both magisterial figures, convincing at the time, and profoundly influential. They were also British. From 1980 on, American English departments had no further call to locate authority on the other side of the Atlantic.⁹ In the sheer American-ness of its allegiances, *Renaissance Self-Fashioning* constituted a declaration of critical independence. No wonder it represented a welcome departure in the United States itself.

## Self-fashioning

'"Keep, ancient lands, your storied pomp!"' enjoins the Statue of Liberty, 'Mother of Exiles', as she holds her torch aloft in New York Harbor. Instead, '"Give me your tired, your poor,/ Your huddled masses yearning to breathe free"'. In 1883, when this poem was written, most of the huddled masses in question would have been made home-less in Europe, driven out by unemployment, famine, racial and religious persecution. When Greenblatt records the remorseless oppressions practised by Europeans, he tells his American readers a story that, in a different guise, they already know.

And what were they to do, these new arrivals in America, now that they were at last able to breathe free? Why, remake themselves, of course. Self-fashioning is another name for the American Dream, exemplified by any number of immigrants whose rags-to-riches stories display the endless adaptability of human beings. Naturalized (strange word) as American citizens, obedient to the flag, assimilated by and to American values, they faced no limits on what they could become. Self-fashioned, self-made, in conformity with American culture, they were free to demonstrate that talent, intelligence and hard work could lead to the acquisition of untold wealth and a corresponding social position or, in other words, a new identity.

Of course, it wasn't always quite like that, and by the 1970s, when Greenblatt was writing *Renaissance Self-Fashioning*, the American Dream was an object as much of critique as it was of wonder. Among other questions it raised, just how high was the price of success in these terms? And exactly how free were the subjects of American culture? Greenblatt's book is not naïve. On the contrary, most of its stories of self-made men do not end happily. More is executed, Tyndale chooses exile, Wyatt ends up talking, in effect, to himself. Marlowe and Spenser were both in their antithetical ways disappointed. Only Shakespeare, who managed to keep his opinions to himself, can be said to have succeeded in what he set out to do.

And the ending of Greenblatt's own book? Its Epilogue is by any standards a brilliant piece of writing. The ponderous and question-begging 'we' of the preceding text ('as we shall see'. But what if I don't?) gives way to an 'I' who is altogether more vulnerable, more uncertain. Meanwhile, the anecdote about the anxious passenger, told in the first person, ironic, self-deprecating, disarming, for once owes nothing stylistic to Foucault, but resembles instead the personal narrative that opens Geertz's account of Balinese cockfighting. In the Epilogue the story comes into its own as the central issue: an author of a book on self-fashioning as role-play finds himself unable to gratify a troubled father by playing, even for a moment, the role of a man who wants to die. The episode testifies to the ambiguity that haunts the book from the beginning. 'My starting point is quite simply that in sixteenth-century England there were both selves and a sense that they could be fashioned' (1980: 1). On the one hand, anthropology stresses the cultural construction of the self; on the other, the American Dream insists on the individual as origin of that construction. And the Epilogue, personal, empirical, evades the obligation a more summative conclusion might impose to resolve the difficulty. The anthropological framework has impelled certain recognitions: 'In all my texts and documents, there were, so far as I could see, no moments of pure, unfettered subjectivity' (256). On the contrary, there were cultural artifacts. But the protagonists of *Renaissance Self-Fashioning* do not know that and cling to a sense of the self as origin.

There then follows a very puzzling sentence: 'For the Renaissance figures we have considered understand that in our culture to abandon self-fashioning is to abandon the craving for freedom, and to let go of one's stubborn hold upon selfhood, even selfhood conceived as a fiction, is to die' (257). It is not clear what these Renaissance figures are doing in 'our' culture, at least in a historicist work which insists that we best understand them in the light of their own. Nor is it clear, as least to me, why a *craving* for freedom constitutes a virtue. The proposition that to give up selfhood is to die seems rather extreme. But strangest of all, even anthropology does not call a constructed self a 'fiction' or withhold from the 'self' that results from the union of culture with biology the entitlement to feelings, deliberate actions, choices – in short, agency – however subject it might be to conditions that are not of its own making.

But we murder to dissect. The confessional manner of these pages discourages theoretical analysis. Instead, the key to the Epilogue is to be found three pages earlier in the account of Shakespeare, the only truly successful self-fashioner of his time, who nothing affirms, nothing denies: 'Shakespeare's language and themes are caught up . . . in unsettling repetitions, committed to . . . shifting voices and audiences, with their shifting aesthetic assumptions and historical imperatives' (254). Not a bad precedent, we might think. It worked for him . . .

## Notes

1  Although I differ from it in substantial ways, I have learnt much from Pieters 2001.
2  I am grateful to Andrew Belsey for access to this pamphlet.
3  Writing from the perspective of what she calls 'the American academic establishment', Karen Raber brings into focus the influence of collaboration on Foucault's account of power, but she has almost nothing to say about the French resistance, except that it 'failed' (Raber 2004: 64).
4  It was published in *Glyph* 8 (1981), 40–61, and in revised form in Dollimore and Sinfield 1985: 18–47, and Erickson and Kahn 1985: 276–302.
5  Greenblatt would later ascribe the anecdote to the influence of Geertz (1997: 15), but the style is Foucault's.
6  Later still, resistance had 'always' been integral to new historicism, but now it dislocates people from their historical moment itself, 'somehow pulling out and away' (Gallagher and Greenblatt 2000: 16–17).
7  Greenblatt's are not French either (1988b: 7–8). In fact, his purchase on post-structuralist vocabulary seems altogether shaky. With Catherine Gallagher he confides that, despite a 'passionate interest' in Althusser, they have not adopted terms like 'Institutional State Apparatus' (2000: 2). I should hope not (see Althusser 1977). The pair also distance themselves from their own eccentric interpretation of 'deconstructionism' (sic) (2000: 14).
8  The link is textual and inventive, namely, Freud's observation that civilization treats sexuality as elites do the oppressed or the colonies (Greenblatt 1980: 173–74, 180).
9  Other new historicists confirmed this widening of the Atlantic by hiving off British 'cultural materialism' as a separate development, and then characterizing it as preoccupied by the institution of English studies in the present (Montrose 1986: 6–7), thus leaving the serious historical scholarship to the Americans (Wilson 1995: 55–56).

# 3
# ... And I'm the King of France

Michael Bristol

My father-in-law is just like King Lear. A statement like this might express a certain exasperation over what I take to be unreasonable behavior on his part. Or I might be thinking that his daughters aren't being very nice. Either way I would be applying insights derived from reading Shakespeare's play to my present situation. One way to describe this is to say that *King Lear* is the "source domain" (what I already know) that I am using to map the "target domain" (something I'm trying to understand). This might not be such a good idea, especially if any of my wife's relatives were to hear about what I've been saying, thus making the situation even more King-Lear-like than it already is. But really. My father-in-law is a man with three daughters who has left all his real estate in a trust. And he can be quite demanding at times, as any one of his daughters would tell you. I'm married to the youngest. Well OK. He isn't really altogether like King Lear and it's not very nice of me to say that he is, but sometimes the comparisons are hard to ignore. And it's not like I'm the only one to ever have such thoughts (Denby 1994).

King Lear is just like my father-in-law. This is not quite the same thing as saying my father-in-law is like King Lear, since here I would be applying insights taken from my own everyday experience to help me understand a complex literary text. I would be using my father-in-law as an example of the behavior or the psychology of aging parents to inform my interpretation of a play written in the early seventeenth century. Here the "source domain" is my present-day understanding of older people and the "target domain" is Shakespeare's *King Lear*. Strictly speaking it is this second situation that should count as "presentism," though in practice the first situation is also included. This would be risky in a different way than saying King Lear is like my father-in-law; disapproval would come not from my wife's relatives but from my professional colleagues, who are constantly reminding us not to "read things into" literary texts, especially things that are part of our ordinary everyday experience. Many critics would describe "presentism" as a systematic practice of reading things into the texts of Shakespeare's works, and they would regard this practice as wrong-headed, perverse, and probably reactionary.

As I've already told the editors of this volume, "presentism" is not an expression I like very much, because the word already means wrong-headed, perverse and indefensible. The "ism" suffix suggests analogues with coinages referring to heresies (Arminianism) or to pernicious ideologies (Nazism) or to various species of intellectual error (historicism). A usage like presentism could evolve into a perfectly self-respecting way for people to identify with a style of intellectual inquiry – as historicism has done in recent years. But historicism did not gain its present respectability because it privileges facts. Historical criticism (the term I would prefer to use) resists the attribution of "anachronistic" ideas that could not have entered into the self-understanding of anyone in the audience for Shakespeare's plays during his lifetime. Historical inquiry is concerned with "bringing out, as vividly as possible, the peculiar and transient idiosyncrasy of the individual or social group under study" (Hampshire 1983: 69). There are good reasons for this constraint. Learning about how people thought and felt in other kinds of societies can help to bring out "the peculiar and transient idiosyncrasy" of our own contemporary ways of doing things. And we might also be moved by ethical considerations here, approaching literary works with the specific goal of trying to understand what its author intended to say. But neither of these concerns would rule out asking "of the past utterance . . . the questions that we have for them, no matter how 'different' from the questions they may have had in mind" (Siemon 2002: 25).

Nor is it quite right to claim that presentism has something to do with a "windy" belief in universality. Concepts like "universality" or "human nature" are well worth serious exploration, though it's not good to be careless or smug about such notions (Habermas 1991; Nussbaum 1993). The way I look at it is that presentism is a commitment to the possibility of making general interpretations about the way people think and act that would be valid in different historical contexts. Finally, I don't like the reference to presentism as a "new kid on the block" – a description that has more to do with hype than with accuracy (Rabkin 1967; Styan 1977). There have always been important presentist critics of Shakespeare, though I would prefer the term vernacular criticism as the rubric for what they're doing (Bristol 2000). Among the more important presentist critics I would include Samuel Johnson and Northrop Frye; Sigmund Freud and Harry Berger; A. C. Bradley and Marjorie Garber; Ralph Waldo Emerson and Stanley Cavell. Presentism is not really controversial and making it seem controversial isn't going to make it important. Presentism is important because it is indispensable. It's a name for what we have to do if we are to read anything at all.

## Why "presentism" is indispensable

Reading a work of fiction like *King Lear* is never merely passive and receptive; it requires skilled engagement with a text of the play. The full complexity of this engagement is usually not apparent as we read, though we may experience a sense of difficulty or frustration as we try to grasp what's going on. That difficulty comes from a kind of multi-tasking, as there are at least three analytically distinct mental actions that take place in reading even fairly simple works of literature. First, reading is a type of problem-solving as we try to figure out what's happening in the story – who did what to whom, when they did it, how and why, etc. Second, we engage in a second order analysis of the story with the aim of semantic modelling or the determination of a meaning for the events that occur in the fiction. Third, we respond to the story in an emotional way, sometimes with surprising intensity. These feelings are often tied to our normative beliefs, our basic sense of good and bad, right and wrong. In practice, of course, these activities are interactive and interdependent; most of the time we're not aware of doing three quite different things at the same time.

Understanding what happens in a fiction looks like it should be relatively straightforward, since the text we're reading is "telling us the story." But it's not really entirely clear how we "get the story." David Lewis maintains that "extraction of plot from text is no trivial or automatic task. Perhaps the reader accomplishes this by figuring out what is true in the stories . . . " (1983: 265). We know, for example, that it is true that Cordelia is King Lear's daughter because the text explicitly says so. We also think that Cordelia had a mother – indeed a mother is briefly mentioned in the text – and that she was born in the usual way that human babies come into this world even though this is nowhere specified in the text. We don't think she was hatched from an egg or found under a cabbage leaf or that the stork brought her. Ignoring these possibilities is part of reading competence, but this competence depends not only on what the text explicitly tells us, but also on what we already know about the way our own world actually works. Competent readers generally understand that salient features of the actual world – the laws of gravity, which way is up, where babies come from – are also basic features of the fictional universe unless we are specifically told otherwise.

Fictional works are like that. Their texts always leave things out and somehow we have to fill in the blanks in order to extract the plot or to figure out what's true in the fiction. Some of the missing information is most usefully ignored, such as Cordelia's birth-weight or the exact number of hairs on her head at the time her father decided on the division of the kingdom. But other blank spaces really need to be filled in some way. If we ask "what did Cordelia say that made her father so angry"? the answer would be "nothing." If we want to understand just *why* she would say such a thing we have to make some kind of inference about her state of mind – her intentions, let's say, or her attitudes to what her sisters have just said, or whether she really loves her father or whether she resents him for spoiling her engagement party. And in order to make this kind of inference we might depend in part on what we already know about interactions between contemporary fathers and their daughters. *If my dad pulled a stunt like that on the day I was going to be engaged to the King of France I'd be pretty pissed off at him* (A-M.K.). Now this looks exactly like what's called "reading something into a text" and it is my professional obligation as an English Professor, I suppose, to try to talk the student out of seeing things this way. But hasn't the student really understood something important here? By reading her own experience into the play Anne-Marie has done some real work in the extraction of the plot. Her insight speaks to the question of Cordelia's motives, but it also brings out the emotional and the social complexity of the famous opening scene of *King Lear* in some really interesting ways. This scene takes place on the day when Cordelia will announce her betrothal, to the King of France, no less. It's an important occasion for her, to say the least, and perhaps she expects much to be made of it. But then it turns out that her father wants to steal the spotlight from her by choosing just exactly this moment to announce the plans for his retirement. Couldn't this have waited, at least a few days? And if, as we have good reason to think, Lear's youngest daughter really does love him, then that only makes matters worse. "He knows I really love him, and that's why he thinks he's going to get away with this."

This student's response corresponds to what David Lewis calls "Analysis 1" where understanding what's true in the fiction can be inferred from "matters of contingent fact" in the world we're living in now (1983: 270). For our purposes this is an aspect of what we're calling "presentism." But it's also possible to look at the collective belief systems in the world in which the author lived as the basis for making inferences about fathers and daughters. *The division of the kingdom is a ceremonial occasion and Cordelia is expected to behave like a princess not like a spoiled brat* (J.B.). This is what Lewis calls "Analysis 2" where the extraction of the plot (understanding what's true in the fiction) can be related to "matters of contingent fact" in the author's world (1983: 273). This lines up very nicely with the practice of "historicism." Analysis 1 and Analysis 2 are treated as equally plausible by Lewis, but in my own view Analysis 1 – or presentism – is actually indispensable in the sense that this aspect of reading simply cannot be dispensed with. What we know about how the world actually works – Analysis 1 – gives us reliable default conditions for understanding what's true in a fiction, and a lot of the time it's all we could possibly need.

The idea that I could somehow delete all contemporary material – beliefs, attitudes, dispositions, feelings, not to mention the basic facts of life – from my mental repertoire and replace it with a full set of beliefs, attitudes, dispositions and feelings current in Shakespeare's time is science fiction. If a mad scientist were to do this to my brain "I" would for all intents and purposes be dead and the living creature who took my place would most likely be institutionalized as hopelessly psychotic. No one could ever do such a thing and no one really wants to. We can and we should assume that things don't fall up, and that the basic physiology of childbirth is always and everywhere the same. But the cultural meanings, practices and beliefs associated with childbirth are emphatically not always and everywhere the same. And the same might be said about the relationship between daughters and their fathers (Jardine 1983). It's exactly here that historical knowledge can be most useful.

Coppélia Kahn has noticed that the three sisters have no mother; and the mother is also absent from the story of Gloucester and his two sons (1986: 35). The absent mother looks like one of those things we can usefully ignore for the purposes of "extracting the plot." But Kahn's discussion of the mother shows that her absence is quite important for the related but analytically distinct practice of determining the meaning of the play. Semantic modelling – determination of meaning – will always reflect the "peculiar and transient idiosyncracy" of the cultural agent who is doing the reading – it could hardly be otherwise. This is a separate skill from extraction of the plot that entails working out more general maxims or explanatory insights over and above what's true in the story. For King Lear this could mean something really crude and basic like *old age sucks* (J.B.) or *life's a bitch* (M-H.S.) – interpretations that seem entirely cogent but not very complex. Kahn's interpretation starts from a puzzling reference Lear makes when he finds the Earl of Kent in the stocks: "O, how this mother swells up toward my heart! Hysterica passio, down, thou climbing sorrow" (2.3.54–56). Kahn has identified "hysterica passio" or "the mother" as an early modern term for a supposed medical condition also known as the wandering womb (1986: 33ff.) Wombs were thought to have the ability to wander around in a woman's body and to cause a range of physical and emotional manifestations.

Lear does not, of course, have a womb, but Kahn interprets the reference as an indication that the King has in some sense internalized his own feelings about his own mother, feelings of longing, frustration, and disappointment that he has projected onto his daughters. This interpretation is made possible by historical research into the collective belief systems in the author's world (Analysis 2) but it is motivated by Kahn's intention to find out what the absent mother means in Lear's inner life (Analysis 1). She points out that his displays of patriarchal authority and power over his daughters suggest a basic insecurity and a need for love that comes from an identification with his mother and a feeling of rage prompted by her loss. Lear's feelings of deprivation of the comforting presence of a mother are what prompts his creepy insistence on having his daughters profess their love for him. His daughters are supposed to compensate him for everything he has ever lost. This discussion is framed by concepts taken from modern psychoanalysis, especially Sigmund Freud and Melanie Klein whose ideas are very clearly not part of the "collective belief world" in which the author lived.

Coppélia Kahn's discussion of the absent mother in King Lear is a brilliant and richly elaborated example of the kind of "mixed reasoning" that must take place whenever we read fictional works. Combining premises taken from a fiction with premises taken from the actual world in the same argument is actually a type of informal fallacy. But in practice this sort of thing not only seems intuitively right, it is often intellectually very productive (Lewis 1983: 269). Kahn's reasoning is also "mixed" in other ways. Her efforts at "semantic modelling" are closely tied in with "extraction of plot" in the sense that part of what counts as determination of meaning also counts as explaining the behavior of fictional agents. Most important for the purposes of this essay, however, is the way Kahn mixes her historical research with modern psychological concepts. The theory of "the wandering womb" looks like a crazy idea that no one needs to worry about now except for a few historians of medicine. Wombs do not wander; they never did. What Kahn achieves in her essay is explaining how such an apparently misguided medical theory matters to our understanding of *King Lear*. That explanation depends not on the depth or the accuracy of Kahn's "historicism" but on the intellectual sophistication of her presentism – that is on her skillful use of modern concepts to illuminate both the story and its historical context.

Kahn's essay does not discuss Lear's doomed attempts to maintain unquestioned patriarchal authority as a theoretical abstraction and there is much more to her discussion than interpretive problem-solving. Her essay reveals an emotional investment as well, one closely linked with a set of complex ethical judgements about meanings discovered through an analysis of the absent mother. Lear's rage is frightening, self-destructive, and finally catastrophic for everyone he has ever touched. For Kahn this feeling is expressed not only in Lear's often spectacular tantrums, but also in his persistent fantasies of mastery, possession, and vindictive triumph over his enemies (1986: 40ff). *Whenever I see rage like that I feel that I'm looking at something very old* (S.D.). The intuition here is that Lear's rage has no connection to his present circumstances, but is instead the present manifestation of archaic harm and injury experienced in a deeply buried past.

Even after they are re-united Lear sees Cordelia as a daughter but not as a separate self with her own needs and her own desires. He clings to the belief "that one good woman like Cordelia can triumph over or negate her evil counterparts, as well as the fantasy that a prison can be a nursery in which Cordelia has no independent being and exists solely for her father . . . " (Kahn 1986: 49). Kahn suggests, moreover, that his delusional outlook is incorrigible. Lear's wishful thinking – "we two will sing like birds in a cage" (5.3.9) – masks his acquiescence in Cordelia's imminent death at the hands of Edmund's grim officer. The king, we would say, is in denial about what's going to happen. What's most striking about Coppélia Kahn's interpretation is its steady refusal to seek out consolation for the emotional devastation expressed in the play's conclusions. This refusal to explain things away is grounded in Kahn's normative assessment of the story, her deep conviction that efforts to maintain patriarchal authority through deceit, bullying, and emotional blackmail is wrong, and somehow it should be resisted, in the fictional world as well as in the world in which the critic is living at the present time.

Feelings are often very prominent in our response to fictional occurrences, a fact that was very puzzling to Hamlet – "What's Hecuba to him or he to Hecuba that he should weep for her?" (*Hamlet*, 2.2.559) – and that still bothers various thinkers to this day. Why should I feel afraid of the dinosaurs in Jurassic Park if I do not have a belief that they can really harm me? One way to understand this apparent inconsistency is the suggestion that strong emotional reactions are correlated with strong evaluations, with deeply held beliefs about what's right and what's wrong (Dadlez 1987: 5). Our feelings about King Lear are implicated not because we have a belief that an old man has just lost his daughter but because we think that a person suffering the loss of a daughter in such circumstances would be impossible to console. Lear is responsible for all the bad things that happened, but even so no one deserves to feel the kind of pain he has experienced. Beliefs like this engage our views about very basic and even universal ethical concerns, which we can not hold dispassionately as pure ethical or ideological abstractions (Nussbaum 1993).

## Rude Cordelia

Many people can ride a bicycle without having any theoretical knowledge of the laws of physics or the principles of neurophysiology that explain why their actions are possible. And many people can read a difficult text like *King Lear* without having any theory to explain the complexity of reading and interpretation. For many such readers the question of "reading something into a text" simply doesn't come up. And if it does they're generally willing to defer to their professors when they tell them not to do it. But not always. *Well, you're always telling us we shouldn't read things into texts, but you never explain what you mean. We'll stop doing it once you tell us what it is and why it's wrong* (A.M.). "Reading things into a text" is a phrase that implies both a constraint on reading and a judgement about reading practices. But the underlying principles to which these constraints and judgements refer are not really clear. What constraints should the reader adopt? And to what aspects of reading should these constraints apply: extraction of the plot – or ascription of meaning – or evaluation of actions – or all of the above?

Historical scholars often suggest that we're not really reading Shakespeare unless we're reading him against the background of his own culture. This entails a constraint on the present, on background knowledge that readers use to understand stories and on ethical values that readers use to make judgements. It also involves a further constraint on emotions, on the immediacy of a reader's felt response. Historicism is a tacit insistence on impersonal and intellectually detached forms of reading and in this sense it can be both arbitrary and quite alienating. But why not just flip over the truism of historical scholarship and say that we're not really reading Shakespeare unless we're taking it personally? Presentism wants to lift the constraint on the present and to enable readers to use all of their available resources to help them understand what they're reading. And presentism encourages readers to take things more personally, and to recognize their own feelings as the point of departure for the exploration of a complex, emotionally demanding text like *King Lear*.

For several years I have been able to teach *King Lear*, *Macbeth*, and other plays in a graduate seminar on "Shakespeare and Moral Agency" and in a course on "Philosophical Approaches to English Studies," (English 317). Philosophers are often interested in literary texts for the way they pose complex ethical questions in concrete form (Cavell 1987; Nussbaum 1993). But in this orientation historical constraints are not only unnecessary, they are also undesirable. Because historicism is functionally equivalent to ethical relativism it makes important philosophical issues vanish. But these issues are often the same ones that most readers, including most students, actually struggle with when they read something like *King Lear*. The rest of this discussion incorporates my student's responses to *King Lear* that they have worked out in the framework of moral philosophy, ranging from Aristotle, Kant, and Nietzsche to Martha Nussbaum, Bernard Williams, and Alasdair McIntyre. The students I have worked with are "naïve" in the somewhat neutral sense of inexperienced. Since they are not familiar with the tradition of critical interpretation and commentary that trails along with *King Lear* for more sophisticated readers their responses may have considerable heuristic value. They experience the story unencumbered by historical background and they make some wild – or inspired guesses – about what's going on in the story. *Does King Lear have syphilis?* (G.L). Actually there is nothing in the text of *King Lear* that would explicitly rule this out. And there are actually some aspects of about this "naïve" suggestion that might help explain a few things, like references to burning and corruption, Lear's apparent disgust with his own sexuality and everyone else's, not to mention his dementia, a development that actually occurs in the late stages of the disease.

Working with naïve hunches and not-so-educated guesses works by acknowledging students' experience so that they are better able to discover sources of their own authority. From here it's not really so hard to move towards more complex articulation of their own pretheoretical insights by relating them to the philosophical traditions they're studying at the same time. But the real advantage of inexperience is not just that students don't have foreknowledge of the critical literature. They don't even know how the story is going to turn out and they can be genuinely shocked by what actually happens. So when Lear asks his daughter "which of you shall we say doth love us most?" (1.1.49) Goneril and Regan reply with somewhat over-rehearsed effusiveness, but in a way this doesn't seem so bad. Maybe they're "genuine phonies" who are used to the everyday currency of bogus and inflated expressions of sincerely felt if somewhat tepid affection for their father. *It's just the usual family bullshit, isn't it?* (A.M.) For anyone who's pretty much used to their own family bullshit the real shocker is not the egregious but evidently harmless phoniness of Goneril and Regan but rather the pointless bad manners exhibited by Cordelia when she says "nothing" to Lear's question to her: "What can you say to win a third more opulent than your sisters?" (1.1.72–73). *Cordelia is just plain rude (G.G.). She's just like my sucky little sister who always pouts when she doesn't get all the attention* (T.W.).

Exactly how and in what way can we describe Cordelia's rudeness? To be rude is to be unlearned, ignorant, unskilled, or without proper knowledge of how to behave. Cordelia's response to Lear is the more deliberate and intentional sense of rude as unmannerly, impolite, or deliberately discourteous. Roger Brown and Albert Gilman have analyzed the specific norms of polite discourse in *King Lear* in considerable detail. Lear's "question" on their account is in fact a direct request.

> "What can you say?" is only grammatically interrogative. As a speech act it is a directive or command having the exact sense of the subsequent imperative "Speak". The question asks about a felicity condition on speaking-so-as-to-win-a-more-opulent-third. Is there something that can be said and if so, what? In inquiring about a felicity condition, it becomes an indirect or polite request. To respond not to the request but to the literal meaning of the question with "Nothing, my lord" is shockingly rude. . . . Everyone reading or seeing the play feels the shock. The cause of the shock is Cordelia's choosing to speak as if she did not understand what every child understands about indirect requests.
>
> (Brown and Gilman 1989: 182)

Given the alternatives of shocking rudeness or purely conventional and empty forms of politeness it may seem that even the usual family bullshit might be preferable to Cordelia's disruptive and ultimately destructive efforts at candor. As a royal Princess Cordelia can certainly be expected to act in the way that "every child understands." But this way of looking at it may in fact be only partially right.

Speaking in more general terms about the "rationality" of politeness, Mark Kingwell wants to argue that our ways of communicating with each other involve much more than merely an exchange of information about our states of mind. " . . . it is also about not hurting other people's feelings, not having mine hurt, not saying all we could say, oiling the wheels of mundane social interaction, and strengthening the ties that bind us together" (1993: 401). What we say to others must be based not on the bare expression of the truth – not even the whole truth – but rather on the larger aims of maintaining trust and openness. But in this sense it seems that the standards of politeness have already been compromised when Lear asks "which of you shall we say doth love us most?"

Given the circumstances of the bidding it is hard to see how the real aims of politeness: tact, modesty, generosity can be satisfied, except perhaps by saying "nothing, my lord." And just as Cordelia seems to mis-read her father's question as a "polite" request, Lear seems unwilling to recognize her silence as a "polite" refusal to play his foolish and sinister game. It may be that real politeness is just incompatible with the family, since it appears that politeness is rational when it really respects boundaries and gives genuine consideration to what is being said. Lear extends the borders of his emotional needs in a way that invades the human dignity of his daughters and he forces them to defend those borders in ways that conflict with any notion of personal integrity. Cordelia's "shocking rudeness" might be construed rather differently then, not as a deliberately offensive affront to the norms of social behavior but as a desperate response to a "face-threatening" action on the part of her father. Unlike her sisters, she is unwilling to submit to emotional blackmail and so she rejects the alternative of continuing the usual family bullshit in favor of something she wants the king to understand as honesty. *She really loves him but she doesn't want to say so if it will look like she just wants to get more of his land* (E.T.).

Kingwell argues that reasonable and harmonious relations with others always depend on maintaining an otherwise precarious and unstable equilibrium. This possibility is always based on a competent grasp of "implication" where we are able to understand what is not said, what is not to be said (paradoxically perhaps) for the sake of maintaining openness and trust. The conventions of polite behavior are in one way tied to a basic linguistic competence in that they entail an intuitive grasp of what one can and ought to say even in novel situations. In this sense having good manners is not so different from using good grammar (Hampshire 1983: 126ff.) But these conventions are also tied in fundamental ways to questions about ethics, especially where the concern is with matters of love and friendship. Good manners are not merely customary and trivial formalities in social life; they have a genuine moral weight, even though or perhaps because they derive their justification only from local traditions, from the transient and peculiar idiosyncracy of a particular way of life.

Cordelia may wish to decline the available option of the usual family bullshit and say something simple and from the heart, but she appears to have an obligation to say something more generous than just nothing. Unfortunately her father's question is so weird that she can't think fast enough about what that something might be. But for readers who view her behavior as rude, obstinate, or unco-operative Cordelia is not trying to express true love by remaining silent – in any event when you pronounce the word nothing you're actually saying something out loud, which can not be construed as silence. Her behavior is not about silence as a way of expressing true love at all. It's really aimed at "showing up" her sisters and exposing their dishonesty. The rudeness doesn't come from being unschooled or maladroit; it has to be calculating and just as malicious in its way as the deceitfulness of Goneril and Regan.

If you happen to have a sucky little sister who always seems to act in a way that puts you in a bad light you might be inclined to think the worst of Cordelia. *She just wants to go off to France with her new husband and avoid the nuisance of taking care of her creepy old father* (A.K.). This is more or less what Harry Berger has suggested in his account of Cordelia's complicity (1997). When Cordelia says "nothing" in return for his offer of "a third more opulent than your sisters" her response might be rude, but even worse, it gives the game away by stating, somewhat obliquely, the actual facts of the situation. It's Lear who is actually offering nothing to his daughters in return for their devotion and care, including supplying room and board to a rather large entourage. They're faced with providing hospitality to an endless parade of house guests and in the meantime all that land has in fact been given to their husbands, who are themselves only trustees for a single beneficiary – the King himself. It's not easy to have kind thoughts about a father who expects to be thanked, praised, and loved unconditionally for doing something like that. Berger thinks Cordelia is fully aware of these considerations and that she acts with deliberate calculation.

> . . . what Cordelia's words imply is that by their bad treat-
> ment her sisters will bring him to uncover his faults and be
> exposed to shame. Whatever she consciously intends, her
> action commits Lear to his other daughters for the punish-
> ment he deserves. Cordelia will ultimately be vindicated by
> the effects of their punishment, without herself having any
> hand in it. They will do the bad things that will bring Lear to
> realize how he has mistreated and misprize the daughter who
> loved him most (p. 44).

So if the flattering sisters are monsters of ingratitude then perhaps
Cordelia is a monster of sincerity and inappropriate candor. In the end,
however, it doesn't really do her any good – she turns out to be as big a
fool as Lear himself. *Cordelia is a fool by virtue of her monstrosity. She is a monster,
from the verb montrer "to show" or "demonstrate" who martyrs herself for the abstract
"unpublish'd" virtues of love and honesty* (J.D.).

Manners are not trivial or merely cosmetic; because they reflect
agreed ways to get along with each other they have a genuine ethical
gravity (Hampshire 1983: 136–37). This is the way Lear sees it and he
doesn't take it lightly. But maybe he should have thought about putting
his own daughter in a position where the only way she can avoid dishon-
oring herself is through a tactless reply. At the same time it's not really
obvious that he should actually prefer the usual family bullshit, which is
never really as benign or innocuous as it might appear. Kind words, not
saying all that could be said, acting politely might be a way to maintain
peace in the family, but they might also be a way to nurture grievance
and conceal murderous intentions. If she's not actually in cahoots with
Lear's own murderous and self-destructive intentions, as Harry Berger
maintains, than it's possible her behavior is designed to protect him from
what her sisters might do. But it's also possible that it's not really about
Lear at all in the final analysis. Saying nothing is an expression of *rapport
à soi*, the relationship of the self to the self. "If I am not for myself then
who will be for me?" as Rabbi Hillel famously put it. This is a risky thing
to say in any circumstances, and even worse if you think about saying it
to a parent. *Saying I love you according to my bond to my Mom would not be a good
idea* (G.G.). But this is what Cordelia does in fact say, right after she says
her shocking nothing.

## Rational Cordelia

You might not have a sucky little sister. You might, as a matter of fact,
have two older sisters who like to bully you and never take you seri-

ously. *They are not evil or selfish, but they do know how to work around my father's irrational behavior. My father once threatened to not love me anymore because I spoke of moving out before I was married* (L.I.). What Cordelia actually says after she says "nothing" is "I love your majesty according to my bond, no more no less" (1.1.92–93). For some readers this is even worse than nothing. It looks like a rather frosty way of saying that love is directly proportional to some clearly specified list of obligations – "you have begot me, bred me, loved me. I return those duties back as are right fit" (1.1.96–97). *I don't want somebody to love me just because it's their duty and then they say, there I've loved you enough, you're not getting any more, go away* (K.C.). Bond is an important word in Shakespeare and it can mean a number of different things. A bond is something like a contract, a signed agreement between consenting parties. But a bond also refers to something that has nothing to do with agreeing and consenting, as in the bond between parents and their children. When a child is feeling particularly put upon by parental insistence on some form of obedience, one of the things often said is "I didn't ask to be born" as if family relationships could only be binding on the parties if there were prior agreement. In one way this is just flat wrong; no one asks to be born, but the obligations of family life, like manners, are not elective, not matters of discretionary choice. In another way, however, not asking to be born expresses some kind of deeper intuition that children, once they reach a certain age, are in fact separate selves whose wishes deserve respect and consideration. The former obligations based on helpless dependency have been superseded by *mutual* bonds based on reasonable balancing of first-personal needs and interests with second-personal concern and consideration.

Bond comes from the verb to bind, and the past participle of bind is bound, a word that refers both to obligation – what I am bound to do – and to boundary – where I stand as a separately embodied self in the sense of a limit, or bourne. A bond is also a pledge or a promise. "According to my bond" seems almost to imply an idea of contract, but in fact there is a condensation here of all the various senses of bond. Cordelia means that she loves her father in ways that are appropriate to the nature of her social role as a daughter. But she also means that "even though I didn't ask to be born, I have entered into an agreement with you and I intend to keep my promises." This is rather more than nothing – a lot more than nothing in fact – but it's definitely not everything. It's no more and it's no less. But there is a real question here about a rather different sense for bond, viz. anything with which one's body or limbs are bound in restraint of personal liberty; a shackle, chain, fetter, manacle. Cordelia will perform her obligations as she is bound to do as a loving and obedient daughter but she will not be bound as a slave. Her bond implies boundaries, separateness, limits on what can be asked and what can be given, even within the fore-ordained constraints of parents and their children.

What is the extent of Cordelia's obligation to her father? How much is "no more, no less"? What does the fifth commandment actually require? What are we saying when we say, "I didn't ask to be born"? Lawrence Becker refers to family obligations as "profound relationships," referring both to depth and to obscurity. His sense is that interactions within families are so frequent and so dense that it is not possible to "settle accounts" or to achieve balance in the give and take of everyday life. Our obligations are "incalculable" – so much is going on that we can never know everything that we have given and everything we have received (1990: 185 ff.) *I guess that means we just have to trust each other to do what we can* (L.T.). Ordinary reciprocity like "I did the dishes so you wash the car" is simply inadequate as a way to express love. "Love stands as an implicit rebuke to the business of reciprocating. That business is crass by comparison – simplistic, superficial, singleminded, overly concerned with obligations and with getting even" (1990: 186). Becker's general maxim of reciprocity is that "we ought to be disposed, as a matter of moral obligation, to return good in proportion to the good we receive and to make reparation for the harm we have done." He also suggests that we should resist evil, but that any true "resistance" should avoid retaliation.

Nurturing a child looks like what is called a "thankless task" because children do not have the resources to make good on everything they get from parents (Tyler 2002). There is an aspect of what's called "pure expenditure" built into the structure of this relationship; Lear's constant complaints about the "ingratitude" of his daughters might suggest that he doesn't actually understand what it really means to be a father. Some goods simply cannot be paid back; their movement is "a serial flow from each generation to its successors" (Cheal 1988: 59). Serial reciprocity is the way love and care that people have received from their parents is given to their own children. But the relationship of parent and child is not always about loving and caring.

> LEAR:   If she must teem
> Create her child of spleen, that it live
> And be a thwart disnatur'd torment to her.
>
> (1.4.281)

Instead of benefits, what is passed on is harm, injury, pain. *Well, maybe our parents really want to get even with us for all the unhappiness we cause them* (G.G.).

Cordelia's shocking behavior can be understood as a refusal or as an inability to act co-operatively with the members of her family in the presence of the King's entourage. But how is she supposed to co-operate with a demand that seems not only embarrassing but downright crazy? Stanley Cavell feels that no one should ever be asked to do what Cordelia has been asked to do. "Lear is torturing her, claiming her devotion, which she wants to give, but forcing her to help him ... to falsify it publicly" (1987: 63). *He wants to be a king without responsibility, a parent without love, a child / citizen without debt or guilt, and, in the final analysis, a man without death* (M.A.). No one can give a parent – or a child for that matter – any of these things. She won't "sell out" to her father by accepting a large "gift" that leaves her perpetually indebted. She will only "return ... what is right fit." In other words she is committed to maintaining her own bounds or psychological boundaries, her own separateness as a person from the emotionally needy and exploiting parent. She is acting in her own more deeply considered self-interest. *On pragmatic grounds there remains no basis for Cordelia's act. However, in expanding the notion of self-interest to include moral interest, a different conclusion may be reached* (K.G-S.). On this view a morally self-interested *rapport à soi* can appear just as reasonable as the most gracious and artful expressions of politeness.

Cordelia's actions look something like what Aristotle calls philautia, self-love – or self-friendship (Aristotle 1953: 273–76). We can also construe this as self-respect. Aristotle thought this disposition would be a virtue when it was genuine love for what is the most admirable part of a person, and for Aristotle this meant the faculty of Reason. Cordelia's responses to her father are not in the first instance governed by social norms of polite speech nor by considerations of reciprocity. Her first consideration is her own rationally considered best judgement; she is "a queen over her passions" (4.3.13–14). But it's not easy to get this right (Frankfurt 2006). She is refusing to abdicate her own dignity in the exploitive auction of her father. She follows the Kantian "maxim of the end in itself: So act as to treat humanity, whether in thine own person or in that of any other, in every case as an end withal, never as means only." *She will not allow her father to commit such an egregious moral offense. Of course, the tragic consequence of her refusal will be Lear's outrage, her banishment, and ultimately the death of nearly every character in the play* (J.M.). Even doing what is most rational from a moral point of view, viz. telling your parents the truth, doesn't get you beyond the usual family bullshit. As Stanley Cavell puts it, "Our actions have consequences which outrun our best, or worst, intentions" (1987: 81). Meditating on Cordelia's words gradually makes it appear that her good will is in some sense the moral equivalent of her complicity in her father's mad project of self-destruction. *The family is not an ethical space, it's about suffering, betrayed expectations, unpaid debts* (M.R.).

Lear was careless when he divided his kingdom and banished the only one of his children who really cared about him. His reckless disregard for what he really felt about Cordelia led to her death and the destruction of his kingdom. And when he dies there is no consolation for anything that has happened. *King Lear* doesn't quite end with Lear's death – there is a little bit more to say, though often the closing lines do not get much attention. Albany, one of the few characters to survive the devastation of this world, puts it this way.

> ALBANY: The weight of this sad time we must obey.
> Speak what we feel, not what we ought to say.
> The oldest have borne most. We that are young
> Shall never see so much, nor live so long.
>
> (5.3.324–27)

Students are young, and they speak what they feel because they don't know what they ought to say. Our feelings are uniquely our own and when we are dissociated from them our mental health can suffer, and our ability to be honest is compromised. The task of reading something like *King Lear* requires not only skilled engagement with a text but also discriminating engagement with our own feelings. That is really what I think "reading things into the text" actually means, but it also suggests why it's indispensable. *Maybe Cordelia didn't ask to be born, but then King Lear didn't ask to get old* (E.Z.). *Perhaps truth screams loudest when it says nothing. Perhaps moral will is not the authoritative father but is always the "naughty" little sister* (C.A.). *Whatever Cordelia is, she deserves forgiveness* (J.M.). *One must be prepared to crack, and to extract their own suffering from this fiction* (K.K.).

ENGLISH 317: 1999–2005
Collyn Ahart
Kristin Ames
Joseph Biestritsky
Kira Costanza
Joanna Donehower

Sharon Dwoskin
Benoît Faucher
Kerah Gordon-Solmon
Gabriel Gorman
Kaspar Hartmann
Margaret Healey-Varley
Linda Issa
Kristin Keerma
Anne-Marie Kendall
Alda Kravec
Griff Leach
Andrew McCarthy
Jonathan Meyers
Emily O'Keefe
Mathieu Remacle
Marie-Hélène Séguin
Johanna Staley
Laura Turner
Rosa Vasconcelos
Tiffany Wong
Erica Zelfand
Emmett Zeifman
Dov Ziegler

# 4

# Shakespeare, and belief, in the future

Linda Charnes

> Human beings seem to have a deep need to have sufficient reasons
> for what they do, and an equally deep aversion to situations in
> which reason gives no clear answer. They often need a belief – some
> belief or other – more than they need a correct belief.
>
> (Jon Elster, Political Psychology)

Several years ago, in his book *Shakespeare After Theory*, David Kastan called
for a renewed commitment to the past, arguing that those of us engaged
in literary analysis "must begin to respond to its significant challenges,
not by producing more theory but more facts" (Kastan 1999: 31).

Calling his approach "The New Boredom," Kastan announced that
we are in "a post-theoretical moment," and that "the great age of theory
is over" (1999: 31). If we do not turn our efforts toward reconstructing
Shakespeare in his own context, then we are betraying the past:

> If the alternative is to ignore the processes and practices by
> which the literary work is produced and read, we are left with
> an honorific and toothless formalism that offers . . . a
> profound lack of consequence for literary study.
>
> (Kastan 1999: 41)

Arguing that the only consequences "profound" enough to be on offer
are those that tell us more about how people in Shakespeare's day

produced, and read, texts, Kastan's claim begs much larger questions. Aside from its reductionist view of what constitutes "theory" and a reluctance to imagine new theoretical directions, Kastan's position exhibits a vague and limited notion of "consequence." It seems to me that the "consequences" of literary study are ultimately bound up with what we use it *to do*. What, if anything, do we "owe" to the texts of the past, and what exactly would the nature of that debt be? Should our obligation to the past outweigh our investment in the present, or in the future? How will we explain to new generations that a figure such as Shakespeare, for example, is still relevant in a world changing at an astonishing pace? How will we make our case if we devote ourselves solely to ever fine-tuning our estrangement from Shakespeare's era – if we neglect contemporary culture because we believe the past is only valuable on and in its own terms? In a nutshell, why do we fetishize our ability to imagine ourselves into Shakespeare's past, but feel so little responsibility for imagining ourselves into Shakespeare's future?

Every generation has its cultural and historical traumas; but in the current state of the world, not to mention higher education, it seems especially urgent that the work of literary study interface with the present in its immediacy. The historicist project of "reconstructing the Renaissance," as valuable as it was, may no longer be the most useful – or even, despite Kastan's assertions, the most ethical – way for us to engage as scholars. After two decades of "new historicist" hegemony, of privileging the material "realities" of the past, we have reached a turning point. What will it take to believe in the importance of Shakespeare in the future?

Before addressing this particular question, I would like to raise a larger and more fundamental one: what does it take to believe in the future, full stop? This may seem a strangely banal question – of course we believe in the future; after all (to paraphrase Polonius) the future will follow, as the night the day. But what must we have in our conceptual, social, political and emotional arsenals in order to imagine *particular* futures, and to believe that they are possible? As we go about our daily lives, we tend to think that the future will continue to look not unlike the present; without such thinking it would be difficult to plan, to strive, or even to proceed. In fact, however, we have no way of knowing what the future will look like. Perhaps now more than ever, we stand (whether American or European) as did the early American colonists, in the midst of nations taking on new and unrecognizable shapes.

The issue of temporality and what we mean when we talk about time is anything but straightforward. As physical creatures moving inexorably toward our own mortality, our experience of time convinces us that it moves in only one direction: forward. As cognitive and affective creatures, our experience of time is vastly more complicated. If psychoanalysis has taught us anything, it is that there are more directions to memory and affect than are dreamt of by our chronology. Only rarely do we "process" or complete a relationship to the past in a way that lets us say to ourselves, confidently, "that was then, and this is now." Despite this fact, certain scholarly disciplines, such as History, have built a methodological church on the porous rock of a biological experience, a church that comes no closer directly to representing "reality" than the dreamwork we undertake each night as we sleep. There is indeed a reason that "history repeats itself," and it is not just that if we fail to remember the past we are doomed to repeat it. We repeat it because human history is always unfolding in multiple directions simultaneously: futures appear before cultures are ready for them, and pasts have nasty ways of popping back up, especially when we think we have laid them to rest. The messy reality of human experience is that past, present, and future are tangled together in ways that will always complicate and even confound our best efforts to "always historicize."

Any effort to discern what Ernesto Laclau has called "the hidden truth behind any history"[1] demands that we acquire a resistance to what Kevis Goodman calls "the disturbing disease of historicity": a syndrome in which scholars remain locked in an imaginary relationship to the past in ways not unlike the affliction of nostalgia, which has more to do with how we want things to have been than with how they actually were.[2]

Historicity can take many forms. Depending upon which epistemology one chooses, history can be determined by a) human primate behavior; b) our relationship to sexuality; c) our entrance into language and the symbolic order; d) the exploitation of capital and the alienation of human labor; and e) "progressive" eras driven by the values of Western "enlightenment." We are all familiar with the theoretical underpinnings of items a)–e): from Margaret Mead and Levi-Strauss to Freud and Lacan, from Marx and Hegel to Weber and Foucault, these have been our primary modes of theorizing history. There is, however, another agent that plays a key role in how histories happen, one to which we have paid too little attention, and that agent is contingency, or chance.

Contingency plays a powerful role in how history unfolds, yet it is consistently undertheorized, denied a legitimate place at the epistemological table. Like the proverbial elephant in the room, we try not to think too much about "chance," since it challenges our belief in our own agency and more importantly, in our predictive authority. As psychoanalyst Adam Phillips argues, in order to acknowledge contingency, we would need to,

> Stop finding or being deities and . . . do something else together. [There is another] choice – which looks as though it's somewhere between belief in omnipotence and the abrogation of that belief – though I think it is something quite different. It is called acknowledgement of contingency. It can be called luck, fortune, accident, coincidence, and is sometimes experienced and described as a kind of non-intentional or random agency. There is actually nothing behind it making it happen – though we can personalize it by projection – and its presence, in and of itself, says nothing about our power. It neither diminishes nor enlarges us, but we can use it to do both.
>
> (Phillips 1994: 20)

Contingency must be taken seriously in any effort to theorize how history happens. As Phillips says, contingency neither diminishes nor enlarges us; yet how we react to it generates some of the most powerful determinants of how futures unfold. But how exactly are we to theorize contingency? How do we incorporate non-intentionality or *accident* into our views of individual and social agency? We cannot predict accidents (and by accidents I mean something quite different from those events that we could and should have predicted and did nothing to prepare for, such as the 9/11 attacks or the collapse of the New Orleans levees, or even the majority election of Hamas).

"History" is something that not only always might have turned out differently, but always still could. Its trajectory is not nearly as overdetermined as our methodologies would make it appear. As Phillips puts the question: "What is the cost of not considering chance to be worthy of determining our fate?"(1994: 20). It is intolerable to us that we should ever be at the mercy of chance. That our futures are ultimately arbitrated by contingency mortifies our western notions of agency and will. How would we prepare for such a future? Is it possible to negotiate with contingency in advance?

To do that we would have to be willing to entertain the possibility (in fact a likelihood) of multiple futures that cannot necessarily be "selected for" in advance. There is a difference between belief in *the* future and belief in *a* (particular) future. Contingency interferes with our personal futures to be sure: its weak effect creates obstacles, its strong effect creates emergencies. But emergencies, as the word implies, are opportunities as well as crises. It is precisely at the intersection where contingency collides with emergency, that the conditions for particular futures arise. What is done with those conditions, the ways in which they are managed or mismanaged, determines which particular future will ultimately coalesce into History. Contingency has a role to play in the production of consequence.

In the political sphere, contingency can be powerful enough to disrupt the normal functioning of entire nations. When emergency and contingency collide on a national level, we are thrown into what Giorgio Agamben calls "states of exception" (Agamben 2005). In a state of exception, the veils that normally cover over sovereign power are abruptly removed, and it stands before us starkly naked: as Edmund Burke has put it (albeit in a slightly different context), "all the pleasing illusions which made power gentle, and obedience liberal . . . all the decent drapery of life is to be rudely torn off" (Burke 1969: 171).

The "state of exception" is the strategy by which the Sovereign reserves for himself extrajuridical powers that are justified solely by the logic of "emergency." In the Roman Republic, Agamben tells us,

> Upon learning of a situation that endangered the Republic, the Senate would issue a [final decree of the Senate] by which it called upon the consuls . . . and, in some cases, the praetor and the tribunes of the people . . . to take whatever measures they considered necessary for the salvation of the state. At the base of this *senatus consultum* was a decree declaring a *tumultus* . . . an emergency situation in Rome resulting from a foreign war, insurrection, or civil war . . . which usually led to the proclamation of a *iustitium* . . . which literally means a "standstill" or suspension of the law.
>
> (2005: 41)

Machiavelli put it more bluntly in the *Discourses* when (sounding not unlike an early modern Alberto Gonzales defending illegal wiretapping) he talked about "breaking the order to save it" ("For in a republic where such a provision [for breaking the order] is lacking, one must either observe the orders and be ruined, or break them and not be ruined" (Agamben 2005: 46)). The problem it would seem is tautological: unless a republic has an explicit legal provision that permits the sovereign to break its order, breaking its order is illegal. Roman historians have always been uneasy about this, Agamben tells us, since for a republic to make such a provision is to build a toehold for tyranny in

advance. A state of exception, or suspension of normal legal procedures, affects the republic at every level, ethical as well as juridical.
Under *iustitium*, many aspects of life in the private, as well as public,
sphere are subjected to the legal "standstill."

Agamben differentiates between the Roman concept of *tumultus* and
that of *bellum*. *Bellum* refers to war with an external enemy, a state of military siege; *tumultus* (which is "related to tumor, which means 'swelling,
fermentation'") refers not to war *per se* but to its experienced effects over
time within domestic society, or the "homeland" so to speak (2005: 42).
Cicero claimed that "there can be war without tumult, but no tumult
without a war" (42). I suppose it depends on what kind of war one is
talking about. There can be such a thing as *tumultus* within the domestic
sphere even if a republic is not under catastrophic siege. But I suppose
it depends on what one means by siege. In certain circumstances, the ratio
of domestic *tumultus* relative to foreign attack can become severely imbal-
anced. The question always to be raised is, at what point should states
of exception be called for, and more importantly, at what point should
they be called off? Should a state of exception be allowed to continue
indefinitely once its original *causus belli* is no longer a genuine threat?

In a republic, when matters of military security are in direct conflict
with the normal and cherished values of civil society, a sovereign who
imposes an *iustitium* or a juridical "standstill" upon citizens must be
very careful, or he will overstep his bounds. Of course, it is these very
"bounds" that a state of exception is designed to overstep. But what
happens when the Sovereign figure leading the fight against an
external enemy is also himself the direct object/cause of domestic
*tumult* (more so than the external enemy)? Can the same figure be both
defender and destroyer of the state?

Lest anyone think I am talking about current American politics, let
us turn now to Shakespeare's *Othello*, a play that starkly foregrounds
the difference between calendar and affective time, exceptionality and
contingency, and the pitting of martial sovereignty against the interests of civil society.[3] "Civil society," a term invented by Scottish
Enlightenment writer Adam Ferguson, connotes the extra-legal "institutions" that occupy the wide ground between clan and state, tribe and
nation, regime and "regime-change." As historian Tom Nairn describes
it, "civil society" is

> the diffuse assemblage of anything and everything which can
> be located somewhere in between politics and state power on
> the one hand, and the family on the other.
>
> (Nairn 1997: 77)

In the context of *Othello*, this bears repeating: "the diffuse assemblage of anything and everything" that lies between state power on the one hand, and the family on the other. Civil society is clearly the turf on which most of our daily social, material, and interpersonal encounters occur. Civil society, in other words, is properly the domain of political psychology. "Nobody," says Nairn, "would deny the existence or significance of such institutions"; and yet,

> In what sense do they compose an overall or corporate entity meriting a title like "civil society"? In what sense are they self-standing or self-directing as distinct from control by Monarchs, politicians, policeman or administrators?
>
> (1997: 77)

The question at hand is this: can the unwritten codes and values of civil society form a "corporate entity" as capable of coercion as state power? And are there circumstances in which the values of civil society should outweigh the interests of sovereignty?

*Othello* begins with a domestic event that creates a major *tumultus* in Venice: we'll call it an unsanctioned state of exception. This event breaks with the institutions of civil society and probably even with the rule of law. I refer to the elopement of Othello and Desdemona, which, when revealed to Brabantio, the duke and senate at large, is perceived to have brazenly attacked the procedures through which marriage normally takes place – as an economic and social exchange between the bride's father and the prospective husband. In addition to thumbing its nose at the legal transfer of property, the marriage is also clearly a blow to the "values" of Venetian society, which would certainly have prohibited interracial marriage as "miscegenation," particularly among the upper classes. By any measure of Venetian, or Shakespearean culture, the elopement of Othello and Desdemona is an outrage.

Thus the play begins with what is experienced domestically as a small-scale insurrection, a "siege" from within the homeland – an isolated instance to be sure, but one which, if taken as precedent, could have potentially metastatic consequences. Before this domestic siege can be reckoned with, however, it is followed hard upon by news of another threat to the state – the Turkish fleet, which is advancing on Rhodes and Cyprus. Faced with the external threat of war ("the general enemy Ottoman"), the Duke imposes an *iustitium* – a "stand-still" or suspension of normal laws and values – in order to deal with what is seen by the Senate as a larger threat (although we have to wonder whether loss of the colony of Cyprus would ultimately be more damaging to Venice than interracial marriage and bi-racial children). A sanctioned state of exception immediately supersedes and occludes an unsanctioned one. Like citizens faced with the dilemma of what to fear the most (for example, a disputed election on the one hand, or a terrorist attack on the other), the Venetian council decides that infidel Turks on the move are the bigger threat to the republic.

This is an understandable position to take, were it not for one huge problem: while normal rule of law must be suspended in order to "close ranks" and secure the state from external threat, the very perpetrator of the domestic insurrection must now be deployed as the commander in chief – the General – of the Venetian army. State sovereignty trumps civil society, at least for the moment, and Othello morphs from "foul thief" to "Valiant Othello," from criminal trespasser to defender of the state. The racist superstructure of the play is more than matched by its political irony, by the fact that the perpetrator of the domestic "insurrection" and the "policeman" of state power are one and the same.

Prior to his marriage, Othello is an exotic element in Venetian society by virtue of being a black Moor; his exceptionality, however, had been accounted for in advance, that is to say, the strictly martial "use" of his body neutralizes the threat its blackness poses to his host culture. He was "oft invited," he tells us, to Brabantio's house, where he provided dinner entertainment with stories of his exotic past.[4] Locked into the "stocks" of what Lacan calls *extimacy* – a position in which one is trapped simultaneously inside and outside the social formation, Othello's difference is acceptable because it serves as a hedge against external threats to the nation. His *extimacy* secures, rather than destabilizes, social order. Once he takes it upon himself to marry a white Senator's daughter, however, without license either from her father or the state, Othello makes himself a different kind of exception. His end-run around Brabantio reveals that he knows, despite his performative disavowals, that he has committed a social crime. We are not given to know whether he has technically broken a law. But as is often the case, in states of exception ("wartime"), issues of legality are bracketed.

Othello knows that the state of emergency will protect him. When warned by Iago that Brabantio is coming after him, he declares:

> Let him do his spite.
> My services, which I have done the signiory,
> Shall out-tongue his complaints.

(2.2.18–20)[5]

Othello's "parts, title, and perfect soul" are all beside the point and he knows it; what matters is that he has done the state some service, will do more, and they know it. There is no evidence that Othello knew, before he eloped with Desdemona, that the Turkish fleet was advancing upon Cyprus; but he certainly may have. When Othello first appears before the council, the Duke says "Valiant Othello, we must straight employ you/Against the general enemy Ottoman" (1.3.50). The moment he hears this, Othello knows that he has won the domestic battle. Consequently he is able, with apparent confidence, to defend himself against Brabantio's vicious accusations of theft and witchcraft:

> That I have ta'en away this old man's daughter
> It is most true; true, I have married her.
> The very head and front of my offending
> Hath this extent, no more.
>
> (1.3.79–81)

The larger state of emergency permits Othello to act, disingenuously, as if his marriage to Desdemona were a non-event. By disavowing the fact that he has penetrated a citizen's home and "ta'en away this old man's daughter" without obtaining a warrant, Othello reveals his awareness that had he followed proper legal procedure, the Venetian FISA (Forbid Interracial Sexuality Act) would have denied him access.[6]

Because the "general enemy Ottoman" makes him an exception to the exception, Othello does not have to confront what he himself believes about his status in Venice. All he requires is that the future continue to unfold like the present. As long as the threat of Turkish terror exists, he can get away with his marriage because states of exception force bitter pills down citizens' throats; and matters of national security can be used to get away with anything, even a marriage that the Duke himself characterized as a "mischief" and a "theft."

In actuality, by eloping with Desdemona, Othello attempts to alter what Michel Foucault called the "biopolitics" of his life in Venice: the "inclusion of man's natural life in the mechanisms and calculations of power."[7] Othello proceeds as if it were possible to include his "natural life in the mechanisms and calculations of power," his life as a man among men. But there is already a biopolitics in Venice, and it is homogeneous and exclusive: similarly classed white bodies reproduce other white bodies, for a polis that is always understood to be white, hierarchical, and Christian. The inclusion of Othello's body as a "part" of the Venetian whole has hitherto been authorized by a kind of tempo-rary parking permit; when he attempts to "naturalize" himself as part of the body politic by marrying into it, he clearly parks his person in a place where it does not belong. In his explanation to Iago, Othello suggests that he married almost unwillingly:

> But that I love the gentle Desdemona
> I would not my unhoused free condition
> Put into circumscription and confine
> For the sea's worth.
>
> (1.2.24–28)

Editors usually gloss "unhoused free condition" as, loosely, "he has up until now lived and slept in tents" and is loath to give up the bachelor life. But to be unhoused and free is also to be homeless. It is not so easy being an "extravagant and wheeling stranger, of here, and everywhere" (1.1.134–35). Othello has, as he says, for nine moons wasted, submitted his person to the strict limits of Venetian biopolitics. Things are about to change. The question we must ask at the end of Act 1, then, is this: what kind of future does Othello imagine for himself, that he now attempts to deploy his body differently? More importantly, does he *believe* in the new future he imagines?

What Othello believes is crucial, for despite his disdain for Brabantio and his pretense that his marriage is "normal," he backpedals away from the new biopolitics he has implemented. Desdemona declares (in front of the entire assembly) her sexual passion for her husband,

> That I did love the Moor to live with him
> My downright violence and scorn of fortunes
> May trumpet to the world . . .
>
> (249–51)

Othello's response is rhetorically to castrate himself, reassuring the senators that he supports her request to accompany him to Cyprus

>     not
> To please the palate of my appetite,
> Nor to comply with heat, the young affects
> In me defunct, and proper satisfaction
> But to be free and bounteous to her mind.
> And heaven defend your good souls that you think

> I will your serious and great business scant
> When she is with me . . .
>
> (1.3.262–69)

Instead of telling the obviously horrified "signiory" to go defend their
own bloody colony, Othello professes a "prompt alacrity," an even
greater eagerness, to renew his body's lease to the state. In return, the
Duke grants him status as a "citizen," with all the rights and privileges
therein, but only if he leaves for Cyprus immediately:

> Be it as you shall privately determine,
> Either for her stay or going: th'affair cries haste
> and speed must answer it.
>
> (1.3.276–78)

In this instance, wartime emergency and its suspension of normal laws
are, paradoxically, what grants Othello a state-sanctioned recognition
of the validity of his marriage, of his rights as a man among men.
Under the provisions of the Duke's "Patriot Act," Othello has "rights"
he would surely have been denied in peacetime. It will take something
very unexpected to make Othello face the fact that he does not believe
in his right to these rights. Of course it is not always easy for any of us
to believe in our right to our rights.

What will determine the course of Othello's history is not Iago –
despite his malicious intentions – but rather, Contingency. The entire
Turkish fleet unexpectedly drowns in stormy seas en route to Cyprus,
thereby foreclosing the battle for which Othello and his troops have been
preparing. He has gone all the way to Cyprus, and the Ottoman WMDs
(weapons of maritime destruction) will not be there. Shakespeare's use
of contingency as the tipping point that facilitates what will follow is
fascinating, for it makes us wonder what would have happened had the
fleet not drowned, and had the battle not been pre-empted. Had the
Turkish fleet landed, Othello might have proven his indispensability to
the state in battle, or he might have been killed. Either outcome would
surely have secured a different future than the one that unfolds. By
depriving Othello of the opportunity to "earn" his Venetian bride in
battle, or to die trying, Shakespeare makes the "success" of this marriage
entirely dependent upon how the couple shall "privately determine"
themselves. If there is no immediate external threat to Venice, then by
what right does Othello trespass on the codes of Venetian civil society?

Contingency suddenly confronts both Othello and Desdemona with
the "truth" of their elopement, the truth of what they were "really"

doing, a truth that neither of them was prepared to face. As Ania Loomba has argued, instead of becoming an "honorary white" by marrying Desdemona, Othello finds himself wed to "an honorary black"[8]:

> Her name, that was as fresh
> As Dian's visage, is now begrimed and black
> As mine own face.
>
> (3.3.389–91)

After all, Desdemona has made an exception of herself by marrying him. With the abrupt cancellation of war, their biopolitics – the issue of what their bodies will mean and the meaning of what their bodies will issue – is now front and center. Although they are relocated on Cyprus, the island is a hothouse version of Venetian culture, one in which gossip, hypocrisy, lying, backbiting, social climbing and racism – everything, in other words, that lies between state power on the one hand and the family on the other – are even more amplified. In this environment, without a war to distract him, Othello seems overwhelmed by the fact that he has, as Roderigo would put it, "carried it thus." With his identity as defender of the state put on furlough, his other identity, the extravagant and wheeling stranger, needs only the tiniest whisper from Iago before his divided self returns to the state of externality from which it had temporarily escaped. Iago's machinations will all take place in the realm of civil society, that implacable "corporate entity" that no state of exception can ever entirely eliminate.

In 1916 Freud wrote an essay entitled "Those Wrecked by Success," in which he "intimates [that there is] nothing like success to show us that we are not quite who we think we are" (Phillips 1994: 48). Othello's "success" against the general enemy Ottoman is achieved by default; and now the future of a marriage that did not have to be "believed in" because it was built on the deferral that war provided has been delivered in advance of its participants' ability to cope withal. In Shakespearean England there is no place for interracial marriage, nor for the "profit's yet to come" (2.3.10). No matter how much a contemporary audience may believe in their "right" to their marriage, Shakespeare probably does not, and most importantly, Othello does not. Success shows Othello that he is not who he thinks he is.

The kinds of futures we believe in (as Adam Phillips has eloquently argued) tell us who we have been in the past, and which, and whose, version of the past we choose to privilege in believing ourselves into our futures. The version Othello chooses to retrieve and carry forward is not Desdemona's but Iago's, and Brabantio's, and the Duke's, a version in which he will always be, no matter how it is bracketed, an old black ram tupping a white ewe. Contingency is strong enough to drown the Turkish fleet, but not strong enough to alter how he sees and will be seen.

Shortly after his arrival on Cyprus, Othello orders a proclamation to be read to the general colony. The Herald announces:

> It is Othello's pleasure, our noble and valiant general,
> that, upon certain tidings now arrived, importing the
> mere perdition of the Turkish fleet, every man put
> himself into triumph: some to dance, some to make
> bonfires, each man to what sport and revels his
> addiction leads him. for besides these beneficial
> news, it is the celebration of his nuptials. So much
> was his pleasure should be proclaimed. All offices
> are open and there is full liberty, from this present
> hour of five till the bell hath told eleven.
>
> (2.2.1–10)

The reiteration of Othello's "pleasure" reminds us that he is not supposed to have any; and the declaration that "all offices are open and there is full liberty" announces that the state of emergency is officially over. Time, now released from its standstill, can be used for sports, revels, addictions, liberties; and, "for besides, it is the celebration of his nuptials." In its older sense, the word "celebration" means a solemn ceremony, a sacrament to be performed publically to honor as a holy day an occasion for public acclaim. But celebration is a banner that should only be hung when a mission has been truly accomplished. Trailing the proclamation like an afterthought, the announcement of his nuptials will not be cause for celebration, and Othello knows it. For in celebrations, and especially celebrations of weddings, the values of civil society – of everything that lies between state power on the one hand and the family on the other – are indisputably sovereign. And in Shakespeare's Venice they are indisputably racist. Those "values," briefly dammed by the levee of wartime, will come flooding back into Othello's life with a vengeance.

An averted external crisis reverts to an internal one; *iustitium* is cancelled but *tumultus* remains. To return now to where this essay began, it is possible to regard everything from Act Two forward as Shakespeare's extended meditation on Othello's inability (and unwilling-ness) to come up with a *new theory* about his life, one that would enable him to believe in a future that could look different than the past. This is, after all, the biggest challenge Othello faces: how to keep a crisis of interpretation from becoming a crisis of belief. By refusing to believe that his future is as important as his past, and perhaps more so, Othello is condemned to reparsing his history with increasing circularity and in oppressive detail. Things he would have preferred to forget are now foregrounded, most notably, Cassio and the role he played in the early courtship. Goaded by Iago into becoming a kind of historicist reader of the very texts he has hitherto spun for others, Othello treats Iago like a research assistant from Hell, charging him with the task of producing more "facts" about Desdemona and Cassio: "Villain, be sure thou prove my love a whore/Be sure of it" (3.3.362–63). Had Othello read more as a presentist and less as an historicist, Iago's preposterous anecdotes might have failed to persuade.[9] If Othello had believed more in his own formidable powers of reinvention and less in Iago's "facts," more in his ability to imagine himself and Desdemona as brave new warriors moving forward together, if he had been willing to produce a new theory of how to read his past differently, he might have been enlarged – rather than so drastically diminished – by contingency.

Although it is highly unlikely that Shakespeare found the idea of interracial marriage acceptable, it is nonetheless true that in his play, it is Othello, and not the state, who destroys his own future, and who destroys it by granting the past more epistemological authority than it deserves. Shakespeare understood (and this is why he was the greatest source of inspiration to Freud and Lacan) that nothing is more important than what we *do* with our histories; that getting them "right" is not as important as deploying them rightly; that choosing a version of the past is a necessary first step in any effort to move forward; but that whatever version of our past we choose, when contingency strikes – and it always does – we must be prepared to theorize it all over again, and with fresh eyes. When states of emergency are called off – and eventually they always are – citizens must believe in their right to their rights. Belief in the future requires it, and the New Boredom is simply not an option.

# Notes

This essay began as a talk that I delivered as a Ropes Lecture at the University of Cincinnati in February, 2006. I am deeply grateful to Jon Kamholz, Bill Godshalk, and the other faculty and graduate students who provided sharp and lively feedback.

1  Ernesto Laclau, quoted in Zizek 2000: 178.

2  I am indebted to Kevis Goodman for permission to borrow this phrase, which
   she used in a talk that she gave, at Indiana University in 2005, from her work
   in progress, entitled "Nostalgia, Or the History and Science of Motion[s]."
3  For a full discussion of what I call "affective time," see Charnes 2006: Chapter
   4 *passim*. But even calendar, or chronological, time is notoriously disjointed in
   the play, as Peter Stallybrass 1986, Ania Loomba 1992, Patricia Parker 1987,
   Joel Altman 1987, and Michael Neill 1989, among many others, have pointed
   out. Anyone who attempts to reconstruct the exact duration of time in the play
   finds herself at a loss, since the "history" of "what happens in *Othello*" is one in
   which the order of events fails to explain mechanisms of cause and effect.
4  For a rich discussion of a phenomenon she calls "eating the other," see bell
   hooks 1992. hooks describes the cannibalization/incorporation of exciting
   "dangerous" elements of black street culture by the white middle class.
5  All references to *Othello* are taken from *The Arden Shakespeare* ed. E.A.J.
   Honigmann, 2003.
6  FISA is the acronym for Foreign Intelligence Surveillance Act.
7  Foucault, cited in Giorgio Agamben (1998: 119).
8  See Ania Loomba's brilliant chapter on *Othello* (1992).
9  Patricia Parker 1987 has written brilliantly on the figure of *hysteron proteron*, as
   has Joel B. Altman 1987.

# Present text
## Editing *The Merchant of Venice*

### John Drakakis

## Theory vs. textual bibliography

Some twenty years ago, just after the publication of *Alternative Shakespeares*, I was interviewed for an academic post, and once the initial pleasantries had been dispensed with, I was asked by a member of the panel, who apologised in advance, the following 'hostile' question: 'Don't you think that, given your interests in Literary Theory and Textual Bibliography, you are in danger of becoming schizophrenic?' My response was immediate, accustomed as I was at that time to having to defend my interests in both these fields of study: 'May I answer in a hostile manner?' My interlocutor nodded his head in polite assent, but he was clearly not prepared for the directness of my response: 'What do you know about Textual Bibliography?' The panel giggled nervously. He did not reply, and I was not offered the post.

But my interlocutor's question haunted me for some time, since I had just completed a large project that involved Textual Bibliography, literary and social history, and Literary Theory. I was at a loss to understand how anybody with knowledge of any of these fields of study, particularly those of Literary Theory and Textual Bibliography, could think that they were, in some fundamental sense, incompatible with each other. The one activity concerned itself with the business of establishing texts, an activity that, by the mid-1980s had already begun to diverge from questions of original authorial intention, and to consider what has subsequently come to be called 'the materiality of the text'. Evidently, my interlocutor was firmly ensconced in the assumption that the role of the textual editor was to produce an 'ideal' version of the literary text; this would have been the text as it was assumed to have existed in the author's imagination before the intervening influence of printers, publishers, and, of course, readers. But also, one divorced from any of the complex social and historical conditions that may have shaped its composition and its subsequent reception. It was a version of textual composition that the film *Shakespeare in Love* (1998) subsequently promulgated. Here, in Stoppard's screenplay, the figure of Shakespeare (Joseph Fiennes) is shown to suffer from a 'writer's block' resulting from an absence of 'inspiration'. His 'creative juices' only begin to flow in the film when he encounters the alarmingly androgynous Viola de Lesseps (Gwyneth Paltrow); after a hazardous pursuit, and an even more hazardous consummation, which provides the blueprint, not for *Romeo and Ethel the Pirate's Daughter*, but for *Romeo and Juliet*, he sketches out the plan for *Twelfth Night*. Stoppard's script plays in a characteristically post-modern way with this 'romantic' notion of 'authorship', even as it panders to our fascination with the origins of these and other Shakespearean texts. The film however plays down its own origins in the 1941 novel by Brahms and Simon, *No Bed for Bacon*.

In contrast, theoretical enquiry apparently disrupts this smooth progression from the moment of inspiration to that of the emergence of the text, and its subsequent a-historic universality. With its allegedly self-enclosed preoccupation with the business of conceptualisation, 'theory' dismantles an assumed progress of textual production. In so doing – so the argument goes – it introduces a series of extraneous considerations, and qualifications into what ought to be the business of establishing an authoritative text whose meaning can be authenticated by tracing the words on the page back to the very moment of the author's inscription of 'ideas' and 'thoughts'. Whatever has taken place in academic debate since, this version of a romantic author is surprisingly resilient, no matter how complex the 'truths' inscribed in the literary text turn out to be.

Thankfully, within the field of Shakespeare Studies things have changed. Stephen Orgel has recently put the case in its most direct form in his insistence that 'When we make our editions of Shakespeare or any other dramatist, we are *not* "getting back to the author's original text." We know nothing', he says, 'about Shakespeare's original text' (Orgel 2002: 5). Orgel's concern is to establish the fundamental 'instability' of theatrical texts, which are, by their very nature, collaborative. In a short chapter that follows his brief investigation of 'What is a text?' Orgel goes on to ask 'What is an editor?' He castigates Charlton Hinman's photo-facsimile of the Shakespeare First Folio as 'an ideal Shakespeare folio' that did not exist, as opposed to the 'real' folio that Jaggard and Blount published in 1623 (Orgel 2002: 15). Indeed, Orgel insists that 'The text in flux, the text as process, was precisely what printing practice – whether for economic or philosophical reasons – preserved' (Orgel 2002: 15). And he goes on to expose the assumption that 'not only the meaning of the text, but the text itself is somehow independent of its material embodiment' (Orgel 2002: 16). Orgel's observations emanate both from his own editorial experience, but also from a much larger context, outlined by Jerome McGann in his book, *The Textual Condition* (1991). McGann wishes to dislodge what he takes to be the following 'illusion': that an edition should aim for an 'ideal' text, that is, in reality, an 'eclectic' text, 'that would work from a basic copy-text in which would be incorporated certain materials from texts other than the copy-text' (McGann 1991: 29). This illusion is sustained by the assumption that the copy-text will be closest to the text over which the writer has the most control. But this, McGann later argues, gives rise to a problem. 'If the eclectic edition is based on a printed version rather than an authorial manuscript version' then 'the result will be to move even further from that moment "when the artist was most in control" of his own work' (McGann 1991: 71). One other facet of the general illusion is that editors 'establish' texts that critics then go on to 'interpret', something that he wishes to contest with the counter-claim that 'All editing is an act of interpretation' (McGann 1991: 27).

McGann's general argument, that draws mainly on texts that have been generated during the last two centuries, derives much of its power from the insistence that a text inscribes within itself variants that may be actualised over time and in the process of reading:

> These variants and antitheses appear (and multiply) over time, as the hidden features of the textual media are developed and made explicit. They appear because even the most "informational" text comprises an interactive mechanism of communicative exchange. Various readers and audiences are hidden in our texts, and the traces of their multiple presence are scripted at the most material levels.
>
> (McGann 1991: 10)

Those 'material levels' comprise both linguistic elements – those with which we normally associate 'textuality' – and bibliographical elements such as page layouts, typefaces, and other para-textual phenomena normally regarded as peripheral to the generation of textual meaning. Taken together, these two elements constitute 'a laced network of linguistic and bibliographical codes' that constitute what McGann calls 'the textual condition' (McGann 1991: 13). Indeed, he goes on to argue that it is a feature of 'works of imaginative literature' that they 'foreground their materiality at the linguistic and the bibliographical levels alike' (McGann 1991: 14). It hardly needs to be added that the process becomes particularly intriguing when details that fall within one category exert influence on the other. I will offer some examples from the First Quarto of *The Merchant of Venice* (1600) shortly in an attempt to amplify some of McGann's claims. For the moment, I want simply to distinguish between the purely formal elements of McGann's argument, and some of the historical questions that it provokes.

## Past and present

A central question involves the nature of the interplay between, let us say, a text printed almost four and a half centuries ago, and for which no known manuscript source exists, and the academic protocols that seek to establish its authority, and the 'interpretation' of its 'meanings'. We have become fond of fudging this interplay, and of emphasising the *difference* between past and present; it is only through recognising this *difference* as somehow constitutive that we can come to an understanding of ourselves. The 'truth' of the past is recovered 'as an object of knowledge' as Catherine Belsey puts it (Belsey 1999: 5), which 'history' then translates into the present. Her elevation of the role of the reader and her championing of the practice of 'history at the level of the signifier' (Belsey 1999: 5) foregrounds writing itself. But writing, as Michel de Certeau observed, performs two functions as part of what he calls 'the historiographical operation': 'Writing speaks of the past only in order to inter it', but this act of 'taking the dead or the past back to a symbolic place is connected to the labour aimed at creating in the present a place (past or future) to be filled, a "something to be done"' (de Certeau 1988: 101). De Certeau concludes, 'Writing gathers together the products of this labour. In this way it liberates the present without having to name it. Thus it can be said that writing makes the dead so that the living can exist elsewhere.' He refines this process further with the suggestion that writing 'receives the dead that a social change has produced, so that the space opened up by this past can be marked, and so that it will still be possible to connect what appears with what disappears' (de Certeau 1988: 101).

This is, in part, presumably, what McGann means when he talks about the kind of dialogue that a text from the past engages in with a 'modern' reader: 'an interactive mechanism of communicative exchange' (McGann 1991: 10). In 1988 Stephen Greenblatt 'dreamed of speaking with the dead', but he came to realise that he had to hear, not one, but 'the many voices of the dead', and that if he wanted 'to hear the voice of the other, I had', he says, 'to hear my own voice' (Greenblatt 1988b: 20). In a similar vein, though a little more guarded, McGann argues that 'texts are produced and reproduced under specific social and institutional conditions, and hence that every text, including those that may appear to be purely private, is a social text' (McGann 1991: 21).

The entanglement between 'past' and 'present', between the actuality of a past and the manner in which we establish history as 'fact' and 'reality', is a complex one. Some ten years before Greenblatt, Hayden White dismissed as a 'dream' any 'historical discourse that would consist of nothing but factually accurate statements about a realm of events which were (or had been) observable in principle, the arrangement of which, in the order of their original occurrence, would permit them to figure forth their true meaning or significance' (White 1978: 123). We must be careful here not to decline the manner of establishing 'fact' as purely factitious. Indeed, the most cursory reading of a text such as Marx's *Eighteenth Brumaire of Louis Bonaparte* provides an insight into some of the ways in which cause and effect 'lose their distinguishing characteristics when they interact', when 'facts' – that 'congeries of contiguously related fragments', to use Hayden White's phrase – 'are put together to make a whole of a particular, not a general kind'. White likens this process of writing history to that of novelists who 'put together figments of their imaginations to display an ordered world, a cosmos, where only disorder and chaos might appear' (Marx 1973: 245). We may feel that in this account White has gone just a little too far. Perhaps Catherine Belsey's careful formulation does something to correct this position and to clarify it. She acknowledges that 'the present informs our account of the past', and that 'we make history *out of a relation, which is always a relation of difference between the present and the past*'. Belsey continues:

> Cultural history, as a relation between present and past,
> is neither a recovery of the past nor an affirmation of the
> present, but an acknowledgement of the gap that divides
> them from each other. . . . We produce, that is to say, a past
> which is both the consequence of our analysis and its motive.
>
> (Belsey 1999: 12)

Belsey's account of 'History at the level of the signifier' insists that documents from the past can be 'read' and that reading and interpretation will depend in part upon our 'familiarity with the signifying practices of their moment' even though we can never 'understand them as native speakers' (Belsey 1999: 13). It is this final caveat that causes the problem. Terence Hawkes, extending the thesis that he first promulgated in his earlier *Meaning By Shakespeare* (1992), lucidly insists that 'Facts do not speak for themselves. Nor do texts.' Hawkes is at pains to acknowledge that 'facts' and 'texts' exist, but, he goes on to say that 'they don't speak at all unless and until they are inserted into and perceived as part of specific discourses which impose their own shaping requirements and agendas.' And he concludes: 'We choose the facts. We choose the texts. We do the inserting. We do the perceiving. Facts and texts, that is to say, don't simply speak, don't merely mean. *We* speak, *we* mean, *by* them' (Hawkes 2002a: 3).

The 'presentism' that Hawkes advocates, and that is alluded to in accounts of cultural history that are familiar to students of Renaissance literature and drama, presents the editor of a text such as *The Merchant of Venice* with a series of dilemmas. On the one hand there exists the urge to excavate 'the specific social conditions' under which it was produced in 1600, which, of course, we cannot entirely separate from the act of interpretation. Also there is the imperative to observe those 'institutional conditions' under which it has subsequently been 'reproduced', including of course, the editor's own input into the process. Only in this way can an engagement with 'the dead' be something other than a naive invitation to take an imaginative leap into the past in order to reconstruct a specific 'history' that is then accorded the status of objective 'fact'. It is not simply a question of establishing, in some limited positivistic sense, the existence of a series of stable and invariant 'facts' that the editor fabricates as a precondition for the process of making the text mean. Indeed, it is now commonplace to regard as fantasy the wish to gain 'unmediated access to an author or to his or her era'. To fail to acknowledge this is, according to Leah Marcus, to risk getting 'caught up in a constricting hermeneutic knot by which the shaping hand of the editor is mistaken for the intent of the author, or for some lost, "perfect" version of the author's creation' (Marcus 1996: 3).

McGann's conclusion is that at the root of all texts is a radical and constitutive instability, or as he puts it, 'Variation . . . is the invariant rule of the textual condition' (McGann 1991: 185). This much is clear, but what is less clear is whether the way forward should be a full Derridean deconstruction of the process of editing – an activity that self-consciously reverses the editorial process, in order to examine its conditions of possibility – or a return to the facsimile edition, that – as in the case of the Norton facsimile of the Shakespeare First Folio – exacerbates rather than eradicates the problem. Perhaps one way forward might be to emphasise the distinction that Walter Benjamin makes between an historicism that 'gives an "eternal" image of the past' and a materialist historiography whose own thought and narrative flow is arrested when it confronts 'a configuration pregnant with tensions'. This is the activity, as Benjamin puts it memorably, that 'leaves it to others to be drained by the whore called "Once upon a time" in historicism's bordello' (Benjamin 1973: 264–65). As a general principle, we cannot divorce the present from the past, whether our primary interest in it might be, like Benjamin's, a recognition of the sign of 'a revolutionary chance in the fight for the oppressed past' (Benjamin 1973: 265), or in seeking to understand the relations of production between writer, theatre, printer, audience and reader as they change through time.

It is, perhaps, worth recalling that the face of Benjamin's 'Angel of history' is turned towards the past but that 'the storm blowing from paradise' gets caught in his wings 'with such violence that the angel can no longer close them. The storm irresistibly propels him into the future to which is back is turned.' 'This storm', Benjamin tells us, 'is what we call progress' (Benjamin 1973: 259–60).

## From principle to practice

Some of Shakespeare's plays are more obviously prone than others to disclose the radical instability that McGann identifies as a basic feature of 'the textual condition' insofar as they are what he calls 'the very events of time and of history itself' (McGann 1991: 186). The texts, like all texts, change over time as the social contexts within which they are interpreted change. Thus plays like *The Merchant of Venice*, or *The Taming of The Shrew*, occupy something of a special position in that the contexts in which they are read, or performed, exert an increased pressure that renders their radical variability more directly visible than might otherwise be the case. The Oxford editors of Shakespeare are reasonably certain that in *1 Henry IV*, performed around 1596, the character that we have come to know as Sir John Falstaff originally bore the name of the Protestant martyr, Sir John Oldcastle, but that this was changed as a result of pressure exerted by the Cobham family, 'one of whom – William Brooke, 7th Lord Cobham – was Elizabeth I's Lord Chamberlain from August 1596 till he died on 5 March 1597'

(Wells and Taylor 1986: 509). In the form in which Wells and Taylor resurrect this detail it is little more than a historical curiosity, a 'fact' that is partly empirically verifiable and partly the result of informed speculation that matters very little, except in a scholarly sense, to a modern audience or reader. We may, of course, interpolate the 'feelings' of a family towards the theatrical representation of one of its members, and this process may, indeed, involve our projecting a whole range of assumptions about the emotional lives of particular social groups. So even this 'fact' cannot be easily separated from our interpretation of its significance. But it is the whole *ethos* of a play like *The Taming of The Shrew* with its apparent justification of male violence towards women that jars with our current thinking, feeling and politics, that perplexes a modern audience. Are we to read Kate's final capitulation as ironic? Or has she been, as Michael Bogdanov's 1976 production of the play insisted, completely and violently crushed? Or, of course, can we read this as a masculine fantasy of control that bears little relation to any social reality? The play becomes more uncomfortable if we begin to investigate Petrucchio's behaviour as a form of sadism or Kate's as masochism, and more uncomfortable still, if we were to speculate in psychoanalytical terms upon the connection between the inflicting of pain and the generation of sexual excitement.

In *The Merchant of Venice*, which is by no means a difficult text bibliographically, there are a small number of examples that require the editor's judgement. The first is a simple one, and arises from an emendation proposed by Nicholas Rowe in 1709. At Act 2 scene 2 Morocco speculates on the gamble that he is about to take as he ponders the choice between the three caskets:

> But, alas the while,
> If Hercules and Lichas play at dice
> Which is the better man, the greater throw
> May turn by fortune from the weaker hand.
> So is Alcides beaten by his rage,
> And so may I, blind Fortune leading me,
> Miss that which one unworthier may attain,
> And die with grieving.

> (2.1.31–38)

The line in question is 'So is Alcides beaten by his rage', and this is the Q1 (1600) reading. That reading is sustained through Q2 (1619), Q3 (1637), and each of the four Folio texts from 1623 onwards. But in 1709, Nicholas Rowe emends the line to: 'So is *Alcides* beaten by his

Page', and this reading is sustained well into the twentieth century in Charles Pooler's Arden 1 edition (1916). J. Dover Wilson's Cambridge edition of 1926 substitutes the following, rather eccentric, 'So is Alcides beaten by his wag' (Dover Wilson 1926: 19). Johnson's edition of 1765 offers the following reason for the emendation:

> Let us look into the Poet's drift, and the History of the Persons mentioned in the Context. If *Hercules* (says he) and *Lichas* were to play at Dice for the Decision of their Superiority, *Lichas*, the weaker Man, might have the better Cast of the Two. But how then is *Alcides* beaten by his *rage*? The Poet means no more, than, if *Lichas* had the better Throw, so might *Hercules* himself be beaten by *Lichas*. And who was he, but a poor unfortunate Servant of *Hercules*, that unknowingly brought his Master the envenomed Shirt, dipt in the blood of the Centaur *Nessas*, and was thrown headlong into the Sea for his pains? The one circumstance of *Lichas's* Quality known, sufficiently ascertains the Emendation, I have substituted *page* instead of *rage*.
>
> (Johnson 1765: 404)

The logic of Johnson's elegant explanation is persuasive, although it depends upon a particular perception of social hierarchy through which the line is read, and it also rests on the disguised speculation that 'the Poet means no more than . . . '. Johnson identifies in the story of Hercules/Alcides and Lychas a social relation with which he is familiar, and which he assumes to be universal. But these lines yield a different meaning and a different emphasis: that if Hercules loses the wager, and also his self control, then he will succumb to 'rage' at the prospect of fortune favouring 'the weaker hand'. The 'fact' of Hercules being beaten by Lychas is, in this reading, subordinate to the effect it will have on Hercules' loss of self control. Thus, we may read Morocco's comparison as an inadvertent exposure of the volatility of his own temperament, and of a pride for whose fall his audience is being prepared.

The issue of self-control arises again later in the play, this time in connection with the character that I shall call for the moment 'Shylock'. At Act 4 scene 1, in the 'trial' scene, Shylock is asked why he persists in his suit against Antonio. He replies:

> Some men there are love not a gaping pig;
> Some that are mad if they behold a cat,

And others when the bagpipe sings i'th' nose
Cannot contain their urine: for affection,
Maistrice of passion, sways it to the mood
Of what it likes or loathes.

(4.1.46–51)

The phrase 'Maistrice of passion' appears in Q1 (1600) and in F2 (1632) as 'Maisters of passion', and in Q2 (1619) and Q3 (1637), and F3 (1663) as 'Masters of passion', a version that both Warburton (1747) and Steevens reverted to in 1778. But in 1709 Rowe emended the phrase to 'Masterless passion', and this was further emended to 'Master of passion' by Johnson (1765). In 1768 Capell emended the phrase to 'Mistress of passion', a reading followed by the majority of nineteenth-century editors and retained in the Wells–Taylor Oxford *Shakespeare*. More recently, M. M. Mahood's New Cambridge edition of the play proposed a further refinement: 'Masters oft passion' (Mahood 1987: 137). The difficulty arises out of the Q1 (1600) spelling 'Maister', usually a form of 'master', that occurs earlier at Act 2 scene 2 when the character that we have become used to referring to as Launcelot Gobbo uses the phrase 'this Iewe my Maister' (2.2.2); indeed the spelling 'maister' is used consistently throughout the play. Of course, we might conclude that the phrase 'Maisters of passion' contains a manifest error, and emend, as many editors have done to 'Master of passion'. Except that in the context of Q1, 'Maisters' is used as a synonym for 'Affection': 'Affection. / Maisters of passion swayes it to the moode.' Clearly the full stop after 'affection.' in QF is an error retained until Johnson (1765) who altered it to a semi-colon, and further emended by Steevens in 1778 to a comma. Of the most recent editors it is only Mahood who alters the sense of the phrase radically by transforming 'masters' from a noun into a verb: 'Masters oft passion.'

The immediate context does not allow us to produce a clear meaning for the phrase, but if we go to Shakespeare's Sonnet 20, we find the following lines:

A woman's face with nature's own hand painted
Hast thou, the master mistress of my passion;
A woman's gentle heart, by not acquainted
With shifting change, as is false women's fashion;
(ll.1–4)

(Duncan-Jones 1997: 20)

The poem makes great play of the opposition between the masculine capacity for control – 'A man in hue, all hues in his controlling' (l.7), and a feminine propensity for loss of control. It is this idiom that Shylock is invoking here, aligning himself with 'Affection' whose main characteristic is an unmanly, and by strong implication feminine, loss of control. As in the case of Morocco, so here, the character is made to disclose his own shortcomings as a way of preparing us for his eventual fate. Indeed, the intertwining of attributes that are both 'masculine' and 'feminine', along with a series of characteristics that identify both figures as 'other', encourages us to adopt a critical rather than a sympathetic stance. The archaic term for what in the play is an hermaphroditic figure is 'Maistrice', a term that although it *connotes* 'mastery' combines orally the words 'master' and 'mistress'. And it is this that, I suggest, the spelling 'Maisters' is designed to convey. Apart from Mahood, editions have oscillated between 'Master' and 'Mistress' in their emendation. What my suggestion attempts is to foreground the *difference* between a modern reading, much more attuned to the *sound* of the word when spoken on the stage, to the political nuance of the process of feminising the act of losing control, and to the Elizabethan commonplace of asserting the feminine nature of passion. It would, of course, be a very brave man, in the present day, who would insist that the act of losing control, of displaying passion, was a defining characteristic of the female of the species.

## What's in a name?

This is the bread-and-butter of editorial practice, of seeking to alter a text in order to produce meanings. That process, of course, embraces the speculation that in the case of these two examples, the manuscript behind the printed text contained the words 'Page' and 'Maisters' and that what was intended in the latter case was the word 'maistrice' spelt as 'Maisters'. But, of course, we do not have a manuscript of the play, and am I not therefore guilty of falling into the trap of speculating about authorial intention? The motivation for 'Maisters' could easily lie with the compositor who for reasons that we cannot fathom added a terminal 's' to the word 'Maister'. It is at this point that it becomes necessary to invoke a larger context as a means of advancing the argument. Hence the brief excavation of both a 'literary' and a social context, and the subsequent measurement of the historical distance between past and present usage. Looked at from the perspective of the present, then, a word like 'Maisters' is anachronistic, but the difficulty really arises when the editor is required to 'modernise' it. What gets lost is the word's function as part of a larger gender psychology to which we, ourselves, no longer subscribe. At this point our reading of the text is resistant on a number of levels. We acknowledge an outmoded psychology, but we also resist the ideological manoeuvring of two characters into subaltern positions in the text. We could extend this last point further to speculate on the possible significance of Salarino's insulting comment at 3.1.34–35, when he contrasts Shylock with his daughter: 'There is more difference between thy flesh and hers than between jet and ivory'. Were the parts of 'Shylock' and 'Morocco' doubled in Elizabethan performance, and if so, what would be the meaning *effect* produced by such a doubling? The only obstacle to that speculation is the speed with which the actor would have needed to change costumes between the end of Act 1 and the beginning of Act 2 (Dando and Hunt 1595).[1] In all of this we need to ask ourselves the following question: what constitutes a 'fact' here? And how separate might it be from the act of interpretation?

This process is complex enough, but in the case of the two following examples the issues involved become even more so. I referred earlier to two characters in the play, 'Shylock' and 'Gobbo', whose names we have come to accept without question as being integral, and in the case of Shylock, central, to *The Merchant of Venice*. Let us consider the case of 'Gobbo' first. The stage direction at Act 2 scene 2 in Q1 (1600) reads '*Enter the Clowne alone.*' We know, of course that the 'the clown' was a specialised role, played possibly in this case by the actor Will Kemp. It is Kemp whose name appears at 4.2.27 in the later play *Much Ado About Nothing*: '*Kemp*. A marvellous witty fellow, I assure you', and a little earlier as 'Andrew' (i.e. 'Merry Andrew'): '*Andrew*. Marry, that I am, and my partner.' (4.2.4). In the following line the character of Verges appears in Q1 (1600) as 'Cowly' – the Richard Cowley whose name appears with 'William Kempt' as part of Shakespeare's company in the First Folio of 1623. The inconsistency of speech-prefixes indicates that the source of the copy for both plays was Shakespeare's 'foul papers' (McEachern 2006: 128–29). If this is so, then it complicates considerably the question of authorial 'origin'. Here origin does not mean authorial imagination, but the dramatist's full awareness of the theatrical competence of particular members of the company. In the case of *Much Ado* we glimpse the actor behind the role, whose skills direct the dramatist's imagination. But there is a further complication in the case of 'the Clowne' in *The Merchant of Venice*. The initial speech-prefix in sig. C1<sup>r</sup> is '*Clowne*' but in the speech that follows the Clown refers to himself as '*Iobbe, Launcelet Iobbe*, good *Launcelet*, or good *Iobbe*' (2.2.3). The names 'Launcelet' and 'Iobbe' recur in this speech, and the speech-prefix varies throughout the scene between 'Clowne' and 'Launce' or 'Launcelet'. For the moment let us note the variations in the initial letter of 'Iobbe' and 'Jobbe', italic 'I' and italic 'J', and let us also note that these variations occur in the first signature of the outer forme of sheet C. In a quarto it would be normal to set signatures C1$^r$, C2$^v$, C3$^r$ and C4$^v$ (pages 1, 4, 5 and 8), which is the outer forme, and C1$^v$, C2$^r$, C3$^v$ and C4$^r$ (pages 2, 3, 6 and 7) which is the inner forme.

Two compositors were involved in setting the play into type and they both adopted similar strategies when faced with type shortages (Kennedy 1998: 191).[2] Already by the time compositor X came to set sheet C he was short of particular type sorts, especially roman capital 'I' types. In some of the pages of sheet B, set by compositor Y, there are shortages of capital 'I' and capital 'W' types. The shortage of roman capital 'I' types was solved by the substitution of italic capital 'I' types (a frequent compositorial strategy). It is the resulting shortage of italic 'I' types that is of interest to us in this case, and will also be of interest to us in another, more sensitive case that I shall come to shortly.

We observed that the Clown's name was '*Launcelet Iobbe*' or '*Jobbe*', where the surname is the Italianate form of the biblical 'Job'. On his initial appearance the Clown identifies himself as the son of Job. At sig. C1$^v$ we have the following stage direction: '*Enter old Gobbo with a basket.*' Sig. C1$^v$ (page 2) is in the inner forme of sheet C, and is likely to have been set into type *after* sig. C2$^v$ (page 4). On sig. C2$^v$ the speech prefix '*Gob.*' is the truncated spelling used, but two lines from the bottom of the page we have '*Gobbe*'. On sig. C3$^r$ (page 5) both versions '*Clowne*' and '*Lau(n)*' appear. On sigs. C1$^v$ and C2$^r$ (pages 2 and 3) the speech prefixes '*Launcelet*' and its abbreviations, and '*Gobbo*' appear.

I have drawn attention to this issue in some little detail, because it is quite clear from the type shortages in this quarto that there is something more at issue than a dramatist who is uncertain about the names of some of his characters. Elsewhere in the quarto, there are shortages of roman capitals that necessitate beginning verse lines with lower case letters, and there are various kinds of substitution made as an attempt to overcome type shortages. Moreover, we know that this is the case from other quartos that were printed in James Roberts' printing shop (Kennedy 1998: 177ff.). The names that have come down to us through editorial tradition are 'Lancelot Gobbo' and 'Old Gobbo'.[3]

I mentioned a moment ago that 'Iobbe' was the Italianate form of 'Job'; but it is not until F3 (1663) and F4 (1685), that the anglicised form 'Job' appears in the Clown's initial speech: 'The fiend is at mine elbow, and attempts me, saying to me, *Job, Launcelet Job*, good *Launcelet*, or good *Job*' (p. 167). Elsewhere the variations of nomenclature that we have already noticed in the first quarto re-appear. Up until now editors have not connected the shortages of type during the printing of this quarto with this particular variation. The forms 'Giobbe' and 'Iobbe' were interchangeable, and I want to argue that that is the case in *The Merchant of Venice*. For some time editors have assumed that the prefix 'Gobbo', meaning 'hunchback' in Italian, may have been a covert reference to the crook-backed Lord Cecil. But if the form is really 'Job' then we will need to think again about the significance of this brief underplot in a play that is preoccupied with fathers and with suffering. In this revised context, the name 'Launcelet', meaning 'a little lance' adds a further layer of meaning in its gesture towards one of the plagues that befell the biblical Job. The son (Lancelet) appears to relieve his ageing and 'sand-blind' father from the suffering that has been inflicted upon him. Those editors who have followed the trail of Gobbo, even to the Rialto of Venice and to the statue of 'Il Gobbo di Rialto', may, if I may be allowed to mix a metaphor, very well be barking up the wrong tree (Mahood 1987: 13–14).

In one sense, the recovery of the inscription of the Old Testament figure of 'Job' within the text of *The Merchant of Venice* constitutes a kind of Elizabethan 'presentism': a means of inscribing within a text from the past a contemporary relevance. What was 'present' to a culture steeped in the Bible, may be, for us, an historical curiosity whose new-found significance allows us to expand our understanding of the structure of the play, and also, to speculate further upon parts of its composition. But in view of our heightened awareness of the current clash of religious fundamentalisms, does not this apparent historical curiosity begin to assume a much sharper focus? To borrow de Certeau's formulation, the restoration of what has been obscured by editorial re-writing, allowed Elizabethan popular culture, *and* us to 'connect what appears with what disappears' (de Certeau 1988: 101) The Italianate 'Iobbe' almost literally, names 'the absent of the household' and inserts them 'into the language of the scriptural gallery' that is also 'equivalent to liberating the apartment for the living' (de Certeau 1989: 101). The text traces something more than a mere scriptural analogy. The compositor's mediation traces an enforced, and perhaps inadvertent, naturalisation of a comic 'Job' and his son 'Lancelet', while at the same time opening up a space for a complex reading, both from the perspective of an Elizabethan present, with its ambivalent attitude towards the republic of Venice, and our own differentially constructed and conflicted present.

The case of 'Shylock' is even more complicated. The variation of the speech-prefix '*Iew(e)*' and '*Shy(l)*' has long been recognised, but editors have always normalised it as 'Shylock'. As in the case of the Clown's reference to himself as '*Iobbe*' so in the case of 'Shylock', when he appears at sig. B2$^v$ (the outer forme of sheet B) the speech-prefix is '*Iew*'. Already in sigs. B2$^v$ and B3$^r$ there are signs of shortage of roman capital 'I' sorts, because a number of substitutions are made in the text of the dialogue. Compositor Y, who set the outer forme of sheet B, seems to have adjusted his practice by the time he came to set sig. B3$^r$; the catchword at the bottom of sig. B2$^v$ is '*Shylocke*', but the first word on sig. B3$^r$ is '*An*', since it is Antonio who speaks. It is conceivable that this minor error was the consequence of the compositor's dilemma about what to do with a speech-prefix that he could not set without depleting his supply of italic capital 'I' sorts further. And so he changed to the speech-prefix '*Shy*'. This was not sustained, and where the availability of type sorts permitted, in subsequent sheets the speech-prefix '*Iew(e)*' re-appears in the work of both compositors. Indeed, at Act 4 scene 1, in a short line, in sheet H, set by compositor Y, we find: '*Iew.* Shylocke is my name' (4.1.169), in which the speech-prefix and the character's name appear in close proximity to each other in the text, in exactly the same manner as that of '*Clowne*' and '*Launcelet Iobbe*' at the beginning of Act 2 scene 2. The conclusion that I draw from this bibliographical evidence is that *either* the speech-prefixes '*Shy(l)*' and '*Iew(e)*' were unstable in the manuscript from which the play was set, or, alternatively that the form '*Iew(e)*' was consistent but had to be changed because of the shortage of particular type sorts. In the case of one explanation the instability is attributed to Shakespeare, but in the other, which is more likely, it is caused by compositorial practice.

In some modern productions of the play, little distinction is made between Shylock and Antonio. Both are deeply embedded in the fiscal practices with which the play deals. Indeed, recently Stephen Orgel has confirmed that the name 'Shylock' was an English name (Orgel 2003: 144ff.), thereby exacerbating the tension between 'character' and 'role' that the speech-prefix '*Iewe*' foregrounds. Paradoxically, however, in this play the Jew is a figure from the past, the resurrection of a medieval stereotype, whose own usurious practice addresses the Elizabethan present, and the future that has become our capitalist present. In this sense the Jew figures Benjamin's 'angel of history' that looks backwards into the future (Cohen 1985: 195ff.; Drakakis 2000: 112). But in this particular case, it is much more than a question of recovering an historical curiosity, since we cannot separate the figure of the Jew in Shakespeare's play from its subsequent history of anti-Semitism. When, in his book, *Shakespeare among the Moderns*, Richard Halpern proposes to read this play 'through the lens of modernism' (Halpern 1997: 163), then the implication is that that lens risks the danger of distortion. But what that lens of modernism does is to bring into focus a history of systematic exclusion, and a discourse of intolerance, culminating in holocaust. To reinstate the speech-prefix '*Iewe*' (in its modern version as 'Jew') as part of the experience of reading the text of *The Merchant of Venice* is to foreground a process of self-alienation that we can read into the play, where our reading is itself over-determined, in large part both by what Shakespeare may have written, but also by a knowledge that we ourselves bring to the text. Indeed, the case of '*Iew(e)/Shy(l)*' is a kind of limit case, the locus of the interaction between the 'words' of the dramatist, the practice of the compositor, and the meanings we generate from them.

The figure of Shylock, an 'English' Jew, a fantasy figure for an Elizabethan audience whose experience of 'Jews' was, as far as we can tell, wholly dependent upon religious prejudice and theatrical representation, fulfils the function of an 'empty signifier' that has been subsequently invested with historical and cultural meaning. Those who seek to argue that Shakespeare's 'Jew' is an authentic representation of a 'real' Jew, are in danger, in this case, of collapsing 'art' into 'life'. A recognition of the distinction by no means ameliorates the discomfort that Shakespeare's play generates. Indeed, to foreground the conditions of the text's production, is, in effect, to expose the fabric of a prejudice whose structure can become the very means whereby past and present are critically re-connected, while at the same time acknowledging an epistemology through whose aegis these connections are made. Indeed, if literary texts, especially those of the distant past, are to have any current social value at all beyond that of the antiquarian 'veneration of monuments' (Jay 1996: 278), then we need to take very seriously the *dialectic* relation between the two, a dialectic that cannot simply be reduced to 'dialogue' (R. H. Wells 2000: 37–38). That is to say, we need to acknowledge what Merleau-Ponty in another context describes as 'the double relationship of continuity and discontinuity between the present and the past' (Merleau-Ponty 1973: 92). By excavating, however speculatively, the fissures in the text of Shakespeare's *The Merchant of Venice*, we bring to critical consciousness a relation between structures and forces, matter and the representational frameworks within which it is mediated, that enables us to identify possibilities of which the text itself could not possibly be aware.

## Notes

1  There are further similarities between these two dramatic characters. Morocco's name is that of a horse that was a phenomenon in London in 1595, and there are numerous references to Shylock's animalistic propensities. See John Dando and Harry Hunt, *Maroccus Extaticus or Bankes Bay Horse in a Trance*, (London, 1595).

2  See Kennedy 1998: 191ff. Compositor X set the title page (A1), sheets C, E, G, I, and sigs K1ᵛ-K2; compositor Y set sheets A, B, D F and H. (p. 191).

3  Capell (1768) prints the speech-prefix 'Clown' throughout, and the Folger Shakespeare edition (1992) of the play prints 'Lancelet' throughout. Both accept 'Gobbo'.

# 6

# Action! *Henry V*

Ewan Fernie

> . . . we players are privileged,
> Tis our audience must fight in the field for us,
> And we upon the stage for them.
>
> John Marston, *Histrio-Mastix*

Marston wrote these lines circa 1599: about the same time Shakespeare wrote *Henry V*. Though they were trained fighters, actors weren't then allowed to bear arms. Thus 'our audience must fight in the field for us' is a flat, factual observation; but what follows modifies and vitalises it, setting up a complex reciprocity between 'realworld' fighting and fighting onstage. It challenges any 'educated' aesthetic distance from plays like *Henry V*, sucking the audience into strangely beholding identification with the terrible action portrayed. But how should we respond to Shakespeare's dramatisation of fierce agency at our own violent historical juncture? What does the presence of *Henry V* in the present mean for us?

After 1980s deconstruction, presence has been avoided as a suspect category that helps secure conventional wisdom and the present social order. But we need a new concept of presence if we are to appreciate the immediacy and power of Shakespeare. I conceive the notion of presence, after deconstruction, in terms of difference rather than essence. Simultaneously with becoming suddenly, overwhelmingly present, a play of Shakespeare's, like another person, becomes intellectually engaging and *mysterious*. Presence actually never becomes knowledge, however close we come. Instead it is experienced as the powerful imminence of sense – ineffably beyond thought, which it nonetheless irresistibly solicits. This is the sort of challenging presence I want to put into presentism. Presentism mustn't merely cater to and confirm present values. But any really responsive engagement with Shakespeare's inimitable and even alien presence in the present will in fact creatively confront, unsettle and transcend routine modes of thinking[1] – as I hope the following reading of *Henry V* will demonstrate.

How to characterise Shakespeare's presence? What does Shakespeare bring into the present? What is his mode of being present? Kenneth Gross has written suggestively of the 'wounding presence' of the actor (Gross 2001: 197), but the actor is only part of a play. What's a play, then? What's its mode of being present? A play's an action: so far, so good, but a number of difficulties arise. A play's *medium* is action, and in the fullest, most physical sense: the action of playing on the stage. But its *subject* is also action: the action such acting portrays – which, in a further complication, ultimately refers back to the historical action of Agincourt in the case of *Henry V*. The interplay between representing and represented action is subtle and changing: acting always conditions the action it represents but sometimes the actor's eyes burn through his role and, as Terence Hawkes suggests, 'the play's own continuity breaks down and it seems suddenly to leap out at us' (Hawkes 2002a: 137). At such points, Shakespeare is 'far more concerned to interact with the material reality of the spectator's world than to impersonate a different "reality" on stage' (ibid.: 111). One example of this we'll consider below is when Hal suddenly, shockingly says 'I know you all' to the audience (*1 Henry IV*, 1.2.190). In moments like this, the medium becomes the message: acting becomes action absolutely and in its own right. Shakespeare is no storyteller, indirectly present to his audience via the mediation of theatre. Theatre is suddenly the very substance of his presence.[2]

But if action is, in this absorbingly complex fashion, Shakespeare's way into the present, another question crops up: what happens to dramatic action under the nib of the playwright with the peerless talent for words? Action in the theatre obviously encompasses speech-acts. Hamlet opposes words to deeds but to imagine his acts stripped of words is to realise it's speech which makes the difference: that Hamlet comes alive only in language; or perhaps that his action is preconditioned, counterpointed, filled out by speech, that it makes itself present in that dissimilar element. In Shakespeare, the relation between words and deeds is often switched, as the actor's text shears off from or exceeds dramatic action proper only to make itself felt as a more delicate, definite and effective form of action in its own right. But what's the relation between words and deeds when action is narrated or recounted on stage? And Shakespeare's specifically a *verse* dramatist. How does dramatic action relate to poetry? How does the dynamism of action relate to the epitomising stillness of the poetic image? As we shall see, the Chorus in *Henry V* worries over exactly these questions. It is also anxiously concerned with the kind of presence *Henry V* is able to achieve in relation to the real historical action of Agincourt.

After twenty-five years of new historicism, criticism is beginning to feel and think about Shakespeare's presence. If action is, at this or any other time, Shakespeare's gratifyingly palpable mode of being present, it should clearly be a central theme of any presentist critical practice. And if presentism also proceeds from the recognition that criticism acts primarily in and on the present, action should perhaps be *the* presentist topic. There are two further reasons why a presentist consideration of action seems especially necessary today. The first is the widespread presumption of disability in recent theory and criticism. At their grimmest, the 'masters of suspicion' unfold a frightening vision of a ghastly, pervasive 'agentless' agency that works through the figment of individuality: human agents becomes puppets of the unconscious, of ideology, of power, of *différance*.[3] Shakespeare critics, from Stephen Greenblatt onwards, have struggled to grab back some furtive creativity.[4] And Anthony Giddens reacts more fiercely against what he calls the '*derogation of the lay actor*' in contemporary thought (Giddens 1979: 71, 57, 56). Not all great theorists diminish or deny the power of the lay actor, of course: as if in anticipation of our agency-aversive phase, Jacques Lacan once wrote, 'Why on the threshold of the modern period would *Hamlet* bear witness to the special weakness of future man as far as action is concerned? I am not so gloomy, and nothing apart from a cliché of decadent thought requires that we should be' (Lacan 1999: 251). As I have suggested elsewhere, *Hamlet* has a special centrality in considerations of action. In the vivid present of its own event, Shakespeare's play epitomises a metaphysics of rashness – an absolute now – wherein everything is gathered and staked upon a deed. Moreover, because this is not performed in the name of the father but inspired by a god of 'rashness' (*Hamlet*, 5.2.7) – 'a divinity that shapes our ends' (5.2.10) – Hamlet's act transcends revenge in favour of justice.[5]

And yet – the other urgent reason for presentist work on action are the horrors of terrorism and the 'War on Terror'. These cast extreme action in a more appalling light, and might very well cause us to recoil into an ethically fastidious denial of our present power to act. Given our recent experience of acts of terror and invasion, surely we should repudiate rash and extreme action? But the degree of obscure justice Hamlet achieves is not its only positive fruit in Shakespeare. Rashness leads Tybalt and Mercutio into death, but it equally generates the doomed but utopian love of Romeo and Juliet. Above all, Shakespeare's plays themselves, indeed all works of art, can be described as the fruits of 'rashness without physical violence' as 'unprecedented, incalculable acts, a crazy wager on the future, and one which actually pays off, bringing something into being that is truly new and valuable' (Fernie 2005a: 183). Perhaps now especially we need to act. Not just to prevent more terror, but also positively: to build stronger, more objective international institutions and – let it be said – a fairer world. And yet, it would be intellectually and ethically dishonest and evasive to treat extreme action as a purely ethical phenomenon. As every thriller, action flick or shoot-'em-up computer game bears out, it is also aesthetically and existentially *exciting*.

At which point let's return to *Henry V*. Olivier's 1944 film of the play famously recognised its potential to inspire and encourage extreme action. But, in our present, *Henry V* has been used to promote the 'War on Terror'. 'As Bush stood atop part of the rubble of the World Trade Center', wrote the Editor of *The National Review*, 'he came as close as he ever will to delivering a St. Crispin's Day speech' (Lowry 2001). Peter Robinson, a Research Fellow at the Hoover Institution, declared in the same place, 'Since the events of September the 11th, [Bush] has undergone a transformation as dramatic as anything in Shakespeare. Gravity, moral seriousness, stature, authority – all have descended upon him like a mantle. Prince Hal has become Henry V' (Robinson 2001). When hostilities against Afghanistan had commenced, David Gergen of Kansas State University opined, 'Now to be sure, he has not won his Agincourt, but he has set sail, and for that the country can be grateful' (Gergen 2001). By the time America and Britain were at war with Iraq, Mackubin Owens, Professor of Strategy and Force Planning at the American Naval War College, was quoting Henry's notorious Harfleur speech with approval. He proceeded, exhibiting wider reading, to offer '[a] modest proposal: if Saddam expects his people to die on his behalf, perhaps we should let them know exactly what this entails. This speech should be printed in Arabic on leaflets and dropped on Baghdad, Basra, and especially Tikrit' (Owens 2002). Moreover, when in March 2003 Lieutenant Colonel Tim Collins of the British Army addressed his troops at Fort Blair Myne, a Kuwaiti desert camp near the Iraqi border, his speech, like Bush's after 9/11, was compared to Henry's rallying cry before Agincourt.[6] During the Second World War, the US issued the Armed Forces Editions of Shakespeare. They went out of print in 1947. But the series was revived in 2002. Surprise, surprise: *Henry V* was one of four plays published first.[7]

All this makes Shakespeare's presence in the present disturbingly vivid and important. *Henry V* dramatises a great heroic victory, but what does it mean to pack an Armed Services Edition of the play in your kit bag? What exactly are Olivier and the supporters of Bush and Blair identifying with or unleashing when they exploit the play's motivational force? What is the professional Shakespeare criticism of recent years failing to confront when it holds the play in sceptical regard?[8] What does *Henry V* really tell us about action? This essay attempts to find out.

## Will in the world

Action begins in intention, and it is carried towards execution and any projected end by will power.[9] As in *Hamlet*, in the second Henriad the fulfilment of intention in action is long withheld. This establishes an interim in which, as Hugh Grady has shown, character liberated from the singularity of action richly flourishes: in Hamlet's life of thought, in his 'antic disposition' (*Hamlet*, 1.5.180);[10] in Hal's wild days and nights with Falstaff.[11] But from the first Shakespeare lends Hal an inexorable will which is bent and tested but never broken, and which is his path to a different mode of being-in-action that culminates at Agincourt.[12]

One problem with this dramatisation of a will that is consummated in action is its exclusionary masculine character. As Jean Howard and Phyllis Rackin observe, women are rigorously removed from the second tetralogy.[13] That said, as we shall see, the end of the play involves a belated solicitation of female agency, one which intimates the possibility of a new relationship between the sexes and perhaps even opens the way for a reshaping of the social order as such. Meanwhile we are treated to an extended, intensive dramatic enquiry into specifically masculine agency. Hamlet's problem of establishing his own identity in action within the scope of the will of his father is shared by Hal. Hal tells us he disappointed his father's hopes at first only in order to fulfil them all the more startlingly and completely. But it seems likely, too, that he defies his father in order to stress it is he, Hal, who subsequently chooses a royal career he makes sure spectacularly exceeds Henry IV's. He is not a puppet or creature of the King's; he has accommodated his own *free* will to his father's. And whereas Hamlet fulfils the paternal mandate in so strange a way as to reclaim his action as utterly his own, Hal provocatively exceeds his dad's desire, accomplishing more than Henry IV ever dreamed of. Hotspur is the kind of son Henry has coveted, remember (*1 Henry IV*, 1.1.77 ff.): Hal leaves *him* sprawling in Salisbury, and soars towards Agincourt.

The second Henriad as a whole dramatises a progressive victory and consummation of will. Richard II is weak of will. As a young man, Bolingbroke is possessed and driven by a will he is strangely unable to own: he doesn't come to decisions, doesn't even declare intentions. When, at the end of *Richard II*, he (now Henry IV) protests to Exton that he didn't intend the slaying of Richard, perhaps we should believe him to the extent that he doesn't really intend anything. He is a perfect willing machine, bypassing the impediments of decision-making or justification. It's increasingly clear to everyone but him that he'll take Richard's crown; he knows what he's doing only in the doing or after. He is like the Macbeth who says, 'The very firstlings of my heart shall be / The firstlings of my hand' (*Macbeth*, 4.1.47–48). One of his utterances suggests an identification with action bereft or purified of expressible content: 'This arm shall do it or this life be spent' (*Richard II*, 1.1.108).

But whereas Richard is too self-preoccupied, Bolingbroke isn't self-conscious enough to be fully or convincingly human. As also is the case with Coriolanus and, for that matter, Hollywood action heroes, he exemplifies the creaking bareness of mere action. Hamlet's 'rashness' (*Hamlet*, 5.2.7) is related to but also represents a significant development of Bolingbroke's. For Hamlet, action minus intention plays host to something beyond the individual and social human sphere. There is no such metaphysics in *Richard II*. Here, by contrast, metaphysics is associated with Richard's suffering. In the *Henry IV* plays, Henry is obliged to cope with the messy consequences of having been the unforeseeing Bolingbroke. If Bolingbroke is a hyperbolical and bathetic agent, Henry IV is more of a patient, tossed about in the wake of the actions of a man scarcely recognisable as his own former self.

This is the context in which Hal seizes a will as powerful as his father's: indeed, the quantity of Bolingbroke's active will remaining to Henry IV expresses itself primarily as yearning desire that his son make good on his own compromised kingship. But Hal possesses and inhabits his will in a way that Bolingbroke never does. He finds his way into its centre. He not only discards his father's will before deliberately taking it up as his; he also pits his will against its opposite by plunging himself, body and soul, into the adverse environment of Eastcheap. This is his most revealing and famous soliloquy:

I know you all, and will awhile uphold
The unyok'd humour of your idleness.
Yet herein will I imitate the sun,
Who doth permit the base contagious clouds
To smother up his beauty from the world,
That, when he please again to be himself,
Being wanted he may be more wonder'd at
By breaking through the foul and ugly mists
Of vapours that did seem to strangle him.
If all the year were playing holidays,
To sport would be as tedious as to work;
But when they seldom come, they wish'd-for come,
And nothing pleaseth but rare accidents.
So when this loose behaviour I throw off
And pay the debt I never promised,
By how much better than my word I am,
By so much shall I falsify men's hopes;
And like bright metal on a sullen ground,
My reformation, glitt'ring over my fault,
Shall show more goodly and attract more eyes
Than that which hath no foil to set it off.
I'll so offend to make offence a skill,
Redeeming time when men least think I will.

(*1 Henry IV*, 1.2.190–212)

'I know you all': as I've already suggested, it's a speech that encompasses the audience in the theatre more immediately than it does the denizens of Eastcheap, who aren't – after all – onstage. And it's a prime example of Shakespeare's concern 'to interact with the material reality of the spectator's world' (Hawkes 2002a: 111). But what exactly is Shakespeare, via Hal, doing here? Most immediately, he's abusing his audience: Hal's preternatural, contemptuous perspicacity slashes through *our* indulgent, theatregoing idleness like the flashing sword he ends with. But this abuse has its point: Hal's life will be a spectacular demonstration to us of the kind of will power which absolutely contrasts with our own aesthetic leisure. The entire kingdom of his future subjects will be a more ideal audience but Hal undresses his will most candidly to us, and he demonstrates to us that his will is even more powerful than they'll know. Because – if he's to be believed here – Hal will not have to overthrow idleness at all. Even though he's completely immersed himself in it, idleness will just make his will more 'glitt'ring': 'like bright metal on sullen ground'.

This seems to flout our specifically twenty-first-century presuppositions. For such nonchalantly incorruptible, absolute will is a scandalous
affront to the prevailing view that human identity is thoroughly historically and culturally determined. Apparently it doesn't occur to the
Prince that what he calls 'this loose behaviour' might change him, that
accustomed idleness with Falstaff might bend him out of shape, might
relax and weaken him a bit, let alone fatally.

It's true that certain ironies cast doubt on the untinctured purity of
will to which Hal pretends here. The sun doesn't, save by pathetic
fallacy, permit its face to be covered by clouds and then burst gloriously
forth. But nor does this slightly mismatched comparison intimate that
Hal is less in control than he says. For the difference between the sun's
behaviour and Hal's action once again isolates and sets off the distinc-
tively human power of will 'like bright metal on a sullen ground'. Hal
proposes his deliberately disappointing casualness will make the majes-
tical king he shall be all the more wonderful, winning over even those
who wish him to fail. But the association with 'holiday' admits the time
with Falstaff is a pleasure to be overcome. This reinforces the thought
that Hal's 'gap-year' in Eastcheap will test his will more than he
pretends. The sudden, unsheathed, sparkling sword confirms his reformation will be violent, emphasising that he is staging a risky, as well as
completely unnecessary, spectacle of will, staking everything on its
power to defy environmental pressure. He will redeem the time himself.
The phrase comes from St Paul, where redemption comes partly by
God's grace (cf. Ephesians 5:16, Colossians 4:5); Hal usurps God's
graceful power over his life. This soliloquy which is addressed so
provocatively to us comes to rest and culminates in the expected word:
'will'. It taunts us with the existential possibility of self creation which
it scornfully insists is beyond our reach; it's a kind of *dare*.

Greenblatt accurately describes 'the triumph of Hal' in terms of 'a
claustrophobic narrowing of pleasure, a hypocritical manipulation of
appearances, and a systematic betrayal of friendship' (Greenblatt
1988a: 42). What this omits from account is the sort of fiercely concentrated agency with which Hal challenges us here, which derives from
an overriding commitment and entails the focussed and intense pleasure of a specific achievement. That sort of pleasure accounts for the
crescendo of 'I know you all' and has its apotheosis at Agincourt. It
also accounts for Hal's weird attractiveness in the theatre, in spite of all
sorts of reasons to disapprove of him.

Shakespeare doesn't shy from the cost of Hal's fierce agency. This
Prince has to cast off his best friend to achieve his end, and much more
besides. When Falstaff says to Hal, 'banish plump Jack, and banish all

the world', Hal answers, 'I do, I will' (*1 Henry IV*, 2.4.473–75): that fearfully emphatic word again, and here in a context which ironically resonates with the marriage service in anticipation of divorce. The rejection will cost everything. In the dialogue that opens *Henry V*, Canterbury describes the change in Hal in terrible terms of a scouring flood (1.1.32–34). But all this sets the seal on Hal's amazing will power. The cost of his project to Hal heightens and intensifies the sheer wilfulness in which he has luxuriated since 'I know you all'. Nor does he just sadly relinquish Falstaff's wildness in a life of boring respectability and cold *realpolitik* and instrumental reason like his brother John's. Rather, he sublates Falstaff's crazy excessiveness – and Hotspur's – into his mad campaign in France. Hal's wild play bears bloody fruit in Henry V's. He is a 'gamester', playing for a kingdom (3.6.111–12), who 'mocks' many a thousand widows out of dear husbands, mothers from sons, castles down (1.2.287–89).

Such suffering is horrible testimony to Henry's dauntlessness. But it's striking that the cost for others of fierce agency in the Henriad is most fully and pathetically worked out not on the blood-soaked battlefield but in Falstaff's suffering and death. On one hand, this is part of a complex distancing of the violence of war which I'll discuss below; but it also testifies to the fact that heroic agency as such involves severance and betrayal as the agent extricates him or her self from unnecessary and distracting relationships. This goes for Ghandi or Lenin as much as for Henry V. A cause is demanding. As Christ puts it, 'If any man come to me, and hate not his father, and mother, and wife, and children, and brethren, and sisters, yea, and his own life also, he cannot be my disciple' (Luke 14:26).

## Fierce agency

*Henry V* can be read in terms of the consummation of a will it has taken four plays to perfect. Action finally, thrillingly flourishes at the end of the tetralogy but in ways that are far from straightforward and which raise disturbing questions about fierce agency. Henry IV advises his son to 'busy giddy minds / With foreign quarrels, that action hence borne out, / May waste the memory of the former days' (*2 Henry IV*, 4.5.213–15). It's tempting to see this as justification for Henry's campaign in France, but no pragmatic reasoning can justify confronting an enemy five times stronger on home turf! As for the rigmarole about the Salic law (1.2.33–95), Simon Palfrey hits the nail on the head when he says, 'Everything about this is parodic (a fact well exploited in Olivier's famous film version): the absurd wealth of precedent, the arcane history and redundant exactitude, the spurious asides and pedantic mastery therein boasted, and the speech's climactic descent into a crabbed and inverted syntax that seems almost wilfully to discard any grammatical object' (Palfrey 2005: 83). Henry, as Palfrey further observes, 'will do it because he *can* do it' (ibid.: 84): capacity seizes opportunity with a compelling and unabashed alacrity. Yet Henry's campaign isn't an original gesture: it wilfully revives and repeats the English victory at Cressy (cf. 1.2.103–14; 2.4.50–64). Moreover, with Henry looking forward to the moment '[w]hen I do rouse me in my throne of France' (1.2.276), we're back with Hal in the tavern pleasuring himself with thoughts of 'redeeming the time' at his accession in England. There may be a hint of Nietzsche's 'eternal return' here, where the will makes its choice so powerfully as to choose it again and again, forever.[14] But there's equally a hint of the evanescence, even tedium, of victory, to which Greenblatt brilliantly pointed in his analysis of Marlowe's plays,[15] and of the theatrical bathos whereby fierce agency is swallowed up in imitation, repetition.

Hal kept us at a contemptuous distance in *Henry IV*, but our participation is vigorously solicited in *Henry V*. Here the strength and fulfilment of Henry's will is measured partly by its sway over the wills of others. This is most triumphantly set off in the inspiring St Crispin's Day speech (4.3.48–67). But it's anticipated in the exhortatory moral Canterbury draws from his observation of bees:

> I this infer,
> That many things having full reference
> To one consent may work contrariously,
> As many arrows loosed several ways
> Come to one mark,
> As many several ways meet in one town,
> As many fresh streams meet in one salt sea,
> As many lines close in the dial's centre.
> So may a thousand actions once afoot.
> End in one purpose and be all well borne
> Without defeat.
>
> (1.2.204–14)

There is a meta-dramatic resonance to this. For, just as Henry attempts by sheer force of will to summon up and guide a ferocious, aggregative will in his men, so the Chorus attempts to conscript our imaginations into Henry's war effort: 'let us, ciphers to this great account, / On your imaginary forces work' (Prologue, 17–18); 'Piece out our imperfections with your thoughts. / Into a thousand parts divide one man / And make imaginary puissance' (Prologue, 23–25); 'Work, work your thoughts, and therein see a siege' (3.0.25), etc. Whereas *1 Henry IV* held us at a disdainful arm's length from Hal's prospective triumph, *Henry V* tries to press us into it as sharers or accomplices, in anticipation of the ways that Olivier and the supporters of Bush and Blair will use the play to capture hearts and minds.[16]

One thing I'm trying to do in this essay is face up to the very real challenge of *Henry V*, partly for the sheer intellectual provocation, partly in the hope that it will cast some light on our own violent history. Jonathan Dollimore has recently called for a certain suspension of critical judgement followed by a subsequent 'reawakening of judgement, inside and after the identification with the work, which the act of identification has enabled'. This allows criticism to become 'a difficult dialectic' wherein 'judgement and work interrogate each other'. Dollimore admits this is probably the way engaged and intelligent students read anyway but amply demonstrates that it's *not* the way the more *a priori* kinds of published scholarship proceed (Dollimore 2001: 163 and *passim*). The Chorus in *Henry V* insists, like Dollimore, on our complicity with the play to the extent that we continue reading or watching at all. At least a degree of identification is involved in any aesthetic experience, and *Henry V* inducts us into an existentially and ethically challenging experience of the fierce agency it dramatises. A subsequent resurgence of judgement facilitates an intellectually honest and complex consideration of that challenge, as I hope to show.

*Henry V* dramatises the thrilling recklessness and hazard of action, which Nietzsche described in terms of affirming the roll of the dice before knowing the outcome.[17] We have recognised the needlessness and risk of Henry's campaign already. The night before Agincourt '[t]he poor condemned English, / Like sacrifices, by their watchful fires / Sit patiently and inly ruminate / The morning's danger' (4.0.22–25). So evidently death-marked are they that to 'the gazing moon' they present a spectacle of '[s]o many horrid ghosts' (4.0.22–28). But Henry does not wish to shorten the odds. The unlikelihood of victory, the mortal danger, concentrates agency, as well as possible glory, absolutely: the next day the English army stake everything on the dice, and their fierce wilfulness miraculously affects the way they fall. By contrast, the prospect of an easy victory – 'A very little let us do / And all is done' (4.2.32–33) – weakens French agency, leaving them vulnerable to such desperate energy.

Henry's ferocious agency is specifically doom-laden: it both wields death and courts it. But the companionable, amorous, bloody death of York and Suffolk (4.5.5–32) crystallises something of the strangely positive appeal of this. Exeter's pathetic description of the passing of these brothers-in-arms suggests that concentrated agency involves an intensification of all life – of love as much as aggression and hatred. The 'death-drive' entailed in Henry's mad campaign carries the impetus of action into death, experiences death more knowingly and perhaps accomplishes a certain limited defiance or even colonisation of its 'undiscovered country' (*Hamlet*, 3.1.81). Hence the paradoxical juxtaposition between an embrace of extinction and the assertion of a second life of perdurable memory.

How does Henry's knee-jerk piety relate to this fierce agency? Of course claiming God's sponsorship is a way of smoothing over and fighting against the essential ambivalence of the campaign, and a way of moralising the English victory. But Henry's insistently expressed relationship with God is also a means of avowing and perhaps partially sublating or carrying back into agency the forces foreign to the self that determine the fate of any action. Agincourt is such an impossible victory that Henry can't just simply take the credit for it. By completely resigning that credit to God, he nests his will in God's to the extent that the two wills become almost indistinguishable and his own will acquires a quality of the absolute.[18]

If Henry's thoroughly secular victory is thereby strangely spiritualised, he is further but more ironically associated with God in his agony the night before Agincourt. This has a resonance of Christ's agony in the Garden of Gethsemane. Whereas Christ struggles to submit his will to God, Henry admits his 'penitence comes after all, imploring after' (4.1.301–2). He gleefully accepts the next day's victory as confirmation of God's blessing. But it remains very possible that Henry's is a demonic triumph.

Still – it's difficult to resist such a sensationally unlikely victory. I say unlikely but of course, equally, we know it's bound to happen. One moment brings this contingency and destiny charmingly together:

KING:          What is this castle called that stands hard by?

MONTJOY:      They call it Agincourt.

KING:          Then call we this the field of Agincourt, Fought on the day of Crispin Crispian.
                                        (4.7.87–90)

Thus is a famous battlefield christened. It's one of those moments in Shakespeare when the specificity, the contingency of drama is charged with tremendous significance. And it resounds with the possibility of efficacious historical action, of finding oneself in the midst of an action which could change, which has changed everything.

## But didn't you say '*Action!*'?

What happens in France? Or, rather, what happens in the play in relation to what we're *told* happens in France? The nearest we get to real fighting is Pistol's bathetic encounter with Monsieur le Fer. Otherwise, our impression of the horrors of war is conveyed in a few barked threats and orders – 'Then every soldier kill his prisoners!' (4.7.37) – and a series of elaborate speech-acts that are far from disinterested or documentary. The first thing in the play is the Chorus's word painting which, with an exhilarating thrust towards burning intensity ('O for a muse of fire, that would ascend / The brightest heaven of invention' (Prologue, 1–2)) and a massive spreading gesture ('A kingdom for a stage, princes to act, / And monarchs to behold the swelling scene' (Prologue, 3–4)) pictures Henry clothed in the mantle of Mars with 'famine, sword and fire' at his feet 'leashed in like hounds' and 'crouching for employment'. But this terrible presence is avowedly what can't be realised in dramatic action. It's stunning but disturbing poetry beyond dramatic embodiment; it manufactures a sort of negative sublime, which is also evident in two similarly visionary descriptions of Edward III standing on a mountain, crowned with the sun, looking approvingly on the specifically maiming and uncreating work of his amazingly violent offspring, the Black Prince (1.2.104–14, 2.4.50–69). These speeches, by Canterbury and the French king, establish the heroic background to Henry's campaign. Their repetition perhaps partly intimates the monotony of valour and the imbrication of fierce agency in imitation, but they also, like Harry's campaign itself, have a touch of the 'eternal return'. The mythical terms of the description share in the essentializing, metaphysical tendency of the Chorus's opening description of Henry.

Harry's famous rallying cry, 'Once more unto the breach', for its part conjures a frightening image of the ideal soldier:

> imitate the action of a tiger:
> Stiffen the sinews, conjure up the blood,
> Disguise fair nature with hard-favoured rage.
> Then lend the eye a terrible aspect;
> Let it pry through the portage of the head

Like the brass canon; let the brow o'erwhelm it
As fearfully as does a galled rock
O'erhang and jutty his confounded base,
Swilled with wild and wasteful ocean.
Now set the teeth and stretch the nostril wide
Hold hard the breath and bend up every spirit
To his full height.

(3.1.6–17)

The tendency of the play to freeze the horrible flux of war into strangely still, heightened images is epitomised by this speech, with its explict stiffening and setting and holding hard in an effort to attain the elemental condition of brass and rock, and with its negative portrayal of the fluidity and movement of water.

Henry's more infamous effort to bludgeon Harfleur into submission also exhibits an essentialist tendency. This serially rehearses then bursts into the centre of a hideous vision of primal rape, infanticide and violation:

> ... *in a moment look to see*
> The blind and bloody soldier with foul hand
> Defile the locks of your shrill-shrieking daughters,
> Your fathers taken by the silver beards,
> And their most reverend heads dashed to the walls,
> Your naked infants spitted upon pikes,
> Whiles the mad mothers with their howls confused
> Do break the clouds, as did the wives of Jewry
> At Herod's bloody-hunting slaughtermen.

(3.3.34–42; my emphasis)

Of course this is particularly horrible, because it brings the victims into focus, but it's not actually different in spirit from the demonic violence positively praised and invoked in the previous examples. It's a rhetorical performance which averts bloodshed but its poetic momentum confirms an immemorial lesson of war Henry is at pains to stress: how readily fierce agency becomes devilish – the 'prince of fiends' actually shows his 'smirched complexion' here (3.3.16–17). Additionally disturbing is the way Henry positions himself in relation to his speech-act. He starts with a demonic sneer: 'What is it then to me' (3.3.15); retreats into qualification and a disclaiming shrug, suggestive of slightly more guilt and anxiety: 'What is't to me, when you yourselves are cause' (3.3.19–20); and, finally, insists he is powerless to resist the tidal wave of violence –

'What rein can hold licentious wickedness' (3.3.22) – and therefore, by implication, blameless. In spite of this recoil and handwashing, he is positively thundering towards his epiphany of rape, smashed heads, skewered babies, etc. Of course he is performing such self-division to extra terroristic effect, but he may equally be growing steadily more frightened of the vivid threats that so completely possess him. Strategy, transgressive compulsion and guilty fear form the tightening knot of this speech.

But, for all of their thrillingly horrible affect, none of the passages discussed are descriptions of real violence, the violence that must be occurring in a war where over ten thousand men are rapidly killed. They are verbal conjurations of masculine ferocity, each attempting to express and epitomise its essence or spirit. The iconic images of Harry as Mars and the frozen soldier ontologise fierce agency as another, indeed a truer form of being. Some such metaphysics of violence is also involved in Henry's extraordinary claim that the English force at Agincourt will be remembered 'till the ending of the world' (4.3.58): here the shock of fierce agency imprints itself throughout time. Its supposed transcendent force also makes some sense of Henry's even more surprising suggestion that 'he today that sheds his blood with me / Shall be my brother; be he ne'er so vile, / This day shall gentle his condition' (4.3.61–63): action, inasmuch as it is another form of being, has the power to undo established differences such as those of class – although, by contrast, it emphasises and underwrites gender difference. The visionary glimpses of the Black Prince offer a scene of primordial violence, and Henry's speech at Harfleur threatens to make a new one in the play's present.

The discrepancy between the violent action the play veils and these tremendous poetic and metaphysical evocations of such action casts the abject self-opinion of the Chorus in a new light. From the beginning the Chorus apologises for the sheer incapacity of 'this unworthy scaffold to bring forth / So great an object' (Prologue, 10–11). By the time the drama's reached its heroic climax, the Chorus is apparently convulsed with embarrassment:

> And so our scene must to the battle fly,
> Where – oh for pity! – we shall much disgrace
> With four or five most vile and ragged foils
> Right ill-disposed in brawl ridiculous
> The name of Agincourt.
>
> (4.0.49–52)

There's comedy in this, and the modesty attractively counterpoints all the bloodshed, glory and derring-do. But it may be more significant than that. We've seen that *Henry V* does not in fact try to realise its matter in embodied action on its unworthy scaffold, that it doesn't afford us even a brawl ridiculous between four or five most ragged foils. This is not just because the spirit, the sense, the meaning of violent action is beyond dramatic representation; *it is beyond action's capacity to represent itself.* Thus: even if we did have 'A kingdom for a stage, princes to act, / And monarchs to behold the swelling scene', we'd need that extraterrestrial thrust of a 'muse of fire' into 'the brightest heaven of invention' to make it *signify*, to make it more than a ridiculous brawl. The poverty of dramatic action which the Chorus bemoans reveals the poverty, the nudity, of action as such. Any interpretation or experience of action – as glorious, as wicked, etc. – is insecurely pitched on that action's meaninglessness, which, because it is irreducible to determinate content, itself becomes strangely ineffable and fascinating. Henry acts. And then in a sort of simultaneous second-order action, he acts to secure the meaning of his acts. But that, the play suggests, can't be done. Any interpretation of action is imported, epiphenomenal. Such interpretations moreover are themselves acts. They supplement the original action's bareness or lack, but they remain fundamentally non-identical with it.

## There is figures in all things

So says Fluellen (4.7.33) and it is a key to reading the play. We have seen that action is always figuratively presented in *Henry V*, and many of the play's characters and scenes reflect and emphasise a specific dimension of Henry's action. Falstaff's name – *fall staff*, interestingly opposite to *shake spear* – is a sign of the impotence which Henry had to shake off. The Dauphin is a ghost of the person Hal was presumed to be; the French prince accuses Henry of foppish ineffectuality, which turns out to characterise himself. Henry's resentful description of 'the wretched slave' (4.1.264–80) actually secretes a Tolstoyan envy of natural, everyday action in the simple cause of subsistence. This is a course barred to Henry by his characteristic excessive agency as much as his royal succession. Williams unwittingly challenges the King, but Henry rewards him by filling his gage with gold, presumably because Williams presents Henry with a living image of just such excessiveness. Henry thereby, perhaps a touch anxiously, confirms his own reward and desert. Fluellen himself, with his pedantic concern with 'the true disciplines of the wars' (3.2.72), represents desirable restraint to Henry: 'Though it appear a little out of fashion, / There is much care and valour in this Welshman' (4.1.84–85). Henry's later avowal to Fluellen that he is Welsh also may be a bit of flattering imperialism, but it is equally an attempt to claim some kinship with Fluellen's valiant carefulness after having wrecked the garden of France.

And yet, Pistol is Henry's real *doppelgänger*. His name, as Henry recognises, suggests that 'fierceness' which is the most terrible attribute of his heroic commander (4.1.64). Pistol of course is a mere braggart, but this provides a parodic confirmation, which is also an intensification, of the strange discrepancy between the 'fact' and the meaning or interpretation of Henry's action as I have explored it above.[19] In addition, the strange scene in which Pistol takes Monsieur le Fer, that iron man, prisoner without a fight emblematises the play's weird failure to provide even a brawl ridiculous.

These shadows of Henry's curiously unsubstantiated campaign are a reminder that we are at a mysterious if not absurd remove from real action in *Henry V*. If there are figures in all things, representation is lost in a deferral of real presence. We are in a hall of mirrors behind which something ineffably singular may or may not be going on. Of all Shakespeare's plays, this one both asserts and withdraws its presence, and it does so in a way that suggests there may paradoxically be something strangely inaccessible in all our experiences of action.

## Love in action

During the long last scene of the play, in which he speaks wooingly to Katherine for nigh on 300 lines, Henry attempts to turn all his fierce agency into love. The French Queen anticipates this but, in the same instant as she gladly beholds his eyes, she imagines them shooting 'fatal balls of murdering basilisks' into a multitude of Frenchmen (5.2.17), and hopes that they've lost their venom. In fact, Henry's fierce agency is not so much lost as transformed into his suit to Katherine. This follows from his effort to win the hearts of his men on St Crispin's Day and throughout his campaign. But it is also related to the Chorus's efforts to capture our hearts for him. Previously *Henry V* has made a play for, and partly from, our more violent instincts; now it attempts to rouse and harness more libidinal energies. Inasmuch as there are figures in all things, Katherine stands for the potentially recalcitrant audience. Henry may not have wooed us directly, but the Chorus has, as his passionately loquacious go-between.

The strange final scene enables us to explore and question the place of fierce agency in love. It's a point in the play where many feel afresh the loss of Hal. Henry's torrent of words is reminiscent of Hal's but entirely lacks its wild freedom. There's plenty of wit, vigour and improvisation in Henry's prose, but it's a form of instrumental action rather than exploratory, self-extending play. All this profuse speech is bent on achieving J. L. Austin's paradigmatic example of a performative utterance that accomplishes its own effects: the marriage vows.[20]

Some commentators recoil from the way the King presents himself to his intended: Colin N. Manlove, for instance, writes of his 'manufactured common touch' (Manlove 1981: 24). But Henry's insistence that he's the kind of man who 'could win a lady at leapfrog, or by vaulting into a saddle with my armour on my back' (5.2.137–38), rather than an ineffably sensitive romantic hero, recapitulates his decisive existential decision to plunge the freedom and possibility of subjectivity into concentrated agency. As the blokeish exchange with Burgundy indicates, the wooing of Katherine is the French campaign in another key, a festive dramatisation of that war, a refracted image of a siege – which, in turn, undresses Henry's ambition to penetrate Katherine physically. The rippling agency whereby violent exertion finally turns into amorous desire in *Henry V* reverses earlier hints that extreme action is wearyingly repetitive. With a desirable sexual partner rather than disembodied honour as its object, the will to prevail, succeed and conquer is reanimated and refreshed.

And in this amorous case there is not the same rupture between the fact and metaphysics of action as there was at war. Of course, the metaphysics of love shear very readily off from the reality of an amorous encounter: think of Troilus's self-pleasuring airinesses or, more positively, of Antony and Cleopatra. But in this last scene of *Henry V* love is immanent in, inseparable from the act of love. If Katherine prevents love's act by refusing to allow and contribute to it, it's love not Henry that will die as a result (cf. 5.2.148–52). Here even the bliss of sex, which often lends itself to rhapsodic flights, is anticipated in earthily active terms: 'If ever thou be'st mine, Kate, as I have a saving faith within me tells me thou shalt, I get thee with scambling, and thou must therefore needs prove a good soldier-breeder' (5.2.199–203).

'Scambling': the Arden editor glosses it as 'struggling, i.e. fighting a war', but in its plainness, vigour and slightly withheld release, it's a great word for sex. Love here is *creative* struggle, a complex union that doesn't dissolve the otherness of the beloved, and magically issues in new life, another quantum of force in the world: 'Shall not thou and I, between Saint Denis and Saint George, compound a boy, half French, half English, that shall go to Constantinople and take the Turk by the beard? Shall we not? What say'st thou, my fair flower-de-luce?' (5.2.189–208). The vigorously repeated rhetorical question, the cheeky franglais, the unabashed brutal implication that love is war at one remove and that it will re-energise war in its effects: these are the exciting provocations of an unconventional lover supremely confident in his ferocious attractiveness. And it isn't simply a violent speech: differences between the English and the French are resolved in Henry's and Katherine's imagined offspring; and if he is to conquer Constantinople as Henry has conquered France, then perhaps he will father a half-European, half-Turkish boy who, in his own person, will unite East and West. One thing especially stands out in the context of *Henry V*'s removal of women from violence: far from casting off his fierce agency to woo a woman, Henry is inviting Katherine to join in.

Of course there are crashingly disturbing notes. Henry's and Katherine's boy will not be a vigorous crusading hero but a weakling and a failure. 'The Turk' makes plain the possibility of victimhood, and Katherine as the struggling lover of a fierce King seems fearfully similar to that imagined victim of outright assault, especially as Henry's vanquished subject. After the multitudinous slaughter at Agincourt, the terror of terrible action underlies and counterpoints Henry's wooing and the picture of sexuality it discloses. If his suit to Katherine is like a siege, that calls disturbingly back to mind the vivid and insistent rape fantasies shouted at the gates of Harfleur. When does 'scambling' become rape? What if Katherine doesn't yield?

But Henry's force and insistency here is bent not on just *taking* his bride. He wants her to want him. Henry's power to coerce the will of others has been amply demonstrated in the war. The loneliness of such a power is glimpsed in the erotic pathos and vulnerability of the moment when he feels Katherine's alien, autonomous choice begin to revolve on him: 'I love thee, Kate . . . I dare not swear thou lovest me, yet my blood begins to flatter me that thou dost' (5.2.218–20). She could rescue him from his monopoly of will.

Henry talks so much as he is to trying to accomplish the delicate task of coaxing, stimulating, bringing on Katherine's will without erasing it. This subtle, extended seeking of consent is also a solicitation of female will and agency in a play that has entirely excluded such things. And it is necessarily an interval of self-consciousness, and male vulnerability, in which Henry tries to commend himself to Katherine's eyes. Apart from the agony before battle, Henry has avoided self-consciousness. It was more securely immanent in the immediate violence of his previous acts. But Henry doesn't tremble under Katherine's gaze, probably because – though he wants her to want him – it's clear he has her anyway. That knowledge, as well as his extraordinary familiarity with achieving his desire, is the platform from which he launches his quest for her love. Hence the darkly ironic humour of the following exchange:

> KING:         . . . wilt thou have me?
> KATHERINE:    Dat is as it sall please *le roi mon père*.
> KING:         Nay, it will please him well, Kate;
>               it shall please him, Kate.
>
> (5.2.243–46)

The paradox of sexual and amorous agency which seeks to compel what it wants to be given freely is dramatised in the last scene: 'Put off your maiden blushes, avouch the thoughts of your heart with the looks of an empress, take me by the hand, and say "Harry of England, I am thine"' (5.2.232–35). Gentleness and responsiveness are braided together with a cruel intensity: 'but, good Kate, mock me mercifully, the rather, gentle Princess, because I love thee cruelly' (5.2.199–200). Inasmuch as a powerful man is harassing a subjugated female, it's offensive. But, once again, isn't Henry's forcefulness, his wilfulness, attractive as well? Can love, can desire, be raised *carefully*? Seduction, copulation, love often attend an individual effort of will. That said, can the impetus of one will, and its will to solicit an answering will in another, bear fruit in genuine mutuality?[21]

As I have indicated already, Henry's paradoxically aggressive seeking of consent expresses his bid for our identification and approval. Inasmuch as *Henry V* is his play, we are no more in a position to refuse him than Kate is, although beyond the moment of identification we may reclaim our free judgement. Nevertheless, there is one moment which crystallises especially attractively the existential promise of fierce agency in love: Henry lustily says, 'We are the makers of manners, Kate', before kissing her in defiance of what, from the perspective of fierce agency, is 'the weak list of a country's fashion' (5.2.266–67). Henry explicitly presents such liberty as proper to a monarch, and in terms which repeat the masculinist prejudice that have unsettled not just the whole scene but the entire play: 'nice customs curtsy to great kings' (5.2.266). And yet, once he has pressed his lips on Kate's, Henry submits to 'the witchcraft of hers' (5.2.273). Yes, it's another misogynist trope. And yet, at the last – if Henry is to be believed – will and agency pulse between him and Katherine in a defiant piece of lovemaking that negotiates the pitfalls and incarnates the possibilities of a fierce agency more attractively than the heroics of Agincourt. But those heroics preceded and enabled this kiss, and the blitzkrieg images associated with them troubling permeate its ardour.

When Henry and Katherine kiss, his will is simultaneously intensified and converted in the face of her opposition, in the opposition of her face to his. As he withdraws from her lips and the play rushes to a close, Henry describes his bride-to-be twice to her father as an obstacle. First, he says, 'he cannot see many a fair French city for one fair French maid which stands in my way' (5.2.314–15). His second, more hopeful suggestion is that 'the maid that stood in the way for my wish shall show me the way to my will' (5.2.322–23). Whereas his ardour for Kate had distracted him from his conquest of France, the French king is now on the point of gratifying him absolutely, by signing over his dominion as well as his daughter. But, in the context of this protracted wooing scene, Henry's riddling words reinforce the complication of will already revealed in the kiss. Katherine has stood in the way not of but *for* his wish. Henry's will splits and opposes itself here. Katherine's being in the way for his wish shows him the way to his will. Because her opposition, as a powerful stimulus to desire, intensely reveals what he wants? Or because what he wants is opposition? As the play dies, as Henry is being satisfied point by point, Katherine discovers within him a countervailing, perverse, insatiate desire to contravene his own will.[22] It must be love! It can hardly be said to compensate for the thousands of lives lost in the play; but, as a present and absorbing dramatic surprise – the discovery of a satisfying tension between separate and even opposed agencies – it perhaps overshadows the losses of Henry VI of which the Chorus reluctantly speaks. To the extent that Katherine is a stand-in for the audience that's subjected to the play, it also intimates the possibility of *critical* identification with Henry's fierce agency, even intimates that this is somehow what Henry wants. Thus perhaps it is in the small compass of a cruel but mutual kiss that this star of England most greatly lives.

## Back to the present

I've been concerned with *Henry V*'s presence in our present throughout this essay, particularly with the challenging experience of fierce agency the play confronts us with. I now wish to place these considerations within the broad contexts of current intellectual history and global politics. If, as I've said, there's been a presumption of disability in much recent theoretical and critical work, the presence of *Henry V* in the present powerfully contravenes it: we've seen that Shakespeare's *grand homme* exercises a will of iron that bears fruit in astonishing achievement. That's why supporters of Bush and the war in Iraq have reached for the play to inspire the troops, encourage the American and (more sceptical) British publics, and borrow a bit of glory. But the great odds Henry faces – which make Agincourt almost a miracle of fierce agency – are absurdly different to the crushing superiority of coalition forces to Saddam's or the Taliban's. Nor is *Henry V* the right play to invoke in a 'war on terror', as it demonstrates how readily extreme action turns terrible. If 'there is figures in all things', the recourse of supporters of that war to *Henry V* just makes the resemblance of their 'War on Terror' to the terrorism it opposes more clear. With famine, sword and fire straining at his leash, Henry is exactly a figure and bringer of terror. And the flattening of Afghanistan or Tikrit is an epitome of terror as well. Moreover, is it really any wonder that the U.N.-defying intervention of Anglo-American leaders released the kind of transgressive agency emblematised in the abuse of prisoners at Abu Ghraib? Not in the perspective of *Henry V*, where insistent intimations of rape and other outrages carry over even into the festive and culminating love scene. Thus Nicholas Hytner's celebrated 2003 production of *Henry V* at The National Theatre in London, with Adrian Lester in the title role, executed French prisoners in hoods in a detail meant to remind audiences of Abu Ghraib and then set Henry's and Katherine's coming together against a background of body bags.

*Henry V* seems uncannily to indict the justification of the Iraq war in terms of 'weapons of mass destruction' in Williams's words:

> [I]f the cause be not good, the King himself hath a heavy reckoning to make when all those legs and arms and heads chopped off in a battle shall join together at the latter day and cry all 'We died at such a place', some swearing, some crying for a surgeon, some upon their wives left poor behind them, some upon the debts they owe, some upon their children rawly left.
>
> (4.1.134–41)

And yet, *Henry V* also suggests that the thrilling experience of action has little to do with its end. Henry's cause is little more than a pretext. Fierce agency's an end in itself. And fierce agency in war is disquietingly similar to fierce agency in love.

The curious split in *Henry V* between an almost ineffable facticity of action and its supplementary or epiphenomenal 'spiritual' or poetic content underlines, in our epoch of terrorism and counter-terrorism, how treacherous any politics of action will be: the meaning of action is always insecurely built on its inexpressible 'real' content. As is well known to any playwright, that's part of its anxious excitement and risk.

And yet, partly in the name of such anxious excitement and risk, *Henry V* emphatically does not recommend a fastidious withdrawal from action. The micro-gestures of a brawl ridiculous among two or three most ragged foils stand for larger historical actions, as the Chorus explains, but equally Agincourt in *Henry V* is converted into a grand gesture: a near miracle of fierce agency which can stand for the thrilling possibility of any human project. Why not a new world order that would redress some of the reasons for terrorism and global discontent? The spuriousness of Henry's supposed cause renders the play remarkably fungible as an exemplum of human action: available in the struggle against fascism *and* in the invasion of Afghanistan and Iraq. As Dollimore has shown, the 'aesthetics of energy' in recent times have generally been associated with fascism (Dollimore 2001); but it would clearly be cutting off our own arms as well as our noses to *resign* heroic energy to the horrible memory of Nazism, and it would risk reinvigorating the fascist cause. The example of Olivier perhaps suggests that the human energy and potential betrayed in aberrant political projects might be redeemed under the right banner. Of course the common denominator between Nazism and Olivier is nationalism but, if there are figures in all things, it is certainly true to say that *Henry V*'s sovereign partly stands for the sovereign human subject's desire and power to act, and the nation in the play could figure any fighting collective. *Henry V*'s strange metaphysics of action that's so much in excess of what is actually dramatised might offend our postmodern sensibilities but it resonates with the phenomenology of action as such. The fiercely concentrated agency of any determined deed – playing sport, writing a novel, making love – approaches absolutism. The metaphysics of action in *Henry V* plugs into the sort of intense desire which drives and is invested in our merely contingent histories. Such desire powerfully enables all sorts of creative as well as destructive projects. As we have seen, *Henry V* isn't just about war; it's also, strangely enough, about love.

When Henry amorously growls, 'We are the makers of manners, Kate', it emblematises the possibility of bursting beyond the given system into a zone of existential and cultural freshness and freedom. At last, the possibility of a female will is glimpsed, as well as the possibility of intense mutuality that's not reducible to the death-drive. And it's closer to action than we get on the battlefield. But, tempting though it is to luxuriate in such positive possibilities, Shakespeare will not let us sentimentalise any such fierce agency from our comfy chairs in theatres or universities. It's not just that female will is countenanced as a separate agency only inasmuch as it coincides with male desire. Henry's and Katherine's kiss is meant to baptise a larger, 'Christian-like accord' between their respective countries (5.2.347), but it's as much enabled and intensified as shadowed and threatened by the war that precedes it. Even the positive fruits of rashness are flavoured with infernal possibilities.[23]

A certain violence is perhaps inalienable from human life. In the preceding remarks I've worried over the ethics of *Henry V*. But maybe the fierce agency the play dramatises is fundamentally and self-delightingly indifferent to ethics. Indeed, Henry bears not a passing resemblance to Nietzsche's 'supreme artist, amoral, recklessly creating and destroying, realizing himself ... in whatever he does or undoes, ridding himself by his acts of the embarrassment of his riches and the strain of his internal contradictions' (Nietzsche 1956: 135). To what extent does any project we cherish or resent depend on such disturbingly unconcerned energy? And yet, in his final, more intimate engagement Henry *is* concerned, concerned to feel the force of another will or agency. Should we recognise the seed of another kind of ethics – one vested in passionate, mutually intensifying and creative assertion – in this?

## Notes

I'm grateful to the editors, Deanna Fernie, Simon Palfrey, Kiernan Ryan and Henry Turner for their stimulating and helpful responses to this essay. I'm also grateful to Emily Hardy for bringing my attention to many of the sources of the present-day political appropriation of *Henry V*.

1 For a full theoretical exposition of this, see Fernie 2005a.
2 For more on the interplay between acting and action, representing and representation, see Weimann 1978 and 2000.
3 For instance, Foucault writes, '[P]ower relations are both intentional and nonsubjective. ... [T]here is no power that is exercised without a series of aims and objectives. But this does not mean that it results from the choice or decision of an individual subject. ... The logic is clear, the aims decipherable, and yet it is often the case that *no one is there to have invented them*' (Foucault 1978: 94–95; my emphasis). A number of postmodern thinkers, such as Bourdieu and de Certeau, have developed operative concepts of agency. And the late Derrida followed Kierkegaard and others into consideration of the kind of action that bursts beyond convention and ethics. Even Foucault rehabilitated a certain self-fashioning agency. For more on these postmodern theories of action, see Fernie 2006. It remains true, however, that postmodern thought as such has seriously problematised where it has not discredited our power to act.
4 Greenblatt's struggle with agency is exemplary. In *Renaissance Self-Fashioning*, he declares 'human actions by themselves are always problematical; they must constantly be referred to an inner state that must, nonetheless, be experienced as the irresistible operation of a force outside the self, indeed alien to the self' (Greenblatt 1980: 111). But he has made efforts to retrieve agency for the human subject up to and including his significantly entitled *Will in the World* (2004).

5  See Fernie 2005b.
6  For instance, in the *Sun*, 20 March 2003, p. 8; and in the National Theatre's programme for *Henry V* directed by Nicholas Hytner in 2003.
7  See Mullan (2003).
8  Some of the crucial statements are Greenblatt 1988a, Dollimore and Sinfield 1992, Howard and Rackin 1997 and Grady 2002. Greenblatt and Grady worry through Henry's – and the play's – charismatic violence. McEachern 1995 makes some guardedly positive observations. But Ruiter 2005's assertion that Henry's success is ethically degenerate sounds the keynote.
9  For an excellent, non-reductive account of intentional action, see Wilson 2000. Wilson writes: 'I approach agency not by means of some account claiming to describe purposive behaviour with objective accuracy in its relation to the structure and meaning of conduct, as if ideology necessarily invalidated the actor's account of what he or she does, but instead with a certain deliberate naiveté' (6).
10 References are to the Arden Shakespeare *Complete Works* (1998). References to *Henry V* are to T. W. Craik's Arden edition (1998).
11 See Grady 2002.
12 Recent criticism has been suspicious of will. See, for instance, Wilson 1993, which is written to 'defy [Shakespeare's] will power' (21). The current essay will explore the ethical and political dangers of will but will equally probe its creative power.
13 See Howard and Rackin 1997: 4.
14 For a revealing commentary on the 'eternal return', see Deleuze 2005.
15 Greenblatt 1980: 193–221.
16 As Jonathan Dollimore and Alan Sinfield observe, the play is preoccupied with rebellious – or potentially rebellious – elements, from Cambridge, Scrope and Grey, to Macmorris, Jamy and Fluellen, to Bardolph and Pistol, etc. (Dollimore and Sinfield 1992). Henry has to placate, convert or defeat such elements to achieve maximum capacity. He also has to overcome any resistance in the audience. And the struggle is genuinely dramatic. The attempt to exercise a collective will on his own is also simultaneously exciting and repulsive.
17 See Deleuze 2005: 25–27.
18 David Evett's notion of 'volitional primacy', whereby the subject 'chooses' the destiny that has been imposed upon it, is relevant here. The exemplar of 'volitional primacy' 'seems . . . to have flung himself, without hesitation, into the waters of experience, letting the current take him where it will in a way that makes its will his will, and gleefully disporting himself in whatever psychological or moral or economic eddies he finds' (Evett 2005: 185).
19 Dekker may have jumped off from this internal parody in *Henry V* when he rewrote the play as citizen comedy, glorifying Shrove Tuesday instead of St Crispin's Day. See Dekker 1979.
20 See Austin 1962.
21 For a powerful analysis of sexual fierceness, which dialogues with a general tendency in modern thought to cast sex in utopian terms, see Dollimore 2001.
22 This goes beyond Evett's 'volitional primacy' where the subject chooses to identify with a force to which (s)he cannot but submit (see Evett 2005).
23 Once again, see Dollimore 2001.

# 7

# Lavinia as 'blank page' and the presence of feminist critical practices

## Evelyn Gajowski

> The hymen is the always folded . . . space in which
> the pen writes its dissemination.
>
> (Gayatri Chakravorty Spivak 1997: lxvi)

> There [seem] . . . to be two things that women are silent about: their
> pleasure and their violation. The work performed by the idealiza-
> tion of this silence is that *it helps culture not to be able to tell the difference
> between the two.*
>
> (Barbara Johnson 1996: 136, emphasis hers)[1]

## 1

Insofar as feminist literary theory and criticism are discursive practices that are rooted in and are informed by late twentieth and early twenty-first century political, economic, and social practices, they are inevitably presentist in nature. Put another way – more succinctly, perhaps, and appropriating Stephen Greenblatt's useful formulation – feminism is *always already* presentist (Greenblatt 1989). It is true that to respond to a Shakespeare text is to enter into a dialogue with the past, whether or not we are prompted, as Greenblatt is, by a desire 'to speak with the dead' (Greenblatt 1988a: 1). Such a conversation means entering into a dialogue not only with Shakespeare and his contemporaries, of course, but also with the tradition of theatrical and critical responses to Shakespeare's texts that has accumulated over the course of four centuries. And these theatrical and critical responses themselves constitute not merely passive responses but also active constructions of meaning in their own right. Yet we are also compelled 'to talk with the living', as Terence Hawkes points out (Hawkes 2002a: 4). Enmeshed in the early twenty-first century as we are, we cannot help but be influenced in our apprehension of Shakespeare's texts by contemporary ideologies and events that constitute us, even as we, in turn, constitute Shakespeare's texts – that construct meanings in us, even as we, in turn, construct meanings in texts.

Situated in the liminal present moment, we occupy a position analogous to that of the classical Janus figure at the doorway – simultaneously looking backward into the past and looking forward into the future. This is nothing new, of course. We have always viewed the past through the lens of the present, as twentieth-century philosophers of history such as Benedetto Croce emphasize when theorizing that 'all history is contemporary history' (Croce 1941: 19–22, 1960: 11–15). In fact, we cannot help but do so, as Hawkes observes:

> None of us can step beyond time. It can't be drained out of
> our experience. As a result, the critic's own 'situatedness'
> does not – cannot – contaminate the past. In effect, it consti-
> tutes the only means by which it's possible to see the past and
> perhaps comprehend it.
>
> (Hawkes 2002a: 3)

At the present moment, our theoretical and critical practices are on the threshold of fully recognizing this crucial factor and deliberately focusing on it. Realizing that we view the past through the lens of our present even as those in the future will, in turn, view us through the lens of their present enables us to gain a heightened awareness of the narrative of human history as an ongoing, imbricated (and imbricating) process. The future will write our epitaph. Questions that naturally come to mind are 'What will those in the future see?' 'How will they regard us?' 'Will it be in the way we would hope or wish to be regarded?' Of course, we can never know the answers. Yet the ethical implications of our actions in the present enter into the picture in a way not possible under the regime of those theoretical approaches that privilege the past at the expense of the present. In other words, amidst the critical practices of fetishizing early modern material objects – or 'antiquarianism', as Hugh Grady succinctly puts it (Grady 2005: 112) – piling up historical anecdotes, and constructing thick descriptions, the present moment has been untheorized. Further, in recent years, the present as well as the past has been unpoliticized, or more accurately, drained of the political content that originally animated cultural materialism and feminism alike – an unfortunate development that Grady also points out.

Because of its rootedness in the political, economic, and social present, a feminist critical practice has a particular responsibility to acknowledge that connection. More so than any other Shakespeare scholar, Phyllis Rackin has appreciated and articulated this responsibility in a series of recent and forthcoming publications:

> Our own experience of Shakespeare's women is conditioned not only by the accumulated tradition of Shakespeare scholarship and reception but also by the present history of the world in which we live: both of these histories help to shape our experience of the plays, whether we study them in an academic setting, see them on stage or screen, or read them in the privacy of our own rooms. Both of these histories will need feminist intervention in the twenty-first century.
>
> (Rackin 2005: 5–6)[2]

Indeed, in deliberately beginning with the material present and using it to set an interrogative agenda, feminism, like presentism, reverses the strategies of historicism. A feminist critical practice intervenes on the past with a heightened awareness of the ways that the present influences the very questions we pose. Inviting us to own up to our 'situatedness' in the present and base our critical practice on an active engagement with that 'situatedness', it does not view the present as a prison to be escaped or an obstacle to be overcome. Instead, a feminist critical practice such as this is capable of constructing transformative readings of early modern English texts such as Shakespeare's *Titus Andronicus* by exploring how its central mutilations are signifiers of patriarchy and female oppression and, furthermore, how the dramatic text is a powerful meditation on these problems.

## 2

In her groundbreaking essay, '"The Blank Page" and the Issues of Female Creativity', Susan Gubar defines the act of writing in a patriarchal society as a profoundly gendered enterprise. Drawing upon the theoretical work of Jacques Derrida, particularly as mediated by Gayatri Spivak (Spivak 1997: lxv–lxvi), Gubar interrogates the paradigm of the 'pen-penis' and the 'virgin page', noting that this configuration participates in and perpetuates a tradition that constructs the writer as male, active, and primary, on the one hand, and the 'page', or text, as female, passive, and secondary, on the other. According to this tradition, woman is reduced to the status of an object that is denied intentionality and lacks autonomy. The unfortunate consequence of this tradition for the putative female writer is, of course, that it systematically excludes her from the act of writing even as it reinscribes her as a text. Woman is not only excluded from the creation of culture – she is reified as an artifact within that culture (Gubar 1985: 295). The patriarchal configuration that man is the writer and woman is 'the blank page' – the text upon which meaning is inscribed and disseminated – is thus a problematic one for women who want to appropriate the pen and become writers themselves.

The body of the female protagonist, Lavinia, in *Titus Andronicus*, the earliest of Shakespeare's tragedies,[3] provides the best early modern stage representation, perhaps, of Gubar's theory of 'the blank page' upon which males in narratives and in history inscribe phallogocentric meaning. Shakespeare dramatizes on the English stage the symbolic economy that Gubar theorizes in a patriarchal society: male inscription of meaning upon a female with the 'pen-penis'. A palpable theatrical presence on the stage, Lavinia's body is a site of contestation upon which the political conflict between her father, Titus, a Roman general, and Tamora, the Queen of the Goths (and later wife of Saturninus and thereby Empress of Rome), is played out. Horridly, the character of Lavinia is subjected to a series of violations during the course of the dramatic action: in Act 1, she is handed over to Saturninus by Titus despite the fact that she is betrothed to Bassianus; in Act 2, after serving as the object of rivalry for another pair of brothers, Demetrius and Chiron, sons of Tamora, she is raped, silenced, and mutilated by them; and, in the end, she is murdered by her own father. Her body is inscribed upon when her rapists inseminate her, even as it is inscribed upon by her own blood when they cut out her tongue and cut off her hands. In this way, more so than any other character in the Shakespearean canon, perhaps, Lavinia is rendered a *tabula rasa*, a cipher, that male characters interpret and give voice to, projecting their meanings upon her. To be a subject is to speak, as Catherine Belsey points out (Belsey 1985: x), as well as to act, to construct meaning. To be an object, on the other hand, is to be silent, to be passive, to have meanings inscribed upon oneself by others. If *Titus Andronicus* is a play about silence (Danson 1974: 12), it is a play that literally and violently silences Lavinia. Shakespeare problematizes male violence toward women and male silencing of women under patriarchy. Before Lavinia dies, however, and despite overwhelming odds, she manages to overcome formidable obstacles, adopt a subject position – and write. She does so to name the crime committed against her – '*Stuprum*' – and to reveal the identities of her rapists.

Intended or attempted rapes abound in early modern English drama. Shakespeare deals with attempted rape, as in the final scene of *The Two Gentlemen of Verona*; threatened rape, as in *A Midsummer Night's Dream* and *The Tempest*; specular rape, as in *Cymbeline*, where Iachimo constructs a pornographic fantasy upon the sleeping body of Imogen; and verbal rape, as in Marina in the brothel in *Pericles*. Together with *The Revenger's Tragedy*, Heywood's *The Rape of Lucrece*, and Fletcher's *Valentinian*, *Titus* is one of four early modern English plays in the period 1594–1612 that dramatize the crime of rape and its consequences for the rape survivor.[4] Among Shakespeare's texts, *Titus* and the narrative poem, *The Rape of Lucrece*, not only confront the subject of rape, they foreground it. An extravagantly bloody play, even according to the standards of Shakespeare's contemporary playwrights, *Titus* can strike twenty-first-century sensibilities as deliberately shocking or grotesque. True to the conventions of Senecan tragedy, violation and violence, although they often occur off stage, are spectacularized on stage. The bloodied text of Lavinia's body is subjected to not only insemination but also the dissemination of meaning upon it by various male characters as it is read, deciphered, interpreted, and given voice, particularly by her uncle, Marcus, and her father, Titus. Within the dramatic world of *Titus*, as within patriarchal societies in history, bodily violence and language fall within the province of heterosexual males. Possessing more power than females, they sometimes abuse it, as Catherine Stimpson points out. Possessing less power than males, females often absorb that abuse (Stimpson 1983: 62). Males inflict violence, in other words, while females are subjected to it; males are granted voice, moreover, while females are not.

The significance of Lavinia's blood in *Titus* resonates with the significance of female blood in Gubar's essay, '"The Blank Page" and the Issues of Female Creativity', and in Isak Dinesen's short story, 'The Blank Page', from which Gubar draws her title. Dinesen's narrative is concerned with an ancient Carmelite order of nuns high in the blue mountains of Portugal who grow flax for a living – flax so fine in quality that it is used in the manufacture of linen for the royal bridal sheets, which the nuns proudly frame, identify, and display after each royal wedding night in a hall in their convent. The nuns in effect convert the wedding sheets into works of art – art which is literally constituted by female bodily fluids – and their hall into an art gallery.

Dinesen's title, 'The Blank Page', refers to the sole sheet on display that is not marked by female blood and does not identify the name of its princess on its nameplate:

> in the midst of the long row there hangs a canvas which differs from the others. The frame of it is as fine and as heavy as any, and as proudly as any carries the golden plate with the royal crown. But on this one plate no name is inscribed, and the linen within the frame is snow-white from corner to corner, a blank page.
>
> (Dinesen 1957: 104)

The blood streaming from Lavinia's mouth, stumps, and genitalia are all symbolic inversions of the blood on the sheets in the virginity test that Dinesen's story interrogates. Dinesen concludes her story by inviting her readers to join with the princesses of Portugal and their companions who stand as if transfixed, speculating on the significance of the anonymous princess's snow-white sheet:

> It is in front of this piece of pure white linen that the old princesses of Portugal – worldly wise, dutiful, long-suffering queens, wives and mothers – and their noble old playmates, bridesmaids and maids-of-honor have most often stood still. It is in front of the blank page that old and young nuns, with the Mother Abbess herself, sink into deepest thought.
>
> (Dinesen 1957: 105)[5]

Gubar takes up where Dinesen leaves off when she rehearses several possibilities for the significance of the blank page. Does the unsoiled wedding sheet mean that the princess bride was not a virgin on the wedding night? Does it mean, therefore, that she was executed or punished in some other way? Does it mean, instead, that she fled the marriage bed and thereby retained her virginity intact? Does it mean that, like Scheherazade, she escaped sexual consummation on the wedding night by narrating stories? Conversely, does it mean that the royal bridegroom was impotent on the wedding night? Because Dinesen does not tell us, we do not know.

Like Dinesen's 'blank page', Lavinia would seem to mean whatever the other characters in *Titus* – and we – want her to mean. Is she a dutiful daughter who obediently succumbs to patriarchal commodification of her in Act 1? Does she object to being so commodified? How does she feel in response to her being handed over to Saturninus by her father, despite the fact that she is betrothed to Bassianus? How does she feel in response to being gang raped, mutilated, and silenced by Demetrius and Chiron? Is she angry? Is she full of self-loathing? Does she, like many survivors in traditional western rape narratives and contemporary society alike, internalize the patriarchal construction of her as shame object? In other words, does she share with her father the belief that she deserves to die because her rape stains the honor of the Andronicus family name? It would seem that we can never know, because, in the first instance, Lavinia is silenced by patriarchal inculcations circulating within the dramatic world of her play, and, in the second instance, she is literally silenced by brutal mutilation at the hands of her rapists.

Lavinia is relentlessly objectified during much of the dramatic action – either she is a silent or a silenced object or else, when she does speak, she parrots patriarchal language. At her initial appearance, she plays the role of dutiful daughter of the patriarchy, speaking ritualistic, scripted lines as she supplies a welcoming chorus to Titus's victorious homecoming with the bodies of his dead sons and her dead brothers in tow: 'In peace and honour, live Lord Titus long: / My noble lord and father, live in fame!' (1.1.160–67).[6] Saturninus selects Lavinia to be his bride and, despite her betrothal to Bassianus, Titus agrees. His foolish absolutist loyalty to the new emperor causes him to play a parallel role of foolish absolutist patriarch, going so far as to ignore his daughter's betrothal and to murder his own son, Mutius, for his commitment to honor that betrothal. Despite the fact that the remaining dramatic action in this scene swirls around Lavinia and centres on her – or rather, on the question of who is the rightful possessor of her – she has only two lines. In response to the rhetorical question which her father tosses at her, almost as an afterthought – 'Lavinia, you are not displeased with this?' (1.1.274) – she responds: 'Not I, my lord, sith true nobility / Warrants these words in princely courtesy' (1.1.275–76).

Before the rape, Chiron's romantic rhetoric and stance exemplify the Petrarchan discursive tradition that circulates throughout late medieval and early modern European society and literature and characterizes the sonnet tradition, in particular. Masculine idealization of woman, although it appears to be the opposite of denigration, is as misogynistic as is denigration. The discourse of courtly love no less than the discourse of misogyny, as R. Howard Bloch points out, participates in the reduction of women to the status of a category (Bloch 1991: 196). While Chiron declares, in a sentence resonant of the grandiose sentiments of many of Shakespeare's male characters, 'I love Lavinia more than all the world' (1.1.570), two scenes later, he makes explicit the male concern with sexual assault that is implied by Petrarchan discourse: 'Drag hence her husband to some secret hole / And make his dead trunk pillow to our lust' (2.2.129–30). Traditional rape assumes that, because the rapist does not perceive that the woman does not want him, she is not violated. 'She had sex. Sex itself cannot be an injury. Women have sex every day,' as legal theorist Catherine MacKinnon puts it; 'sex makes a woman a woman. Sex is what women are for' (MacKinnon 1989: 180–81). The association of woman with the body in a patriarchal society defines her value in terms of her chastity because her ultimate purpose is procreation. The early modern construction of woman as a sexually insatiable creature complicates the issue of consent immeasurably. According to both the classical natural philosophy and the medieval Christian theology that influenced early modern medical discourse, as Barbara Baines notes, carnal pleasure was associated more strongly with woman than with man. Because her pleasure was believed to derive both from the release of her own seed and the reception of his seed, it is greater than that of man's – even greater than that of animals. Woman, *by nature*, therefore, would seem to be incapable of wholly resisting any form of sexual intercourse. Her utmost resolution in the denial of consent is therefore always already suspect (Baines 1998: 81, 91). In his response to Chiron's expressions of desire for Lavinia, Demetrius is brutally matter-of-fact about relations between the sexes: 'She is a woman, therefore may be wooed; / She is a woman, therefore may be won; / She is Lavinia, therefore must be loved' (1.1.582–84). According to Demetrius's circuitous logic, 'wooing', 'winning', and 'loving' a woman are synonymous. Both Chiron and Demetrius thus participate in a deconstruction of Petrarchan discourse, exposing the misogynistic sentiments that underlie the apparent idealization of woman.

When Lavinia and Bassianus come upon Tamora and Aaron in the act of sex in the forest, Lavinia joins in Bassianus's taunts of them (2.2.55–87). She sounds shrewish. Because early modern English women had few other resources, they often used their tongues to retaliate against lapses of manners and custom. Those they insulted might respond by accusing them of scolding or witchcraft; the scolding for which woman is punished is often a minor offence in comparison to the excessive response it elicits. There is a causal relationship between women's unruly tongues and men's impulsive violence, in Fran Dolan's view: shrewishness provokes, and therefore justifies, violence (Dolan 1996: 289, 297). When Demetrius and Chiron not only rape Lavinia and mutilate her but also cut out her tongue, she is literally silenced. Her rape is a political act of revenge as much as it is a psychological act of sibling rivalry.

Tamora is bent on avenging the ritual sacrifice of her son, Alarbus, by Titus in Act 1 – the death that sets off the apparently inevitable chain of acts of revenge that constitutes the dramatic action of this tragedy.

Significantly, it is in the forest outside the walls of Rome that the rape occurs.[7] Even as the penetration of the limen, or the walled boundary of the city, signifies victory for invading forces, so too does the penetration of the female hymen signify conquest. When the exchange of women articulates the culture's boundaries, the woman's hymen serves as the physical or sexual sign for the limen or wall defining the city's limits. Like the ground beneath the walls of Rome, the woman's chastity is surrounded by prohibitions and precautions as Patricia Klindienst points out (Klindienst 1998: 618).[8] Unlike the sibling rivalry of the other pair of brothers, Saturninus and Bassianus, who fight over possession of Lavinia at the outset of the dramatic action, the intense sibling rivalry of Demetrius and Chiron resolves itself in an act of intense male homosocial solidarity – gang rape.[9]

Rape and silence are intricately related to each other in contemporary US law and early modern English law, as in the dramatic action of *Titus*. According to MacKinnon, rape law defines rape as intercourse that occurs 'with force or coercion' and 'without consent'. As she goes on to point out, however, it is redundant to stipulate that force be used and that consent not be granted because presumably, if intercourse occurs without consent, it would by its very nature be forceful or coercive. The idea of female consent to intercourse with a male in a patriarchal society is a vexed one. The custom of female consent is supposed to be different from but equal to the custom of male initiative and is, therefore, supposed to constitute the primary form of control over intercourse that females exert. Theoretically, in other words, man proposes, woman disposes. In a patriarchal society in which men are systematically conditioned not even to notice what women want, however, women's consent fails to provide an effective means of control over intercourse because whether a woman gives it or not has little or no meaning (MacKinnon 1989: 172, 174, 181). The formulation that women's consent is constitutive of their control over intercourse is a flawed one, then, because it is premised upon the exercise of female agency.

In the transition from the medieval period to the early modern period, rape statutes underwent redefinition, rendering the question of female consent a particularly problematic one. In medieval England, rape statutes constructed rape as a crime against property – woman as the property of men, whether father or husband – and therefore as a crime 'between men'. In early modern England, however, rape statutes constructed rape as a crime against a person – the woman herself. She is constructed as property or passive object, on the one hand, yet she is constructed as a person invested with agency, with the discernment and the will that define consent, on the other (Baines 1998: 72–73). When rape statutes try to have it both ways, the result is a crisis in the construction of female subjectivity. Contemporary US rape law defines rape as an act of sex rather than an act of violence. Some feminist theorists, such as Susan Brownmiller, however, have redefined rape as an act of violence rather than an act of sex (Brownmiller 1975: 15). Other feminist theorists claim that the fact that rape is an act of violence does not make it less an act of sex. Considering rape as violence rather than sex evades at the moment it most seems to confront the issue of who controls women's sexuality and the domi-nance/submission dynamic that has defined it (MacKinnon 1989: 173, 178). Rape law in patriarchal societies erases the fact of women's sexual violation. Similarly, even as traditional criticism of *Titus* erases Lavinia's violation by ignoring it, so too does recent criticism that analyzes the rape as an act of violence rather than an act of sex erase her violation.

In its emphasis on not only the crime of rape but also the rapists' accompanying crime of silencing of the rape survivor to prevent discovery of the crime – literally rendering her voiceless – Lavinia's rape narrative in Shakespeare's dramatic text contains obvious echoes of Philomela's rape narrative in Book Six of Ovid's *Metamorphoses*. The Philomela story is one with which Shakespeare was familiar in Arthur Golding's 1565/67 English translation. It plays an explicit role within the dramatic action of *Titus* as the means by which Lavinia eventually begins to reveal and Titus begins to articulate the story of her rape:

> Lavinia, shall I read?
> This is the tragic tale of Philomel,
> And treats of Tereus' treason and his rape –
> And rape, I fear, was root of thy annoy.
>
> (4.1.46–49)

Unlike Philomela's rape, Lavinia's rape is a gang rape; unlike Philomela's rape, Lavinia's rape is an act of political revenge – one that is suggested by Aaron, Tamora's lover, and urged on by Tamora. Demetrius and Chiron cut out her tongue, as Tereus does to Philomela, denying her the power of speech and thereby rendering her incapable of revealing the identities of the rapists. An excised tongue, of course, renders a woman permanently silent. Because rape can be known by the law in a patriarchal society only through the mediating word of the rape survivor, it becomes the event through which the law is forced to confront all of the ambivalence inherent in its cultural construction of woman (Baines 1998: 91). The excision of the woman's tongue is, therefore, a crucial plot element in both rape narratives. Finally, unlike Philomela's rapists, Lavinia's rapists cut off her hands so that she is not able to reveal their identity by weaving a graphic representation of her rape, as Philomela is given the power to do. Capability in the craft of weaving – a craft traditionally associated with women, as descendants of Arachne, in classical mythology – serves as Philomela's means of communicating the crime and identifying the perpetrator to her sister, Procne, and therefore constitutes her path to revenge. This means of publicizing the crime and the criminal is denied Lavinia. Her fate is worse than that of Philomela, as Marcus immediately notices when he discovers her in her raped, mute, and mutilated state and forces a comparison between the two: 'Fair Philomela, why she but lost her tongue, / And in a tedious sampler sewed her mind; / But, lovely niece, that mean is cut from thee' (2.3.38–40). Lavinia's rapists, brutal though they are, are cleverer than Philomela's rapist, as Marcus notes: 'A craftier Tereus, cousin, hast thou met, / And he hath cut those pretty fingers off / That could have better sewed than Philomel' (2.3.41–43). Indeed, it is Aaron's knowledge of the Philomela narrative from classical mythology that is the reason that Demetrius and Chiron cut off her hands as well as cut out her tongue: 'This is the day of doom for Bassianus, / His Philomel must lose her tongue today, / Thy sons make pillage of her chastity' (2.2.42–44).

When Demetrius and Chiron not only rape Lavinia but cut out her tongue and cut off her hands, moreover, they deconstruct the Petrarchan convention of the *blazon*, or the male anatomization of the female. They literally take her apart, accomplishing physically that which Petrarchan discourse performs rhetorically. The dramatic world of *Titus* is scattered about with pieces of Lavinia's morcellated anatomy: her maidenhead, her tongue, her hands.[10] Caught in the crossfire between idealizing and denigrating discourses, then, Lavinia is literally and figuratively *undone*. And it is in this male two-step between Chiron, the putative romantic lover, and Demetrius, the more obvious misogynist – in other words, between the manipulative sufferer, on the one hand, and the axe wielder, on the other – that her undoing lies.[11] Their mutilation of Lavinia literalizes the metaphor, or makes the rhetorical anatomization of the female body a palpable physical presence on stage. As Linda Woodbridge has demonstrated, the colors red and white are deployed in different patriarchal societies in different historical periods as part of a semiotic code visible throughout human history, worldwide, which encodes seasonal fertility ritual and individual rites of passage (Woodbridge 1987: 247). Robed in white and stained with blood, Lavinia embodies a grotesque inversion of the red-and-white standard of female beauty that Petrarchan discourse codifies, reproduces, and celebrates. Within the politics of reproductive ritual, the virginal blood that is spectacularized within the dramatic action of *Titus* marks Lavinia as forever stigmatized and excluded from her proper female role in reproducing the patriarchal line, as Charles Frey points out. Rape denies the rape survivor her participation in the reproduction, biologically, of the species, and, socially, of patriarchy (Frey 2004: 83).

The effect of the horrible spectacle of Lavinia's entry on stage is heightened by Demetrius and Chiron, who savagely employ speech to taunt her, rhetorically representing on stage the physical torture of her that they have just perpetrated off stage:

> DEM.   So, now go tell, and if thy tongue can speak,
> Who 'twas that cut thy tongue and ravished thee.
> CHI.   Write down thy mind, bewray thy meaning so,
> And if thy stumps will let thee play the scribe.
>
> (2.3.1–4)

Because of Lavinia's silenced state, it is left to her male relatives, Marcus and Titus, to put the event of her rape into words. Both read the text of her body and speak, attempting to interpret what has happened to her (2.3.13–57, 3.1.67–136, and 3.2.1–45, respectively). 'Shall I speak for thee?' Marcus asks upon discovering her (2.3.33), while Titus vows that he will devote his life to interpreting her needs and giving voice to them:

> Speechless complainer, I will learn thy thought.
> In thy dumb action will I be as perfect
> As begging hermits in their holy prayers.
> Thou shalt not sigh, nor hold thy stumps to heaven,
> Nor wink, nor nod, nor kneel, nor make a sign,
> But I of these will wrest an alphabet
> And by still practice learn to know thy meaning.
>
> (3.2.39–45)

Lavinia's voicelessness is underscored by the rhetorical bombast of Marcus and Titus upon discovering her in her raped, mutilated, and mute state. Titus speaks at length in traditional patriarchal fashion about his own status as the primary injured party in 'the traffic in women', or the political economy of sex, as feminist anthropologist Gayle Rubin puts it, upon which patriarchal societies depend for their existence (Rubin 1975). If Titus's hand is his most powerful weapon as a soldier, Lavinia's tongue is her most powerful weapon as a woman. The dismemberment of both forces an equation between the two characters – and specifically the loss of agency on the part of both. Why does Titus ask Lavinia, though, to carry his hand in her mouth: 'And, Lavinia, thou shalt be employed: / Bear thou my hand, sweet wench, between thy teeth' (3.1.282–83)? In both Jane Howell's and Julie Taymor's cinematic texts, Lavinia looks like a dog when she has Titus's hand in her mouth; in other words, Titus's hand hangs out of her mouth, replacing and representing her own excised tongue. Taymor exploits the visual image of his hand in her mouth to emphasize how he and other male characters have been speaking for Lavinia throughout, how their hands have been controlling her tongue, how she has been a puppet of the patriarchy throughout.

Because rape takes place *inside* – psychologically and physically, according to Mieke Bal – it exists as experience, as memory, as image translated into signs (Bal 1994: 81). This difficulty in representing rape results in a displacement of its depiction – onto suicide, as in the story of Lucrece, or murder, as in the stories of Virginia and Lavinia. Surpassing Lavinia's rapists, Titus subjects her to the ultimate violence: after discovering that she has been raped in addition to having been silenced and mutilated, he murders her in the name of patriarchal honor, proclaiming, 'Die, die, Lavinia, and thy shame with thee, / And with thy shame thy father's sorrow die' (5.3.45–46). He does so, in large part, because her rapists have despoiled her chastity: 'Both her sweet hands, her tongue, and that more dear / Than hands or tongue, her spotless chastity, / Inhuman traitors, you constrained and forced' (5.2.175–77). He also murders her because she has become a daily reminder of the blemish, the 'stain', upon the honor of the Andronicus family name. As the exchange between Titus and Saturninus regarding another famous classical rape, that of Virginia, makes clear, it is the rape survivor in a patriarchal society rather than the rapists who comes to bear the burden of signifying that blemish, that 'stain':

TIT.          Was it done well of rash Virginius
               To slay his own daughter with his own right hand
               Because she was enforced, stained and deflowered?
SAT.        It was, Andronicus.
TIT.              Your reason, mighty lord?

>SAT.      Because the girl should not survive *her* shame,
>           And by *her* presence still renew *his* sorrows.
>                                    (5.3.36–41, my emphasis)

Likewise, it is Lavinia, the rape survivor, rather than Demetrius and Chiron, the perpetrators of the rape, who comes to bear the burden of signifying the crime. The fact of having been raped completely obliterates a woman's previous claims to virtue; she is forever defined by one sexual experience (Stimpson 1983: 61). The central meaning of rape is that it denies woman's equal participation in procreative life (Frey 2004: 83). According to the patriarchal system of primogeniture, however, sexual intercourse within the institution of patriarchal marriage is itself concerned only with the procreation of male identity through a male line of heirs – in this way it, too, denies a woman's equal participation in procreative life (Frey 2004: 83). Lavinia's complicity in her own murder, furthermore, which both Jane Howell's and Julie Taymor's cinematic texts emphasize, may not be easily understood by contemporary readers and viewers. Yet when we take into consideration a society that either ignores or silences a rape survivor's voice or else questions her consent – now as then – we come closer to understanding how she might be driven to suicide or complicity in her own murder. Given such conditions, she could not better affirm the reality of the rape that the suspicion of consent might deny, nor could she better protect what Shakespeare calls, in *The Rape of Lucrece*, 'the name of "chaste"'.[12]

Although Lavinia is relentlessly constructed as an object throughout much of the dramatic action, it would be a mistake to deny those moments when she is granted agency – moments that would seem to offer the potential of challenging the generic imperatives of tragedy. Because the first leads to her rape and the second to her murder, however, these moments have the effect of reinforcing generic imperatives rather than destabilizing them. Lavinia's woman-to-woman appeal to Tamora is the first point in the text where she is a subject – that is, where she speaks her own thoughts and feelings rather than serving as a choric handmaiden of the Roman patriarchy: 'O Tamora, thou bearest a woman's face'; 'Sweet lords, entreat her hear me but a word'; 'O be to me, though thy hard heart say no'; 'O, let me teach thee for my father's sake'; 'O, Tamora, be called a gentle queen'; ''Tis present death I beg, and one thing more' (2.2.136–78). It may be stretching credibility to claim that Tamora genuinely feels for Lavinia. It would not be, however, to suggest that she is threatened by the power of Lavinia's eloquence and, fearing that she may give in to her appeals, she repeatedly tries to prevent her from speaking. She cannot silence her, however; in fact, she can do little more than command her removal: 'I will not hear her speak; away with her!'; 'I know not what it means; away with her!'; 'Therefore away with her, and use her as you will'; 'What begg'st thou then, fond woman! Let me go!' (2.2.137–72). Despite Tamora's efforts, Lavinia does speak and speaks powerfully at this point in the text – only to be literally silenced when Demetrius and Chiron cut out her tongue. 'Nay, then, I'll stop your mouth' (2.2.184), Chiron says as he covers her mouth in an on-stage rehearsal of the permanent silencing of her that will soon occur off stage. The failure of Lavinia's eloquence in preventing the rape provides a significant contrast with early modern English prescriptions for female behavior, according to which a chaste woman was supposed to be capable of dissuading a man from rape, as Jocelyn Catty points out (Catty 1999: 99), despite relentless prescriptions of female silence in conduct books, household manuals, and marriage sermons of the time.

## 3

The rape narratives in Western literature exemplified by Philomela and Lavinia have not lost their viability in contemporary Western society and literature.[13] We bear silent witness as the raped women of Darfur, the Congo, and Bosnia populate our television screens on the nightly news. Maya Angelou, in *I Know Why the Caged Bird Sings*, tells of her rape as a child and of her silence, or muteness, for years following the incident. Maxine Hong Kingston, in a defiant cultural and creative act, deliberately narrates the rape of her aunt, 'No Name Woman', in 1920s China – a woman whose story, as well as her name, is forbidden to be spoken of ('You must not tell anyone') in Kingston's family (Kingston 1975: 3). Blanche DuBois, the female protagonist in Tennessee Williams's *A Streetcar Named Desire*, is, like Philomela, raped by her sister's husband. Unlike the rapes of Ovid's Philomela and Shakespeare's Lavinia, however, Stanley Kowalski's rape of Blanche is a spotless act: Blanche – the 'white', 'the blank page' – is silenced by her rapist psychologically rather than physically. Instead of the lurid spectacle of a butchered tongue and limbs, the audience is offered the sordid spectacle of a woman whose fragile grip on sanity has been forced loose by her rapist. It is true that, unlike her literary predecessors, Lavinia and Philomela, the character of Blanche retains the power of speech. Horridly, however, no one listens. The narrative of her rape that she is able to articulate to her sister, Stella – the one person in whom she confides – is wasted upon her. Stella's denial of Blanche's rape silences Blanche no less than the rapists' excisions of

Lavinia's and Philomela's tongues silence them. Stella's decision to remain in her marriage to Stanley constitutes, moreover, her betrayal of Blanche. In fact, the only way Stella can remain in her marriage to Stanley is, tragically, by denying Blanche's rape. Stella's remarks to Eunice make explicit the conflict she internalizes between Blanche and Stanley: 'I couldn't believe her story and go on living with Stanley' (Williams 1974: 133). In high contrast to Procne's solidarity with Philomela, Stella's betrayal of Blanche contributes as much as the violation and the violence of Stanley's rape to pushing Blanche over the edge.[14]

Insofar as Philomela enjoys the solidarity of her sister Procne in exacting revenge for the crimes of rape and mutilation by Tereus, the classical rape narrative would seem to offer an emotionally satisfying conclusion from the perspective of contemporary feminism. Female solidarity occurs, moreover, without the imperatives of the tragic action demanding the death of the rape survivor, as is the case with Shakespeare. Lavinia, conversely, is granted no solidarity with any other female character; instead, Tamora emphatically crushes any possibility of such solidarity when she deliberately turns a deaf ear on her pleas. Furthermore, Lavinia is not only raped, mutilated, and silenced, but, as I have mentioned, is – as soon as her father exacts revenge upon the rapists – murdered by him in an attempt to exorcise the shame of her rape from the family name of the Andronici – in the *name* of patriarchal honor. Lavinia's murder by her father constitutes, of course, the ultimate patriarchal silencing of woman. Shakespeare's rape narrative offers, therefore, a less emotionally satisfying conclusion from the perspective of contemporary feminism. The twentieth-century rape narrative offers no less bleak a conclusion. While Blanche DuBois is not murdered, whatever incipient female solidarity that may have existed between the two sisters is sacrificed at the altar of Stella's marriage to Stanley. Uniquely among the three rape narratives, no one within the dramatic world of *Streetcar* listens to, cares about – or tells – Blanche's story. No revenge is possible. *Streetcar* concludes with Blanche being led off stage to an asylum as Stella stands by, wringing her hands with guilt. Furthermore, the final stage emblem is that of male camaraderie: Stanley awaits impatiently as Mitch deals out yet one more game of 'stud' in yet one more poker night.[15]

Dominance can only contain but never successfully destroy the woman's voice, as Patricia Klindienst points out (Klindienst 1998: 615). In the end, Lavinia – despite that fact that she is raped, mutilated, and silenced – possesses the ingenuity, determination and wherewithal (and, dare I say, heroism) to hold a stick between the bloody stumps of her arms and in her mouth to name the crime of rape and identify her rapists by inscribing their names in the sand: '*Stuprum* – Chiron – Demetrius' (4.1.78). In so doing, she inverts Gubar's metaphor of 'the blank page' by relinquishing the passive, female position and adopting the active, male position – using the stick, the 'pen-penis' to inscribe meaning upon 'the blank page' of the sand.[16] Eventually Gubar works her way out of the patriarchal bind of the male 'pen-penis' and the female 'blank page' in her essay, 'The Blank Page and the Issues of Female Creativity', by theorizing a new paradigm, that of woman as life-giver – a paradigm that enables women writers to inscribe meaning rather than having it inscribed upon them, giving them a metaphorical point of entry into the act of writing rather than excluding them from it. For Shakespeare, Lavinia is empowered to write when she intervenes in the male paradigm, seizing the stick and revealing the identities of her rapists by writing their names in the sand. For Gubar, on the other hand, the female writer is empowered to write when she discards the male paradigm and replaces it with a female paradigm that configures the act of writing as analogous to the act of giving birth. For Dinesen, 'the blank page' is radically subversive, the result of one woman's defiance that must have cost either her life or her honor. Neither a sign of passivity, innocence, or purity, this 'blank page' is a 'potent act of resistance'. Woman has been defined symbolically in patriarchy as a *tabula rasa*, a lack, a negation, an absence. But blankness in Dinesen's story, 'The Blank Page', is a defiant, dangerous, and risky refusal to certify purity. The resistance of the princess allows for self-expression, for she makes her statement by not writing what she is expected to write (Gubar 1985: 305–6).

As 'blank page', Lavinia inevitably recalls the status of woman under patriarchy; as rape survivor, she is 'painfully emblematic of the plight of women' under patriarchy (Stimpson 1983: 62). Even as male characters within the dramatic world of *Titus* disseminate meaning by violently inseminating and bloodying Lavinia and reading the text of her violated, voiceless body, heterosexual males in history erase women from 'his-story' and construct fantasized categories of 'woman' – whether as love object, as in Petrarchan discourse, or sex object, as in Ovidian discourse, or as demonized object of hatred, as in misogynistic discourse.[17] The patient struggle to read the body of the text of the oppressed and silenced – the 'still practice' that Jane Marcus eloquently theorizes in her essay, 'Still Practice, A/Wrested Alphabet: Toward a Feminist Aesthetic' – offers a model for feminist criticism and theory at the present moment. The rape narratives of Philomela, Lavinia, and Blanche reinforce a vision of a primal scene in the history of women in which both their sexual power and their art are attacked and destroyed. Their procreative and their creative powers are intimately related in their suppression. They weave cloth or write on sand for the reader who is capable of seeing something other than the printed page as a text (Marcus 1987: 80–81). Despite centuries of deafness and deliberate, systematic muting, one of the concerns of feminism is the right of women to be heard. It is incumbent upon feminist theorists and critics at the outset of the twenty-first century to undertake the responsibilities of 'still practice' and 'wrest an alphabet' out of the bloodied, silent pages of 'his-story', displacing it with 'her-story'. This patient effort on the part of those whom the crone narrator in Dinesen's story, 'The Blank Page', calls 'the faithful' reads those who have gone before and who have been silenced and attempts to insure that the voice of silence – the voice of the shuttle, the voice of the stick writing in the sand – will finally be heard. Only then will those who have themselves emerged from silence into language perform the work of undoing the silence of those who are voiceless still. Only then, through the efforts of 'the faithful', as Dinesen's crone narrator emphasizes, will silence finally speak:

> Where the story-teller is loyal, eternally and unswervingly loyal to the story, there, in the end, silence will speak. Where the story has been betrayed, silence is but emptiness. But we, the faithful, when we have spoken our last word, will hear the voice of silence.
>
> (Dinesen 100)

## Notes

This essay is dedicated to Lynda Boose, who not only understands the significance and the value of 'bearing witness' but whose outstanding scholarship on Shakespeare and early modern English culture is animated by that understanding.

1  I am grateful to Barbara Johnson for bringing her article to my attention and suggesting its relevance to my study of Lavinia and patriarchal silencing.
2  In three recent and forthcoming publications, Rackin develops her critique of historicism vis-à-vis feminism (2000): 'Misogyny is Everywhere', in Dympna Callaghan, ed., *A Feminist Companion to Shakespeare*, Alden, MA: Blackwell, 42–56); interrogates feminism's rootedness in the present (2005: *Shakespeare and Women*, Oxford: Oxford University Press); and explicitly considers its relationship to presentism (forthcoming: 'Dated and Outdated: the Present Tense of Feminist Shakespeare Criticism', in Evelyn Gajowski, ed., *The Presence of Shakespeare, Sexuality, and Gender*).
3  Shakespeare may have written *Titus Andronicus* as early as 1592. Textual scholars believe its first quarto, published in 1594, derives directly from Shakespeare's manuscript.

4 See Suzanne Gossett (1984: 305–6) for a comparative analysis of the innova-
tions of several plays that foreground rape in the seven-year period 1617–23:
Fletcher's *The Queen of Corinth*, Rowley's *All's Lost by Lust*, Middleton's *Women
Beware Women*, Middleton's and Rowley's *The Spanish Gypsy*, and Massinger's
*The Unnatural Combat*.

5 See Karen Paige and Jeffery Paige (1981: 90) for an analysis of the politics of
virginity tests and other reproductive rituals in different patriarchal societies in
different time periods.

6 All citations of Shakespeare's *Titus Andronicus* are from The Arden
Shakespeare, 3rd series, edited by Jonathan Bate, and are cited by act, scene,
and line number in the text of the essay.

7 Traditionally critics have constructed the forest in Shakespeare's texts, and
especially his comedies, as a pastoral green retreat, as in the Athenian wood in
*A Midsummer Night's Dream*, the Forest of Arden in *As You Like It*, and Bohemia in
*The Winter's Tale*. For female characters, however, whether they travel alone or
accompanied, it is also a locale saturated with the danger of rape – for Lavinia
in *Titus*, as for Julia and Sylvia in *The Two Gentlemen of Verona*, Helena in *Dream*,
and Rosalind in *As You Like It*.

8 Patricia Klindienst derives the title of her article on Philomela from the
striking phrase, 'the voice of the shuttle', that Aristotle uses in *The Poetics* to
describe Philomela's tell-tale tapestry.

9 See René Girard's analysis of power relations in the traditional erotic triangle
of European high culture. He views the bond between male rivals as more
intense than the bond between either of the so-called male 'lovers' and the so-
called female 'beloved'. When Eve Kosofsky Sedgwick theorizes male
homosocial relations in her groundbreaking book-length study, *Between Men*,
she draws upon the work of Girard.

10 See Nancy Vickers (1985) on Lucrece and Mary Fawcett (1983) on Lavinia in
this regard.

11 I am adapting Barbara Johnson's remarks from her discussion of another text
that is deeply concerned with both female silence and female mutilation, the
contemporary cinematic text, *The Piano*, directed by Jane Campion and starring Holly Hunter: 'It is in this male two-step – the axe wielder and the
manipulative sufferer, *both* of whom see themselves as powerless – that patriarchal power lies' (1996: 147, emphasis hers). Significantly, as Johnson notes,
every female actor who has been nominated for playing the role of a mute –
Jane Wyman (*Johnny Belinda*), Patty Duke (*The Miracle Worker*), Marlee Matlin
(*Children of a Lesser God*), and Holly Hunter – has gone on to win an Oscar.

12 I am drawing on Barbara Baines here (1998: 89).

13 In a related contemporary crime epidemic on and off university and college
campuses across the US, rapists administer the drugs rohipnol or GHB, the so-
called 'date rape' drugs, to women, debilitating them by rendering them not
only passive but also unconscious.

14 Significantly, Elia Kazan alters the ending of Tennessee Williams's dramatic
text in his 1951 cinematic text (starring Vivien Leigh as Blanche, Marlon
Brando as Stanley, Kim Hunter as Stella, and Karl Malden as Mitch). Even
though Blanche is led off to an insane asylum at the end, as in Williams's text,
insofar as Stella twice rejects Stanley, both physically and verbally, her character is endowed with an agency she does not possess in Williams's text. When
Stanley reaches out to her, she pushes him away, proclaiming, 'Don't touch

me – don't you ever touch me again!' After she watches the car holding
Blanche pull away, Stella picks up her baby from the carriage as Stanley,
having returned to his poker game, calls out, 'Stella! Come on, Stella!' from
within the flat. She responds by clutching her baby to her shoulder as she
quietly declares with grim determination – 'I'm not going back in there again!
Not this time! I'm never going back! Never!' – and runs up the stairs in one last
escape to Eunice's flat. There are grounds in this interpolated blocking and in
these interpolated lines for audience members to believe that Stella has left
Stanley for good in the end. Stanley's refrain – 'Hey, Stella! Hey, Stella!' – is
also interpolated into the ending in a reprisal of scene three, however. These
words are the last words audience members hear on the soundtrack, and their
repetition from earlier in the text reminds them that earlier marital conflicts
have melted under the pressure of sexual desire; Kazan suggests, therefore,
that Stella's decision to leave Stanley may not be so permanent, after all.

15  It is significant that Tennessee Williams's original title for *Streetcar* was *The Poker
Night*. After Stanley has rent asunder both the heterosexual bond between
Blanche and Mitch and the female homosocial bond between Blanche and
Stella, Williams's text concludes with the reassertion of male homosocial
bonding as symbolized by Stanley's poker game.

16  The phallic significance of Lavinia's act of writing cannot be denied. I
disagree with critics such as Clark Hulse (1979: 116) and Douglas Green (1989:
325), however, who emphasize the violent erotic connotations of Lavinia's act
of writing by asserting that she both enacts fellatio when she takes the staff in
her mouth and re-enacts her own violation. Instead, it is crucial from the
perspective of contemporary feminism to emphasize that – despite the fact that
she dies and, as contorted as her physical appearance is and as primitive as her
tools are – she does indeed manage to write.

17  See my *The Art of Loving* for in-depth, chapter-length analyses of Petrarchan,
Ovidian, and Orientalist discursive traditions (Gajowski 1992).

# 8

# *Hamlet* and the present
## Notes on the moving aesthetic 'now'

Hugh Grady

'Of all the characters of *Shakespeare* that of *Hamlet* has been generally thought the most difficult to be reduced to any fixed or settled principle' wrote the Scottish novelist and essayist Henry Mackenzie (1780),[1] and his observation continues to ring true two and a quarter centuries later. But our era and the earlier one react quite differently to this common view of *Hamlet*. For Mackenzie and his contemporaries of late Enlightenment Europe, the difficulty of conceptualizing the character Hamlet was a problem, and even a growing scandal, one that released a flood of discourse attempting to make good the perceived *lacuna*. In the early twenty-first century, the resistance to unification of both the character and the play of the same name serves instead as a disclosure about the nature of literary texts and of the more rationalistic discourses that attempt to interpret them. *Hamlet* has escaped the nets of all the critics who have attempted to ensnare it, and it will continue to do so. Theodor Adorno believed that such a critical history revealed something important about the nature not only of *Hamlet* but of all forms of art: 'Although no artwork can be reduced to rationalistic determinations . . . each artwork through the neediness implicit in its enigmaticalness nevertheless turns toward interpretive reason. No message is to be squeezed out of *Hamlet*; this in no way impinges on its truth content' (Adorno 1997: 128). Many aesthetic theorists have pointed to the quality of art that Adorno renders here as its 'enigmaticalness', but not all of them concluded, as Adorno does here, that the work implies a concept-resisting 'truth-value' which must be reinterpreted from generation to generation, as culture, language, values, and assumptions evolve and change over time. We can never, as I have previously argued, abstract a 'timeless' meaning of the text underneath the changing play of historical interpretations,[2] but we can and must posit an objectivity of the text which, however, is not directly and unproblematically available to us, but which reveals itself negatively, in the text's resistance to certain interpretive schemas (Grady 2002: 83–84). In what follows I want to trace the workings of these interpretive dynamics in the history of *Hamlet* criticism in a selective survey of its interpreters from the earliest to the latest critics, observing the impact on interpreting *Hamlet* of changes in ideas of aesthetic form and the nature of art which make up what I have termed 'aesthetic paradigms' (Grady 1991: 24–27; 75–81). Aesthetic paradigms have a paradoxical relation to temporality – they always construct art in the present for us in a form peculiar to the specific era of cultural history in which they are situated. But each age forms a specific relationship with earlier eras, and that relationship defines its interpretations of works from the earlier era. In the process, we can observe the reality of the inevitable 'presentism' of all critical discourse as we watch interpretations of *Hamlet* embody successive moments of evolving aesthetic paradigms. As I will argue by way of conclusion, the openness of literary texts to such changing interpretations is a corollary of their status as aesthetic objects, as cultural creations that surpass linear, cognitive rationality.

It still seems to be true that more has been written about this play than about any other work of literature. *Hamlet* thus remains a test-case of critical methodologies *par excellence* because it has been interpreted and re-interpreted for over three centuries without any sign of exhaustion. It is an ideal vehicle to illustrate the resistance of Shakespeare's works – and ultimately, of all cultural productions worthy of the name 'art' – to definitive interpretation. Instead, works like *Hamlet* are reinvigorated and re-interpreted from one age to the next as societies, culture, and aesthetics change in an interconnected historical process. For example, for the critics of the Restoration and early Enlightenment, the age of Shakespeare was 'barbarous', and its origins within barbarism were cited as reasons for what almost all critics of the time saw as *Hamlet*'s flaws. For Modernist critics in the early and mid-twentieth century, however, the age of Shakespeare had been reconceptualized as a cultural golden age, an age of an organic society the loss of which had maimed the twentieth century but cast a new shine on the surviving documents of a better time. More recently yet, Shakespeare's age seems to have become neither completely barbarous nor golden, but mixed, conceived as a simulacrum of our own time, and in that way open to a different presentist allegorization, as a period of transition at the beginning of modernity that mirrors our own age of transition into an uncharted postmodernity. But whether the past is constructed as Other or as our own, it is always defined by its relation to ourselves and our self-understanding. Indeed, the re-reading and re-thinking of classic literary works is one of the chief means we have for charting our own changes, our own insights into the way we live now.

It is for these reasons chiefly that, as I have written before, there can be no historicism without a latent presentism (Grady 2005: 115). The past continually changes its shape and meaning for us as we move further into the future, gain new experiences and new perspectives, and research, re-think, and re-evaluate the past. That is to say, then, that our attitude towards the past governs our approach to the artefacts of that past, and that attitude is a function of our present specific social and historical situation. While there are a number of histories of *Hamlet* criticism available, I hope in this account to make a new contribution by highlighting the specific influence of changing aesthetic paradigms in how we have perceived the play over time. For reasons of space, and because the topic has been perceptively explored over the last twenty years in four very different studies of the history of *Hamlet* criticism (Hawkes 1986: 73–91; Foakes 1993: 12–37; Kinney 2002; Hawkes 2002b: 79–120), I will leave the considerable and variegated political impact on the history of *Hamlet* interpretation unaddressed, except in very broad terms.

## Early reactions to *Hamlet*

For all the recent emphasis on re-creating the vanished space of Shakespeare's plays' first reception, we continue to know very little about how the original audiences reacted to the play. We know that *Hamlet* was exceedingly popular and that both the Ghost and the theme of madness created a buzz among early modern London play-goers.[3] We know that the Elizabethan courtier and scholar Gabriel Harvey thought that Shakespeare's *Hamlet* – and his narrative poem *The Rape of Lucrece* – 'have it in them to please the wiser sort'. We know that the play continued to have enough currency to spark the insider joke in the 1605 play 'Eastward Ho', which introduces a servant named Hamlet, apparently for the sole purpose of another character's line, 'Hamlet, are you mad?' According to Anthony Dawson, there were revivals of the play at court in 1619–20 and in 1637 and an amateur performance off the coast of Sierra Leone on William Keeling's ship the *Dragon* in 1607–8 (1995: 30–31). Thus *Hamlet* was among the four Shakespearean plays that were still in production during the eclipse of Shakespeare's reputation in the Caroline period, and likewise it was among the first of Shakespeare's plays revived after the Restoration (Dobson 1992: 25). But none of this takes us very far into the highly contested issues of the play's meaning.

*Hamlet*'s popularity in the Restoration era was attested to in one of the earliest recorded post-Restoration remarks on the play in 1710, when Anthony, fourth Earl of Shaftsesbury, wrote of Shakespeare's then century-old play: 'That Piece of his, The Tragedy of HAMLET . . . appears to have most affected *English* Hearts, and has perhaps been oftenest acted of any which have come upon our Stage' (qtd. in Furness 1877: 2, 143).

Shaftesbury was in fact much more positive in his approach to Shakespeare than many of his contemporaries – certainly so in comparison with the strict neo-classicist Thomas Rymer, for example – although Rymer chose *Othello* rather than *Hamlet* as his chief example of Shakespearean incompetency (Rymer 1693). Shaftesbury, after attesting to the popularity of *Hamlet*, went on to praise it in the terms that were most on the minds of critics of his era: it is, he wrote, 'almost one continu'd *Moral*; a Series of deep Reflections, drawn from *one* Mouth, upon the Subject of *one* single Accident and Calamity, naturally fitted to move Horror and Compassion' (qtd. in Furness 1877: 2: 143). This praise of *Hamlet*'s aesthetic unity and moral probity is high indeed, especially when re-set in the context of his opening list of Shakespeare's 'faults': 'his natural Rudeness, his unpolish'd Style, his antiquated Phrase and Wit, his want of Method and Coherence, and his Deficiency in almost all the Graces and Ornaments of this kind of Writings' (ibid.). As all students of the history of Shakespeare's reception in the eighteenth century know, such mixed reactions were decidedly typical of the time.[4] Under the strictures of the neo-classical literary theory that had slowly developed over the seventeenth century in England and was then established as dominant with the return of a monarchy and its court from Classical France, Shakespeare's plays could only appear barbarous, irregular, and ignorant of the proper rules of dramatic construction. Shakespeare ignored the 'three unities' demanded of tragedy by neo-classical theory – the unities of time (twenty-four hours or less), place (a single, unchanging locale), and action (a causally linked plot without subplots) that had been culled from far less prescriptive language in Aristotle's *Poetics*, the neo-classical Bible for tragedy. He further violated neo-classical standards by mixing comic and tragic matter, by stretching what the age considered to be rational standards of probability, and by often violating the codes of politeness and decorum that had developed in the interim. A strict neo-classical critic like Rymer used such categories to devastate Shakespeare. Many neo-classical critics, however – even Voltaire (1961), who was more steeped in the system of neo-classicism than any of the less system-worshipping English – found redeeming features in parts of the plays, especially in the tragedies. Shakespeare slipped through the neo-classical nets through one of its most prominent loopholes: the idea of the 'natural', unschooled poet. Shakespeare's friend and rival Ben Jonson, the father of English neo-classicism, had first defined this idea in reference to Shakespeare in the early seventeenth century, and it was reproduced repeatedly throughout the neo-classical age.

Beneath the appearance of an unchanging neo-classical paradigm, however, there was in fact considerable change of opinion on Shakespeare's value over the course of the eighteenth century. As Michael Dobson has demonstrated in detail, Shakespeare's reputation grew steadily from decade to decade, under a number of impulses, including a growing anti-French English nationalism; an increase in the number of women reading, discussing, and writing about the arts, including drama; and a growing empirical consciousness that refused to accept the neo-classical 'rules' as absolute (Dobson 1992: 99–222). By the time Samuel Johnson came to edit his own critical edition of Shakespeare (published in 1765), the century's earlier strict interpretation of the three rules of classical unity had loosened enough that Johnson, instead of condemning *Hamlet* for its mixture of comedy and tragedy or its violation of the unities of time, space and action, positively praises the play:

> If the dramas of Shakespeare were to be characterized, each
> by the particular excellence which distinguishes it from the
> rest, we must allow to the tragedy of *Hamlet* the praise of
> variety. The incidents are so numerous that the argument of
> the play would make a long tale. The scenes are interchange-
> ably diversified with a merriment and solemnity; with
> merriment that includes judicious and instructive observa-
> tions; and solemnity not strained by poetical violence above
> the natural sentiments of man.
>
> (Johnson 1968: 8:1010–11)

After this, however, Johnson went on to list a series of criticisms, based on his perceptions of probability and the eighteenth-century concept of poetic justice, which held that rewards and punishments should be distributed at the end of a tragedy in accordance with moral ideals. He is thus still working in the judicial neo-classical critical framework, but he has, reflecting the evolution of opinion in his age, considerably modified earlier ideas about ideal dramatic form.

## From neo-classicism to organic unity

In late eighteenth- and early nineteenth-century Germany, however, in the wake of the development of Kantian and post-Kantian aesthetics, neo-classical unity gave way to Romantic organic unity, and what neo-classicists had seen as *Hamlet*'s alleged faults melted away while the play was celebrated repeatedly as a nearly perfect drama that challenged readers to comprehend its assumed unity rather than as the 'irregular' product of natural genius in a barbarous age. Like all cultural processes, this one was uneven and long-term – but it is precisely historical hindsight that allows us to clarify the overall trend.

*Hamlet*'s rise to world stature – its transformation from the great if flawed masterpiece of the English national poet to perhaps the greatest work of all world literature – was complexly interconnected with the epochal literary and philosophical revolutions that produced German Idealist philosophy and German Romanticism – and much of the content of aesthetic theory. Central to this movement were two crucial concepts – aesthetics and subjectivity. Both were also central to the reception of *Hamlet* that ran parallel to (and was a consequence of) the more general critical revolution. For philosopher Immanuel Kant, as Andrew Bowie argues, one of the central problems of post-Hume philosophy was how to unify the 'sensuous manifold' of human perception, to conceptualize a unitary sensibility, not only in art-works but in human identity itself (Bowie 2003: 16–17). How is our sense of lived continuity, of ourselves as the same person even as we change over time, possible? How can our self-consciousness be described and accounted for?

This problem of unifying the multifarious subjective flow into a sense of personhood is recognizably cut from the same cloth as late eighteenth- and nineteenth-century attempts to conceptualize the character Hamlet as a unified, comprehensible figure. Interpreting *Hamlet* in this period becomes in that sense a simulacrum for solving the age's great philosophical problems of knowledge and personhood. No wonder there was cultural obsession with the play, above all, but not exclusively, in Germany. In fact, as the nineteenth century progressed, the image of the Romantic Hamlet of hesitation, indecision, and moral sensitivity was evoked as a metaphor for pre-unification Germany. Germany itself became Hamlet in a famous, much cited poem,

'Germany Is Hamlet', by Karl Marx's friend Ferdinand Freiligrath, which states in part:

> So he endures, thus dreamily,
>     With secret self-contempt, his pain
> . . .
> No deed from all his talk he hatches.

> (Freiligrath 1844)

The change from a politically conservative, neo-classical, adjudi-cating approach to art to a politically progressive, Romantic, exalting, and, if I may put it this way, submissive approach to 'great works', intu-ited as such and interpreted through a concept of 'organic unity', is nowhere more visible than in Johann Wolfgang von Goethe's prototyp-ical *Bildungsroman*, the 1795–96 *Wilhelm Meister's Apprenticeship* (*Wilhelm Meisters Lehrjahre*). Among many other things, the novel is a milestone in *Hamlet* criticism. It is most famous in that regard for the short passage, long taken to be the quintessential expression of the 'Romantic' reading of *Hamlet*, in which Wilhelm presents the fruits of a long medi-tation on that play's central character and compares the Prince to a delicate vase in which was planted an oak tree. For Goethe's Wilhelm, Hamlet was an otherwise admirable character on whom had been imposed a task for which he was constitutionally unfit, and as a result Hamlet 'sinks beneath a burden [he] cannot bear' (Goethe 1905: 7:223). This was the seed of the 'Romantic' Hamlet that was later cultivated by A. W. Schlegel and Samuel Taylor Coleridge, among many others. But here I want briefly to examine how the play *Hamlet* functions in the novel as a vehicle to describe the transition from neo-classical to Romantic interpretation and becomes a defining instance of the inter-related categories of the aesthetic and subjectivity.

Significantly, Wilhelm is introduced to Shakespeare in the context of his sycophantic praise of seventeenth-century French classical dramaturgy to a German nobleman who idealizes the French tragedian Jean Racine. His acquaintance Jarno (who will later prove to be a more valuable friend than Wilhelm realizes at this moment) pointedly says to him, 'Have you never . . . read one of Shakespeare's plays?' Wilhelm replies as a devotee of French classicism that 'all I have heard of these plays has excited no wish to become acquainted with such extraordi-nary monsters, which appear to set probability and dignity alike at defiance.' Jarno advises him 'to make a trial, notwithstanding . . . I will lend you a volume or two; and you cannot better spend your time, than by casting every thing aside, and retiring to the solitude of your old habitation, to look into the magic-lantern of that unknown world. . . . One thing only I require, – you must not cavil at the form: the rest I can leave to your own good sense and feeling' (1905: 7:165).

After some hesitation Wilhelm takes the suggestion, and the narrator assures us that 'as may be easily supposed, the stream of that mighty genius laid hold of him, and led him down to a shoreless ocean, where he soon completely forgot and lost himself' (1905: 7:166).

As his reading of Shakespeare progresses, Wilhelm becomes both fascinated with and a champion of the aesthetic excellence of *Hamlet*. When he gets agreement from Serlo, the manager of the theatre where Wilhelm has signed on as an actor and writer, to put on a performance of the play, the issue of how to cut and adapt it soon comes to the fore. Serlo, the manager, is still under the influence of neo-classical attitudes: 'his acute understanding could usually discern in any work of art nothing but a more or less imperfect whole' (1905: 7:264). Like the neo-classical adapters of the Restoration and Augustan English theatre before him, Serlo believed that Shakespeare (and in this instance *Hamlet*) could only be improved through a judicious re-write in order to separate 'the wheat from the chaff'. Wilhelm is indignant and counter-poses the nascent Romantic concept of organic unity: '"It is not chaff and wheat together," said he; "it is a trunk with boughs, twigs, leaves, buds, blossoms, and fruit. Is not the one there with the others, and by means of them?"' (Goethe 1905: 7:264).

The change which Goethe fictionalizes for us in *Wilhelm Meister's Apprenticeship*, the shift from a concept of what henceforth would be thought of as 'mechanical form' to the notion of organic form, entailed far more than a change in how to conceptualize the aesthetic unity of an art-work; it amounted to a revolution in attitude to the work. It meant that each work was aesthetically unique, and the challenge it made to the interpreter was less one of measuring the success or failure of the work in conforming to some ideal type than in submitting oneself humbly to the spell of the work itself as something beyond mere conceptual thought. Shakespeare was the major example whose work, achieving greatness in defiance of what a century or more of neo-classical theory had held to be the natural rules of dramatic creation, proved the insufficiency of external rules for comprehending art. Shakespeare thus became the prototype of what Kant called in his *Critique of Judgment* 'the genius', 'the talent (natural endowment) that gives the rule to art' (1790: 174), for, as he argues:

> the concept of fine art does not permit a judgment about the
> beauty of its product to be derived from any rule whatsoever

that has a *concept* as its determining basis, i. e., the judgment
must not be based on a concept of the way in which the
product is possible. Hence fine art cannot itself devise the
rule by which it is to bring about its product.

(Kant 1790:175)

And Kant adds, 'It cannot be couched in a formula and serve as a
precept, for then a judgment about the beautiful could be determined
according to concepts' (1790: 177). The genius cannot explain what
she has wrought and can only communicate her aesthetic ideas
through her works themselves, arousing 'similar ideas' in an apt student
– although Kant adds, 'How that is possible is difficult to explain'
(1790: 177). The form of the work is not to be sought in any external
guide; it can only be discerned, and never fully conceptualized,
through the study of art-works themselves.

Of course, the rise of this new idea of the aesthetic as resisting
determinate conceptualization never put an end to rationalistic attempts
to conceptualize the play. Kant allowed that 'the rule [governing the
artistic purpose of the work] must be abstracted from what the artist
has done, i.e. from the product, which others may use to test their own
talent' (1790: 177). In the case of *Hamlet* in particular, such attempts,
already prolific in England, became even more prolific in Germany in
the nineteenth century.[5] This nineteenth-century moment of Shakespeare
(and especially of *Hamlet*) criticism still dominates much of the public
perception of Shakespeare, despite nearly a century of Modernist and
Postmodernist counter-arguments and critiques. Such cultural staying
power is a testimony to the impact of the ideas of the aesthetic and the
subject that emerged in the late eighteenth and early nineteenth centuries.
To be sure, there was never a consensus as to an interpretation of *Hamlet*
in this period. Instead, rival theories proliferated to the point even of
scandal, revealing that the idea of organic unity functioned primarily
as a limit-concept, an ideal towards which critics strived but which they
never reached.

Samuel Taylor Coleridge was the main conduit of the new German
ideas and evaluation of Shakespeare back into England, and his debt
to the German synthesizer and popularizer A. W. Schlegel – verging
on, perhaps constituting, plagiarism – is well known. Whatever the
nuances of interpretation that might justify an independent place for
Coleridge in the history of *Hamlet* criticism, he is clearly indebted for
his vastly influential ideas about organic unity in Shakespeare and in
literature generally to Germany. As we shall see, the notion of organic
unity was central not only for Romanticism but for Modernism as well.

The culmination of the Romantic tradition (for the English-speaking world at any rate) was undoubtedly the highly influential lectures on *Hamlet* in A. C. Bradley's 1904 *Shakespearean Tragedy*. Bradley has been treated as the first of the new wave of twentieth-century Shakespeare critics in many accounts (e.g. Kinney 2002: 34), but it is in the expansiveness of his discourse and his emphasis on concrete textual evidence rather than in his interpretive ideas themselves that he can be accounted part of twentieth-century Shakespeare critical culture. In his conviction that the neo-classicals were blind to critical obviosities (1904: 94–95), in his fixation on problems of character interpretation (1904: 95–97 and throughout), and in his homage to Hegel's aesthetic philosophy (1902: 32–33), he is very much a product of nineteenth century Shakespeare studies. His Hamlet – and his analysis of the play is essentially an analysis of its central character – is a selective synthesis of insights from Goethe, Schlegel, and Coleridge, however much he criticizes specific aspects of each of these predecessors. The chief difference from his predecessors is his insistence that their description of a hesitating Hamlet who is the victim of his own intellectualizing cast of mind misses the point that Hamlet was not always thus, but had become so through his depression or melancholy (1904: 108–26). But, for example, he continues the general Romantic ideas that Hamlet could not have meant the horrifying things that he said in sparing Claudius at prayer (1904: 133–34), that he never fell completely out of love with Ophelia (1904: 147–53), and that 'though Hamlet hates his uncle and acknowledges the duty of vengeance, his whole heart is never in this feeling or this task' (1904: 135). Bradley is a Romantic chastened by the aesthetic of realism, but one who manages to combine the two rather than replace the first with the second.

## The transition from romanticism to modernism

The beginning of the end of the era when debate about the meaning of *Hamlet* was a central cultural pre-occupation is marked by two iconoclastic interventions in the discussion: Sigmund Freud's interpretation of the play as a prescient demonstration of the power of the Oedipal complex – the idea first appearing in print in his *The Interpretation of Dreams* (Freud 1900);[6] and T. S. Eliot's 1919 essay 'Hamlet and his Problems'. As if to illustrate the principle of uneven cultural development and co-existing rival paradigms at moments of cultural transition, the dates when Freud worked out his views on *Hamlet* are approximately the same as those of A. C. Bradley's work on tragedy and Shakespeare. And indeed, the two share important concerns. Both

Bradley and Freud are hyper-aware of the nineteenth century's extensive archive of writing on Hamlet's character, and each sees himself as working within this tradition – and in fact solving its long-standing problems. But whereas Bradley uses the term 'melancholy' as found in a contemporary, unnamed 'work on mental diseases' (1904: 120) to provide a unified concept for Hamlet's personality, Freud introduced his radical notion of Hamlet as exemplifying a character split between conscious and unconscious parts of the self, thereby decentring Hamlet and inaugurating a new discursive approach within *Hamlet* criticism. In the long run, Freud's intervention within the *Hamlet* debate served to move it out of the cultural centrality it had occupied for about a century. Once Freud's stature as a twentieth-century icon had been established, no critic offering a 'psychological' interpretation of *Hamlet* could afford to ignore him, and no one could compete with him. In effect, Freud ended the debate over the central question of nineteenth-century *Hamlet* criticism: what was it about the personality of Hamlet that caused him to hesitate? Just what kind of character is Hamlet? Freud's theory, if it did not convince all critics, seemed at least to have caused them to decide to change the subject.

In a recent essay in *The New York Times Book Review*, critic Lee Siegel argued that Freud's influence had in fact 'spelled the death of psychology in art', wearing away, as he put it, 'the specificity of fictional character' (8 May, 2005: 29), substituting instead a panoply of impersonal categories (ego, id, superego) that were universal and abstract, but powerfully explanatory. The result, Siegel argues, is the disappearance in our time of the great characters created in the novels of the eighteenth and nineteenth centuries.

What Siegel fails to take into account in this perceptive analysis is the much larger, more inclusive influence of the Modernist aesthetic revolution, for which Freud should be seen as an important source and to which I will turn shortly in reference to Eliot and his aftermath. But if the hypothesis is perhaps too sweeping for the complex case of the late twentieth-century novel, I believe it captures something crucial about what happens to *Hamlet* criticism after Freud and after the aesthetic-paradigm shift to Modernism. The character analysis, for this and for the other Shakespeare plays, more or less disappears.[7] The play – as poem, as dramatic structure, as myth – comes to the fore.

Another major influence on the relative decline in cultural prestige of *Hamlet* in the twentieth century was undoubtedly T. S. Eliot's well-known essay 'Hamlet and His Problems'. First published in 1919, the essay was a part of Eliot's attempt to make a name for himself in the wake of his 1914 re-location to England from America and the success of his 1917 *Prufrock and Other Observations*.[8] In a letter dated 1921 (two years after the appearance of 'Hamlet and His Problems'), Eliot spoke explicitly to his correspondent Richard Aldington of 'my general programme of literary criticism which must by this time be fairly obvious to you', a programme which he links to a de-valuation of 'the nineteenth century in general' (V. Eliot 1988: 460). The specific critique of *Hamlet* by Eliot is very much a part of this attempted devaluation. In shifting attention from Hamlet the character to *Hamlet* the play as a source of the many 'problems' critics had been debating for more than a century, Eliot targeted Goethe and Coleridge as the chief culprits for what he now declaims to be vastly influential but misleading interpretations – 'the most misleading kind possible', he says. (Eliot 1920: 95). In a hermeneutic shift that was indeed a kind of re-assertion of the neo-classical critical values he later identified with – but which was refunctioned for both conservative political and aesthetic Modernist purposes[9] – Eliot claims that the reason why the debate about Hamlet's motivation has gone on for so long is rooted in the aesthetic failure of the play, not in the subtleties of its characterization. But instead of evoking the panoply of neo-classical ideals of correct dramaturgy, Eliot alludes instead to two disparate figures, each of whom figures prominently in the accelerating professionalization of Shakespearean criticism: the American professor and literary historian E. E. Stoll and the English autodidact J. M. Robertson.[10]

Eliot lingers over Stoll only briefly, praising him for his critique of the assumptions of the Romantic interpreters (1920: 96) who are Eliot's principal target as well. But there is a much longer discussion of Robertson, an heir of the Victorian disintegrators who developed their search for co-authors of Shakespeare's work to encompass the entire Shakespearean canon through his own metrical analyses (Robertson 1930), and who had found *Hamlet* to be a palimpsest of different versions of the story of Hamlet (including hypothetical treatments by Kyd and perhaps Chapman) that Shakespeare had imperfectly incorporated into the text(s) we know. As a result of his accepting this (highly questionable) composition process as described by Robertson, Eliot concluded that the play was an incoherent mixing of Shakespearean and 'cruder' materials – and famously, that it was an 'artistic failure' (T. S. Eliot 1920: 96–97; 98). *Hamlet*, unlike the later tragedies, failed to find the 'objective correlative' of the emotions which the play, in spite of this lack, somehow in fact expresses (Eliot 1920: 98–100). *Hamlet* thus for Eliot never emerges 'in the sunlight'. It is, Eliot asserts, 'full of some stuff that the writer could not drag to light' (1920: 100). The essay in this diagnosis uncannily complements Freud's interpretation, sharing with Freud the conviction that Hamlet the character is obsessed with his mother's guilt for obscure reasons which seem to be 'in *excess* of the facts' (1920: 101) and stemming from psychic matter 'which Shakespeare did not understand himself' (1920: 103). Despite this commonality, however, Eliot never embraces Freud's view that the play exhibits symptoms of an origin in the unconscious, an orientation, Freud would assert, characteristic of all art. It is not clear, in fact, that Eliot was familiar with Freud's views on the play: he mentions Robertson as the source of the insight into the importance of Hamlet's feelings towards his mother (1920: 99–100), and a number of earlier critics had noted it as well. In the absence of the Freudian idea of an aesthetically productive influence of the unconscious on the art-work, Eliot instead maintains the provocative but ultimately non-coherent view that Hamlet's emotions both are and are not communicated in the play. How, we might ask, are we conscious of such apparently self-canceling feelings? Eliot himself expressed puzzlement over this question:

> And when we search for this feeling, we find it, as in the sonnets, very difficult to localize. You cannot point to it in the speeches; indeed, if you examine the two famous soliloquies you see the versification of Shakespeare, but a content which might be claimed by another, perhaps by the author of the *Revenge of Bussy d'Ambois*, Act V, sc. i. We find Shakespeare's *Hamlet* not in the action, not in any quotations that we might select, so much as in an unmistakable tone which is unmistakably not in the earlier play.
>
> (1920:100)

Putting aside the curious assured tone in the reference to the style of the 'earlier play' – that is, the hypothesized version by Kyd and possibly Chapman which Robertson claimed he could glimpse in certain portions of Shakespeare's *Hamlet* – a play which does not now and perhaps never did exist – we can see Eliot here straining towards a theory of impersonal 'objective' art which was one of the marks of an emerging Anglo-American Modernism, one famously shared, for example, with James Joyce. *Hamlet*, Eliot implies, fails to provide the objective images to 'contain' its unleashed subjectivity.

Terence Hawkes is surely right in his assessment that Eliot's verdict on *Hamlet* is best explained as part of his political-literary 'programme' for a new, more conservative English literary canon – one based on the denigration of the Romantics in favor of a seventeenth-century Anglican tradition exemplified for Eliot by Donne or Lancelot

Andrewes. 'Even today,' Hawkes writes, 'it seems an astonishing judgment, certainly one which strikes an unrepentant "foreign" note' (Hawkes 1992: 93–94). And certainly among Shakespeare critics of Eliot's time, it is difficult to find enthusiastic seconders of Eliot's devaluation of the play. Even the Eliot admirer E. M. Forster dissented (Forster 1936: 112; cited in Hawkes 1992: 94).

And yet, in the long run, as R. A. Foakes has succinctly but clearly established, *Hamlet* was indeed knocked from its perch at the summit of the Shakespeare canon and replaced by *King Lear* – this ranking becoming a majority position, according to Foakes, by about 1960 (1993: 1–11). To be sure, this is very far from the triumph of Eliot's 'astonishing judgment' that *Hamlet* fails artistically; it is a matter of the play's moving over a few steps to make room for the new champion, rather than falling to the bottom. But it is a significant phenomenon, and I'm not sure that the many narratives of the history of *Hamlet* criticism have well defined it.

## Modernist *Hamlet* critics

At the beginning of the Modernist period of Shakespeare criticism – which lasted from about 1930 to 1970 (Grady 1991) – *Hamlet* was in a peculiar position. The motifs under which the play had been culturally central for the previous hundred years or more, when it was repeatedly celebrated for its iconic hero who was a figure of intellectuality, alienation, and indecision – had become dated, no longer adequately embodying a new era's values and its new perceptions of the play, especially in the Anglo-American world.[11] Freud had given a convincing and paradigm-shifting answer to the long debated issue of why Hamlet hesitates, and Eliot had thrown up his influential hands at the same questions, suggesting that the play itself was the problem. In the context of the profound aesthetic shift that took place over the Western world just before and after 1910, creative of new forms and conceptions of art, these two interventions in the discussion effectively vitiated the old approach to *Hamlet*, and a new one had to be invented. The 1912 production of *Hamlet* in the Moscow Art Theater which used Cubist motifs (a collaboration between Edward Gordon Craig and K. S. Stanislavsky) seemed at first to enlist *Hamlet* into the cause of Modernism, and the twentieth century in fact saw a plethora of Modernist-inspired *Hamlet*s. In the more sheltered groves of academia, however, the critical reception of the play was much less avant-garde, and the responses to the new situation for *Hamlet* criticism were cautious. Foakes saw one key reaction against the nineteenth-century view of the play, developing mainly in the 1950s, to be the substitution of a heroic, action-taking Hamlet for the earlier image of an ineffectual intellectual. Partly under the influence of the new professionalism in the discussion of Shakespeare, but also embodying the cultural and political changes brought on by a half-century of war and other catastrophes, the character Hamlet was reinserted back into the play, and a number of different ways to reconceptualize him as an 'active hero' emerged. If Hamlet were Germany, the play as much as the nation needed to be radically reconsidered after the triumph of Nazism. Lawrence Olivier's 1947 film version, for example, for all its allusions to the Romantic and the Freudian Hamlets, presented through Olivier's gestures, diction, and body language an athletic and decisive hero in this mold. Several critics moved in a similar direction, rethinking Hamlet as a much more decisive hero than before: Peter Alexander (1955), Harry Levin (1959), and E. A. J. Honigmann (1976) all switched the focus so that *Hamlet* was a play about a corrupt society rather than a problematic hero (Foakes 1993: 30). Of these Levin's work was the best developed. Levin applauded Alexander's earlier defense of Hamlet as a hero but went further, attacking an often misplaced and misunderstood doctrine of Aristotelian 'tragic flaw' and replacing emphasis on Hamlet's excellencies rather than his faults.

But more radical and more responsive to the shifting aesthetic tides of Modernism were two influential interpretations by G. Wilson Knight (1930) and Maynard Mack (1952). Knight deployed his newly worked out strategy of 'spatialization' in reference to *Hamlet*, conceiving the play as, in his words, 'set spatially as well as temporally in the mind' (Knight 1930: 3) and pursuing this spatialized text through a study of imagery, symbols and motifs in the play rather than in character and plot, finally seeking to unify the imagery into a thematically connected field expressed by a central symbol.[12] In *Hamlet*, Knight decided, the central theme was death itself, and Hamlet served as death's 'ambassador', bringing into an otherwise healthy world 'the poison of negation, nothingness, threatening to a world of positive assertion' (1930: 41). This interpretation reversed the moral vectors not only of Goethe's Hamlet – that otherwise noble and admirable Prince whose sensibility was crushed beneath the burden of duty in a cruel world – but also of the slightly later emerging figure of a positive, action-taking Hamlet. Knight's analysis may have interested other critics for its methodology, but few accepted without qualification its overall characterization of the play. Morris Weitz (1964), for instance, making *Hamlet* his case in point in a study of the various then extant modes of literary criticism, was scandalized by Knight's interpretation:

'At least one thing must be said immediately', Weitz wrote. 'His entire criticism, both in theory and practice, is not true' (1964: 32). Knight's view of Elsinore as healthy, according to Weitz, is 'perverse', and the notion that Hamlet is the centre and source of the play-world's sickness 'makes a moral mockery of [the play]'. If there is any truth in Knight's account of Hamlet's symbolism, it is narrow, partial, and patently inadequate (1964: 33). On the other hand Kinney, writing almost fifty years later, pronounces Knight's interpretation of *Hamlet* 'more successful' than Eliot's because Knight found the 'objective correlative' that Eliot thought was missing in the play in the symbols and images of the central motif of death (Kinney 2002: 37).

Maynard Mack's influence seems mainly to have been restricted to within the borders of the United States, but his essay, centered on the concept of what he calls *Hamlet*'s 'world', has impressed many and scandalized far fewer than did Knight's. Another Modernist attempt at the spatialization of the play, Mack's analysis relies less on poetic imagery and more on trying to conceptualize 'the imaginative environment that the play asks us to enter when we read it or go to see it', a world 'made of people, actions, situations, thoughts, feelings, and much more, but unlike our own in being perfectly, or almost perfectly, significant and coherent' (Mack 1952: 503). To try to make this more concrete, Mack chooses three inter-related 'attributes' to focus on: 'mysteriousness' (1952: 504), 'the problematic relation to reality and the relation of reality to appearance' (507), and the 'powerful sense of mortality' (1952: 514). True to his era, Mack sees image patterns of the sort defined by Wolfgang Clemen, Caroline Spurgeon, and G. Wilson Knight as a means of expression of these attributes, but his approach is more inclusive than theirs, encompassing the motif of questioning and riddles, the theme of madness, the atmosphere of Machiavellian intrigue, and the repetition of key words, among several others. In retrospect, it seems one of the most successful of the Modernist readings of the play, which may have departed from the Romantics in their strategy of 'spatializing' the text, but were continuous with them in their embrace of the idea of organic unity.

## Postmodernist *Hamlet*

A key transitional work between Modernism and Postmodernism – one showing both impulses at once – was Walter Benjamin's 1928 *The Origin of German Tragic Drama* (1977). Although its focus is on the seventeenth-century German baroque dramas called in German *Trauerspiele*, there are scattered remarks on *Hamlet* throughout the work, and it makes a central claim that organic unity is not the organizing principle of these dramas (including *Hamlet*), but that they rather follow the fragmenting, dissonant aesthetics of allegory defined in a special Benjaminian sense that has much in common (but is not identical) with later Postmodernist approaches to aesthetic unity. Part of a larger German and Anglophone project of linking the baroque with Modernism beginning in the 1920s, the work was little known in the English-speaking world until the 1970s, when it was widely interpreted as being prophetic of structuralist and poststructuralist insights.

In the English-speaking world, however – perhaps because the highly original, late Modernist theory of Northrop Frye played such a key role in Shakespeare studies well into the 1970s (Halpern 1997: 114–58) – Postmodernist criticism came relatively late to the field in comparison with other areas of literary studies. Many theories of aesthetic Postmodernism trace its advent to the period immediately after the Second World War, in such new forms as confessional poetry or the *nouveau roman*; or to the mid-1960s – the age of pop-art and new wave cinema – at the latest. If we take the rise of 'theory' in literary studies as the mark of Postmodernism's emergence within academic literary studies, we could see Postmodernist criticism emerging in France in the 1950s and 1960s and take the date of 1969 (the year of the celebrated conference at Johns Hopkins University that introduced structuralism/poststructuralism to US literary scholars) as the time of its first visibility within American academia. But Shakespeare studies resisted the tide another ten or fifteen years. The dike was finally broken with Stephen Greenblatt's *Renaissance Self-Fashioning* (1980), and the flood began in earnest with the appearance of a number of key critical anthologies in 1985 and the years immediately following. The new Postmodernist aesthetic paradigm broke decisively with the Romantic and then Modernist idea that an art-work was necessarily characterized by organic unity – the view so well articulated by Goethe, and accepted as essential by such Modernists as T. S. Eliot and G. Wilson Knight. The new Postmodernist paradigm, once established in the field, almost immediately produced new analyses of *Hamlet*. Because virtually all previous interpretations since the Romantics had assumed organic unity to be an aesthetic *sine qua non*, and because *Hamlet* so notoriously resisted such unification, it seemed to many in the new critical generation to be a perfect object on which to test the new interpretive ideas. For example, Patricia Parker and Geoffrey Hartman's milestone *Shakespeare and the Question of Theory* (1985: 273–332) devoted an entire subsection to the play, and any number of other essays and books followed; new treatments of *Hamlet* were an essential feature of the critical revolution in Shakespeare studies in the 1980s and beyond. Here I want to focus briefly on a very few representative studies of the play in various critical modes influenced by the new impulses of Postmodernism: two from central theorists of Postmodernist poststructuralism, Lacan's 'Desire and the Interpretation of Desire in *Hamlet*' and Derrida's *Specters of Marx*; and three works squarely within Shakespeare studies – Terence Hawkes's 'Telmah' (1986: 92–119), Marjorie Garber's *Shakespeare's Ghost Writers* (1987: 124–76), and Stephen Greenblatt's *Hamlet in Purgatory* (2001). While these represent only a fraction of the archive of Postmodernist-influenced writings on *Hamlet*, they each represent a different facet of a complex methodology.

Jacques Lacan, like Walter Benjamin, is a transitional figure whose career overlapped the period of both Modernism and Postmodernism in France, but, as has become widely recognized, his writings developed some of the key ideas and procedures of a poststructuralism later developed more explicitly by theorists like Derrida and Foucault. Lacan in effect contributed to a Postmodernist approach to aesthetic unity in the guise of re-writing Freud on the relations among desire, the Oedipal complex, and language. For Lacan our social identity is formed as a result of the Oedipal complex, when an unconscious is created for repressed Oedipal desires in the same movement that throws the individual into a world conceptualized as a set of linguistic signifiers, as language – what Lacan calls the Symbolic Order. The resulting 'I' is a truncated being, symbolically castrated and experiencing a self-constituting 'lack' which in turn results in a constant play of desire over an interminable chain of linked but distinct signifiers within ordinary language. What we call desire is essentially a futile search for objects to fill up the lack of the loss of a now forbidden love.

It is in this theoretical context that Lacan analyzes *Hamlet* in a famous essay first presented in his weekly seminars of 1959, 'Desire and the Interpretation of Desire in *Hamlet*'. Lacan immediately names Ophelia as a desired object: 'As a sort of come-on, I announced [in the previous seminar] that I would speak today about that piece of bait named Ophelia, and I'll be as good as my word' (1977: 11). But as the essay develops, Ophelia is only the first term in an extended series of objects of desire, expressing the concept of the phallus, in Lacan's special sense of the term as a signifier more than a physical organ. He traces a chain of such desired objects throughout the play, defining a structure of continual deferment, as Hamlet attempts through a series of ineffectual activities (pretending madness, commissioning a drama, killing the wrong man) to find the missing phallus, the object of desire – which we know is in some sense 'really' embodied in Claudius, but which is also, as Lacan says, 'a ghost' which cannot be touched (1977: 50). Accordingly, if we might develop Lacan's ideas in a direction which is implied but not spelled out in his essay, *Hamlet* lacks 'organic unity' because it is never complete, because it shares the structures of interminable desiring. And this insight becomes one of the foundations of many Postmodernist readings of the play.

Jacques Derrida came to *Hamlet* considerably later, in his *The Specters of Marx* (1994), a work devoted to assessing the status of Marxism in the post-Communist world. But the book devotes a surprising amount of space to Marx's favorite author William Shakespeare (and his play *Hamlet*) as well, because Derrida decides that the best way to conceptualize the legacy of Marx today is through the famous image that opens *The Communist Manifesto,* that of the spectre that haunts Europe. And he finds the Ghost of Hamlet's father to be the best vehicle for an investigation into this trope:

> *What is* a ghost? What is the *effectivity* or the *presence* of a specter, that is, of what seems to remain as ineffective, virtual, insubstantial as a simulacrum? Is there *there,* between the thing itself and its simulacrum, an opposition that holds up? Repetition *and* first time, but also repetition and last time . . . Altogether other. Staging for the end of history. Let us call it a *hauntology.*
>
> (1994: 10)

Through writing like this, as Margreta de Grazia described in an essay tracing *Hamlet*'s image of the old mole (and related issues) in Hegel, Marx, Lacan, and Derrida (1999), the play resumes something of the cultural import it had possessed in the nineteenth century. *Hamlet* seems to be a play much more amenable to Postmodernist aesthetic assumptions than it was to Modernist ones. In this case Derrida has used *Hamlet* to supply the concepts to reformulate and enrich his earlier discussions of the play of absence and presence, and through this use *Hamlet* and Shakespeare have regained something of their philosophical reputation (or what amounts to the same thing, their philosophical usefulness) to think the present and grasp its paradoxes. Accordingly, something of its slipped cultural prestige has been recuperated after the paradigm-shift from Modernism to Postmodernism.

Terence Hawkes had earlier made central use of some of the younger Derrida's key conceptions in one of the pioneering works of Postmodernist interpretation of *Hamlet,* 'Telmah' – Hamlet spelled backwards.[13] Hawkes proceeds to read the play 'against the grain' (as

Terry Eagleton would later put it), discerning within the text the potential to be interpreted as the tragedy, not of the Prince, but of his 'mighty opposite', Claudius. 'I propose' wrote Hawkes, 'the sense of the text as a site, or an area of conflicting and often contradictory potential interpretations, no one or group of which can claim "intrinsic" primacy or "inherent" authority, and all of which are always ideological in nature and subject to extrinsic political and economic determinisms' (1986: 117). Hawkes's manifesto for radically indeterminate readings was a signal that a new paradigm for the interpretation of *Hamlet* (and of literature generally) was well underway.

If Hawkes developed Derrida, Marjorie Garber made central use of Lacan to forge another of the most deft and sophisticated readings of the play in our time, in her chapter on *Hamlet* in *Shakespeare's Ghost Writers* (1987). Ranging in her discussion over ideas from Freud, Nietzsche, Lacan, Derrida, and de Man, Garber discloses *Hamlet*'s complexity as a drama about memory and forgetting, fathers and sons, writing and absence, and the influence of the unconscious on an unstable, decentred text. Ultimately psychoanalytic in her orientation, Garber showed early in its history the potentiality for hybridization in the new Postmodernist critical methods by linking the philosophical, the psychoanalytical, and the political in a rich texture of commentary.

Stephen Greenblatt deals with some of these same themes within the Postmodernist critical paradigm, but in a very different, much less theorizing mode in the climactic chapter of his late new historicist work *Hamlet in Purgatory* (2001). It is a study very much rooted in the historicist rather than the presentist side of Greenblatt's methodology, one that confronts us with the Otherness of the beliefs about Purgatory and the dead in the late medieval and early modern periods. There are, however, some telling presentist moments in the book: the personal subtext underlining the entire study is clearly explained in the 'Prologue' as stemming from the death of Greenblatt's father and his son's mixed response to the father's bequest for the saying of the Jewish prayer for the dead, the kaddish (Greenblatt 2001: 6); there is an allusion to Derrida's notion of 'hauntology' (Greenblatt 2001: 297 no. 17); and Greenblatt sketches a haunting account of resemblances between the dreams depicted in Shakespeare's *Richard III* with those of participants in Germany's Nazi era (2001: 164–80).

Beyond these presentist moments, what makes the book a part of Postmodernist culture is that the 'exotic' mentality from pre-modernity – even though the doctrine of Purgatory continues in contemporary Catholicism, the lore about it which Greenblatt unearths will be unfamiliar to all but a few specialists – is manifestly still emotionally accessible to us – something we discover as we realize that the medieval desire to aid the dead has strong resonances with modern, even atheist, experiencess of mourning.[14] Greenblatt interprets *Hamlet* as, in effect, resulting in an aestheticization of the complex emotions of mourning tied up with the belief in Purgatory and the opportunity which that belief supplies for a continuous, intimate connection with departed loved ones. The process of transformation is a telling example of the kind of 'Shakespearean negotiations' Greenblatt had defined in his earlier work of that name (1988a), a transformation which is secular in its logic – the formerly sacred becomes the material of an essentially secular drama – but one which avoids conceptual commentary on doctrine in favor of a mobilization of powerful cultural memories and defunct practices.

The work of art that is produced in this transaction is one that defies – has defied for four centuries – a crystallizing focus of its energies behind some clear concept, but by that very quality makes its lost context available to subsequent ages, in constantly regenerated and re-organized forms as history develops. Greenblatt's embrace of an essentially post-structuralist, Postmodernist idea of the play's textuality, its openness to a multiple, unending series of interpretations and reinterpretations, makes his reading of the play simultaneously a work of (incomplete) cultural restoration and a contribution to the culture of Postmodernism.

It is, of course, always thus with *Hamlet* (and any other art-work that 'transcends' – that is, constantly re-negotiates throughout its after-life its relationship to) its historical moment of origination. A work of art always exists in the present to the extent that it remains a work of art, and it is precisely for this reason that presentist criticism is inevitable, if it is sometimes disguised (as late it has been) as historicist criticism. In any art-work, as Ewan Fernie has emphasized in his recent writing, there is an unavoidable presence – and *Hamlet* is a perfect example: 'Like Shakespeare's ghost, *Hamlet* breaches and disrupts successive presents', he writes (2005b: 169). In art there is always a renewability within the flux of time that creates a complex kind of temporality negotiating between past and present. After two decades of trying to avoid a recognition of this presentness of the work of art, it is time to embrace and make it our own again, as we create the contours of the new moment of historical transformation that we are now entering.

# Notes

1  I have corrected the erroneous date of 1770 given in Hoy's citation of this essay. My thanks to Dan Traister of the University of Pennsylvania Furness Rare Books and Manuscripts Collection for establishing the correct date of 1780.

2 This is to say that the distinction posited many years ago by E. D. Hirsch (1967) between a work's timeless 'meaning' and its changing 'significance' is untenable because the 'meaning' will always turn out to be intertwined with the 'significance' and vice versa.

3 See Ingleby *et al.* 1909 for a still unsurpassed listing of contemporaneous reactions to Shakespeare from his contemporaries and their immediate descendants up to 1700. *Hamlet* elicited the greatest number of these allusions to Shakespeare, with the figure of the Ghost and the motif of madness being the most prominently mentioned topics associated with the play.

4 Sayre N. Greenfield is at this time of writing undertaking a computer-aided search for allusions to *Hamlet* in the later seventeenth and eighteenth centuries. In an interim report on this work at the 2005 Annual Meeting of the West Virginia Shakespeare and Renaissance Association, Sayre found a set of parodic allusions to the play in its immediate aftermath (similar in spirit to the one in *Eastward Ho* mentioned above), then a relative silence until about 1630, when *Hamlet* began to be seen more as a work of literature than a theatrical performance; and a continuing and accelerating set of allusions after the Reformation into the eighteenth century.

5 One index of this geographic shift of discursivity can be seen in the large quantity of German writings on Hamlet in the critical extracts in Furness 1877: 2: 267–380.

6 Tracing the evolution and publication of Freud's psychoanalytic analysis of *Hamlet* is a complex business. In one sense, the theory appears in complete form only with the 1949 publication of Freud's disciple Ernst Jones, *Hamlet and Oedipus*. But scholars find that Freud first conceived of Hamlet as in the grip of an Oedipal complex as early as 1897 when Freud outlined the theory in a letter to his friend Wilhelm Fleiss (Freud 1985a: 272–73), but the notion doesn't appear in print until 1900, in Freud 1900.

7 Of course there were continued character analyses, like Charlton 1948, and Bradley's *Shakespearean Tragedy* has never been out of print. My point is that such analyses began to seem old-fashioned, however and were no longer representative of the hegemonic critical approach to Shakespeare.

8 See Hawkes 1992: 90–120 for an account of Eliot's strategies of making a mark in England in this period.

9 Eliot's most famous declaration of his allegiance to 'classicism' (along with royalism and Anglicanism) appeared in Eliot 1929 (originally published in 1928). In the essay under consideration here, Eliot signals this allegiance to neo-classicism through a footnote which proclaims that he had never 'seen a cogent refutation of Thomas Rymer's objections to *Othello*' (Eliot 1920: 96 no.1). Rymer, as mentioned above, was the strictest and most anti-Shakespearean of the Restoration neo-classical critics.

10 See Grady 1991: 69–75 for thumbnail discussions of Robertson and Stoll in this connection.

11 See Foakes 1993: 12–44 and Kinney 2002: 27–44 for two useful accounts of critical reactions to *Hamlet* which show that the 'Romantic' reading of Hamlet persisted in Europe throughout the twentieth century while the English-speaking world elevated *King Lear* above it and fiercely critiqued the Romantic reading of the play.

12 See Grady 1991: 92–108 for a more detailed analysis of Knight's critical innovations as incorporating Modernist aesthetic suppositions.

13 I am citing the essay as it appears as Chapter 5 of Hawkes 1986; earlier versions appeared in Hawkes 1983 and in Parker and Hartman 1985: 310–32.

14 See Fernie 2005b for an insightful reading of the theoretical implications of Greenblatt's *Hamlet in Purgatory* (2001) and its intersections with themes of the late Derrida which, as mentioned above, Greenblatt alludes to in passing.

# 9

## *Troilus and Cressida*
## The perils of presentism

### Kiernan Ryan

### 'Prodigious nondescript'

No play testifies more powerfully than *Troilus and Cressida* to the need for an approach to Shakespeare frankly anchored in the present. Shakespeare's 'mysterious and magnificent monster of a play' (Swinburne 1880: 199) begs to be read as a scathing parable of our modern plight, tricked out as an ancient tale of blighted love in Homer's Troy and couched in the alien idiom of the Elizabethan stage. The play was never at home in its own time, which plainly had no idea what to make of it. The title-page of the revised 1609 Quarto dubbed it 'The Famous Historie of Troylus and Cresseid', while the anonymous blurb in the same edition, cryptically addressed by 'a never writer to an ever reader', hawked it as 'passing full of the palm comical' and stiff competition for Terence and Plautus (Shakespeare 1998b: 120–21).[1] In the First Folio, however, the play is entitled 'The Tragedie of Troylus and Cressida', although the title does not appear in the 'Catalogue', or table of contents, and the text lies stranded between the histories and the tragedies, marooned in the generic twilight zone it has haunted ever since. To make matters murkier, the title page of the first 1609 Quarto bills it as acted at the Globe by Shakespeare's company, 'the Kings Maiesties servants', a claim contradicted in the second edition by the 'never writer', who assures the 'eternal reader': 'you have here a new play, never staled with the stage, never clapper-clawed with the palms of the vulgar' (Shakespeare 1998b: 120). Nor is there any record of private performance at the Inns of Court, at Whitehall or anywhere else, which would mean – if the 'never writer' is to be trusted – that *Troilus* was 'never staled with the stage' for three hundred years, and that Charles Fry's production at the Great Queen Street Theatre in 1907 was its British premiere.

It is hard to think of another play in the Shakespearean canon hamstrung by such a puzzling provenance or cold-shouldered by the English stage for so long. Dryden thought it a defective apprentice-piece, whose construction, characterization, language and conclusion required major surgery before it was fit to be seen on the Restoration stage. Dryden's decorous redaction, subtitled *Truth Found Too Late* (1679), which 'undertook to remove that heap of Rubbish, under which many excellent thoughts lay wholly bury'd' (Dryden 1984: 226), made *Troilus* palatable for a time. But it did so by twisting Shakespeare's play into a sentimental romantic tragedy, at whose close a faithful Cressida dies vindicated and a wrathful Troilus, apprised too late of her fidelity, kills the dastardly Diomede in revenge before being slain by Achilles. Dryden restored to the principal characters the heroic stature and grav-itas Shakespeare had denied them, cut Thersites down to comic size, and defused Pandarus by demonising him. He reconstructed the play to rationalize its distribution of scenes and bring its handling of space and time to heel. He combed out the knots of obscurity in which he found the play's language tangled. And he substituted for its unresolved ending, in which the lovers are left alive and Cressida goes unpunished, a denouement that delivers poetic justice and commends political conformity. In the last line of Shakespeare's *Troilus*, Pandarus promises to bequeath us his diseases; the final line of Dryden's drama urges subjects to learn obedience to their kings. Dryden's tasteful mutation gives us the measure of the original's delinquency and determination to vex its audience. Even his sanitized version, however, could not save Shakespeare's mongrel tragicomedy from languishing in theatrical limbo until the dawn of the twentieth century.

Not that the great Shakespearean critics who flourished in the interim proved any more adept at coming to terms with *Troilus*. Dr Johnson had nothing of note to say beyond a few trite plaudits and animadversions. Hazlitt was obviously discomfited by 'one of the most loose and desultory of our author's plays', which 'rambles on just as it happens' (Hazlitt 1930: 221), and, notwithstanding his acute compar-ison of Shakespeare's art with Chaucer's, failed to get a fix on it. Coleridge found himself likewise at a loss, because 'there is none of Shakespeare's plays harder to characterize'. Despite his conviction that 'Shakespeare calls forth nothing from the mausoleum of history' without 'eliciting some permanent and general interest', the only thing that clearly interested Coleridge was Thersites, whom he immortalized as 'the Caliban of demagogues' life – the admirable portrait of intellectual power deserted by all grace, all moral principle, all not momentary purpose' (Coleridge 1969: 271, 272). Around the same time in Germany, however, Heinrich Heine, Hermann Ulrici and G. G. Gervinus were beginning to tune in to the vision of *Troilus*. The play's 'clamorous bitterness' and 'withering irony' struck a chord in Heine's strife-torn country long before they resonated in its author's native land. Heine recognized that '*Troilus and Cressida* is neither a comedy nor a tragedy in the usual sense; it belongs to no special kind of poetry, and still less can it be judged by any received standard'. Indeed, its eccentric hybridity made the play, paradoxically, 'Shakespeare's most characteristic creation'. Beyond that, there was little the critic could say about *Troilus*: 'We can acknowledge its great excellence only in general terms; for a detailed judgement we should need the help of that new aesthetics which has not yet been written' (Martin 1976: 44–45).

That new aesthetics had still not been written in Britain by the close of the nineteenth century, but its first stirrings could be discerned in the *fin-de-siècle* fans the play won among poets, playwrights and critics. Swinburne hailed it as a 'prodigious nondescript or portent of supreme genius', which 'defies and derides all definitive comment' (Swinburne 1880: 199). George Bernard Shaw, never one to fight shy of a definitive comment, applauded Shakespeare for having 'treated the story' of the ill-starred Trojan lovers 'as an iconoclast treats an idol'. Shaw took *Troilus* as an assault on the jingoistic glamorization of war enshrined not only in Chapman's Homer, but also in *Henry V*, the 'mistake and failure' of which Shakespeare wished 'to expose and avenge'. At the same time, Shakespeare 'had ceased to believe in Romeo and Juliet and in bullies like Petruchio', and so was equally intent on dispelling the mystique of romantic love he had helped to foster; hence his 'enchanting' creation in the inconstant Cressida of 'Shakespeare's first real woman' (Shaw 1969: 203). In the age of Ibsen, Strindberg and Shaw himself the play that had left critics stumped and the stage repelled for centuries started to make sense. So much so that F. S. Boas felt confident enough to classify it, along with *All's Well That Ends Well*, *Measure for Measure* and *Hamlet*, as a 'problem play' (Boas 1896: 345), whose generic instability, disillusioned mood and lack of resolution required the invention of the special category in which it has been quarantined ever since.

The tide had turned at last in favour of *Troilus and Cressida*. The features that had once been deplored as its vices were embraced as the virtues that made it, in Jan Kott's phrase, 'Amazing and Modern' (1964: 61). Shaw's view of *Troilus* became the starting point from that day to this, as directors and critics amplified its resonance with current attitudes to warfare, *Realpolitik*, the sexual revolution, and the erosion of ethical absolutes. Audiences had no trouble hearing in *Troilus and Cressida* the echo of their own moral exhaustion and political cynicism in the wake of the first and second world wars. But during the 1960s and 1970s, when comparisons between the protracted Trojan war and both the relentless conflict in Vietnam and the interminable Cold War became compelling, *Troilus* came into its own as an anti-war play, and since that time it has become a staple of the repertoire, performed almost as often as *Hamlet* or *As You Like It* in the UK and North America. Nor has its burgeoning popularity been exclusively due to its indictment of war and political duplicity. There were four major British productions of *Troilus* in the 1990s alone, one at the National Theatre and three at the Royal Shakespeare Company, making it the most frequently performed Shakespeare play of the decade at those venues. The success of these productions owed much to the prominent sexual politics of Cressida's predicament and, in at least one case (the 1996 RSC production), to the camp homoeroticism of the warriors and the dark hints of AIDS evoked by Pandarus's terminal disease. These productions were all, moreover, eclectic in conception and design, creating through fusions of tribal antiquity with late modernity a postmodern sense of the collapse of history, which the text of *Troilus* does nothing to discourage.

Modern critical accounts of the play have kept pace with, and as often as not paved the way for, theatrical perceptions of the play. Critics weaned on modernist and, subsequently, postmodernist aesthetics lapped up the qualities of *Troilus and Cressida* that had alienated their precursors: its formal fluidity, its decentred dramatic narrative, its ironic manipulation of myth and intertextuality, and its fragmented, deferred denouement. In recent decades, riding the tidal wave of theory that broke in the 1980s, a host of feminist readings have set out to solve the riddle of Cressida's character (Greene 1980; Adelman 1985; Hodgdon 1990; Bowen 1993); it has become *de rigueur* to discern in the play's verbal and literary self-consciousness a master class in deconstruction *avant la lettre* (Freund 1985; Kopper 1988; Scott 1988); and persuasive readings have been produced to prove that *Troilus* secretes not only a profound grasp of postmodern subjectivity (Charnes 1993), but also a prescient Marxist critique of reification (Grady 1996). To trace the play's performance history from Fry's groundbreaking 1907 production through to the 2004 production in

Boston that drew parallels with the current Iraq conflict and the prospect of a perennial War on Terror, is to realize why *Troilus and Cressida* has come to be regarded by so many scholars, critics and directors as 'Shakespeare's play for the twentieth century' (Shirley 2005: 1), and why it shows no signs of losing its grip on the present in the first decade of the twenty-first.

## 'Small pricks'

The reception history of *Troilus and Cressida* is instructive, because it demonstrates with singular force the validity of reading Shakespeare's drama from a presentist perspective. Such an approach is anathema to the kind of historicism that has prevailed in Shakespeare studies for the last quarter of a century. Few adepts of that historicism are so naïve as to believe any more that Shakespeare's texts can be restored to their original contexts undistorted by the distance that divides them from the modern scholar's time and mind. But they all share with their antiquarian forebears an insistence on the priority of the past, a conviction that Shakespeare's world should call the shots when it comes to making sense of Shakespeare now. Indeed, when even historicists as hip as Stephen Greenblatt (2004) and James Shapiro (2005) can be found exhuming the same old topical links between the work and its world (*Macbeth* and the Gunpowder plot, *Henry V* and Essex's Irish campaign), one might be forgiven for wondering how new, deep down, the new historicism really is. It would certainly be unjust to accuse the historicist *nouvelle vague* of striving to reconstruct the plays' early modern matrix *wie es eigentlich gewesen*, although the endless studies bent on shackling Shakespeare to everything from maps and money to cooking and cosmetics often make it seem that way. But it is open to the charge of sacrificing textual analysis to the analysis of surrogate discourses, and of pursuing the cultural study of the plays from a skewed perspective, which privileges their point of origin over the process of reception. In this respect the historicist critic resembles nothing so much as the strange, arthritic creature Arthur encounters at the castle of Orgoglio in *The Faerie Queene*:

> But very uncouth sight was to behold,
>     How he did fashion his untoward pace,
>     For as he forward moov'd his footing old,
>     So backward still was turnd his wrinkled face,
>     Unlike to men, who ever as they trace,
>     Both feet and face one way are wont to lead.

> This was the auncient keeper of that place,
> And foster father of the Gyant dead;
> His name *Ignaro* did his nature right aread.
>
> (Spenser 1978: I.viii.31)

Locked like Ignaro in a trance of retrospection, today's historicists are condemned by their thraldom to a fetishized past to face forever backwards as they move forward, to remain immured in what Coleridge calls 'the mausoleum of history'. To stretch the allegorical analogy a little further, it is also apt that 'the auncient keeper of that place', as his name suggests, knows nothing about what goes on in it and can answer none of Arthur's urgent questions; although he holds 'the keyes of every inner dore' (I.viii.30), he can open none of them, and only when Arthur wrests the keys from Ignaro's grasp is he able to unlock the secrets of the castle and release the dying Redcross Knight from his imprisonment.

To cast presentism as the heroic Prince Arthur in this scenario would perhaps be to stretch the allegory too far. The keeper of Orgoglio's castle does provide, however, a vivid caricature of historicism's blindness to the key quality of Shakespeare's plays, the quality that presentism is primed to take in its stride: their anachronism. By that I mean their refusal to make complete sense – or sometimes any sense at all – in terms of Shakespeare's time, because their vision is not only moulded by the culture that cradled them, but also possessed by 'the prophetic soul / Of the wide world dreaming on things to come' (Sonnet 107, 1–2).[2] *Troilus and Cressida* offers us the most extreme instance of the estrangement of Shakespeare's drama from its era, which is why it struck Heine as 'Shakespeare's most characteristic creation', whose comprehension must await an aesthetic of the future. *Troilus*, needless to say, bears the imprint of its late Elizabethan origin in every line. To grapple with the contortions and obliquities of its verse and prose today is to grasp how deeply it is entrenched in its historical moment, and to feel its resistance to being engaged on any terms but its own. No critical approach to any Shakespeare play could make much headway, let alone carry conviction, unless it was grounded in solid historical knowledge of the language, forms and conventions of his drama. Without such knowledge criticism could never arrive at the point of basic comprehension where the task of interpretation begins. But the assumption that the more fully Shakespeare's plays are embedded in their early modern milieu, the more intelligible they will become, could not be more misguided. In fact, as Shapiro's *1599: A Year in the Life of Shakespeare* (2005) shows, the more detailed the reconstruction of the plays' genetic contexts, the more completely those contexts eclipse the plays that furnish their pretext, and the more difficult it becomes to see what connects the plays to them at all. Under the pressure of this past-bound brand of interdisciplinary historicism, the aesthetic singularity of the plays dissolves, and their difference from their time, their incongruity with their culture, dissolves along with it.

The poverty of the current historicist approach is exposed by the precocious modernity of *Troilus and Cressida*. The incomprehension and neglect from which the play suffered for three hundred years was not the result of historical ignorance. It was the result of the play's being not merely out of sync with its time, but so far ahead of its time that it took three centuries for the theatre and for critics to catch up with it. In its contempt for the premises on which historicism rests and the imperatives that steer its critical practice, *Troilus* demands a radical rethinking of the relationship between Shakespeare's texts and their past and present contexts. If the hallmark of Shakespeare's drama, the feature that makes it more potent in our time than it could ever have been in his own, is its uncanny prescience, then modern appropriations of the plays cannot be dismissed as wilful misreadings that have no historical warrant. If it is not presentist criticism but Shakespeare's dramatic imagination that is anachronistic, then the feminist, Marxist and deconstructive readings that *Troilus and Cressida* has attracted are not only more in tune with the text, but also *more truly historical*, than either old or new historicist accounts of it. For such readings, provided they are close and consistently confirmed by the text, activate implications historically inscribed in the language and form of *Troilus* at the moment it was composed. By doing so, they reveal that all along this play knew more in its time about times to come than historicist criticism deemed it capable of knowing. To release those prospective implications is to expand the play's historical significance, and thus transform our perception of the vanished past that prompted its creation.

Such readings secure anchorage in the text and prove persuasive because they explicate in the critical idiom of the present what has been stored for centuries in the theatrical and poetic idiom of the past. *Troilus and Cressida* always housed these insights into gender, language, power and subjectivity, but it housed them *in a different form*. So when modern critics appropriate these insights genetically encoded in the play, and articulate them in the idiom of our time, they are not riding roughshod over the constraints of history and the text. On the contrary, they are empowering the play to speak to us for the first time of matters that were always on its mind, but that could not be apprehended until now. It is, after all, not so surprising to find Shakespeare dramatizing problems that were embryonic in early modern England, but whose mature form he was already in a position to envisage. Presentist criticism of Shakespeare that proceeds on this understanding, tracing in his visionary dispatches from his epoch the lineaments of life in ours, has no need to tout itself as the implacable foe of historically grounded criticism, which it can beat at its own game.

If it requires a precedent, this conception of presentism need look no further than Shakespeare himself, who provides impeccable authority for it both as an attitude to the past and as a creative and critical practice. The *Sonnets* are shaped throughout by the proleptic cast of Shakespeare's imagination. Poem after poem transports us into the remote future, fore-telling what shall come to pass and eerily anticipating its own fate:

> Your monument shall be my gentle verse,
> Which eyes not yet created shall o'er-read,
> And tongues to be your being shall rehearse
> When all the breathers of this world are dead.
>
> (Sonnet 81, 9–12)

In Sonnet 106, however, Shakespeare adopts the role of the reader of poetry of a bygone age – the same role that we adopt when we read him now. What is remarkable about the poem is not just its awareness of past literature's power to foreshadow the present, but its appreciation of the part played by present-day readers in deciphering that prophetic legacy:

> When in the chronicle of wasted time
> I see description of the fairest wights,
> And beauty making beautiful old rhyme
> In praise of ladies dead and lovely knights;
> Then in the blazon of sweet beauty's best,
> Of hand, of foot, of lip, of eye, of brow,
> I see their antique pen would have expressed
> Even such a beauty as you master now.
> So all their praises are but prophecies
> Of this our time, all you prefiguring,
> And for they looked but with divining eyes
> They had not skill enough your worth to sing;
>   For we which now behold those present days
>   Have eyes to wonder, but lack tongues to praise.

The poem might almost have been written with Shakespeare's own presentist art, and *Troilus and Cressida* in particular, in mind. For what else does *Troilus* do but cull from 'the chronicle of wasted time' the *Iliad*'s heroic tale of the Trojan war and Chaucer's 'beautiful old rhyme / In praise of ladies dead and lovely knights', and discover in the dramatic splicing of ancient Greek epic and medieval romance nothing less than 'prophecies / Of this our time', which not only prefigure the 'present days' the dramatist beholds, but also tell the story of the present with a 'skill' that poets of the present 'lack tongues' to emulate?

We in turn are invited to discover in Shakespeare's Trojan play a displaced representation of his world, containing 'prophecies / Of this our time' in the twenty-first century. There is no disputing that the man Ben Jonson hailed as the 'soul of the age' of Elizabeth and James is still telling the story of our age with a power and eloquence no living dramatist can match. That Shakespeare remains our contemporary owes nothing, however, to the widespread delusion that human nature is immutable and much to the fact that, as Shakespeare recognized, one of the best ways to illuminate the present is to view it in the vatic light of the past. The rationale for this practice is placed in the mouth of Warwick in *2 Henry IV*:

> There is a history in all men's lives
> Figuring the natures of the times deceased,
> The which observed, a man may prophesy,
> With a near aim, of the main chance of things
> As yet not come to life, who in their seeds
> And weak beginnings lie intreasurèd.
> Such things become the hatch and brood of time;
>
> (3.1.75–81)

*Troilus and Cressida* has itself become 'the hatch and brood of time' by prefiguring in its depiction of 'the times deceased . . . the main chance of things / As yet not come to life', which can now be owned as ours. Or as *Troilus* prefers to put it:

> in such indexes, although small pricks
> To their subsequent volumes, there is seen
> The baby figure of the giant mass
> Of things to come at large.
>
> (1.3.344–47)

## 'The present eye'

Although presentism enjoys Shakespeare's imprimatur, it would be unwise for it to conclude prematurely that it had got the measure of *Troilus* or of Shakespeare. If presentist critics were content to find their current concerns foreshadowed in *Troilus*'s plot, language and form, and behold in every play a mirror of modernity, they would fall far short of doing justice to Shakespeare's drama. In fact, they would find themselves satirically foreshadowed in Malvolio's struggle to decode Maria's cryptic *billet-doux*:

> MALVOLIO:    'I may command where I adore.' Why, she may command me. I serve her, she is my lady. Why, this is evident to any formal capacity. There is no obstruction in this. And the end – what should that alphabet ical position portend? If I could make that resemble something in me. Softly – 'M.O.A.I.' . . . This simulation is not as the former; and yet to crush this a little, it would bow to me, for every one of these letters are in my name.
>
> (*Twelfth Night* 2.5.113–18, 134–36)

The elephant trap that yawns before the most circumspect presentist critics is the narcissistic urge to turn resistance into resemblance: to crush Shakespeare's text a little to make it bow to them, screening out the irksome obstructions that baulk at being yoked to their agenda. Omnivorous assimilation – the complete colonization of then by now – is the peril that presentism must avoid at all costs. The greatest strength of presentism is its recognition that the present is the place from which critics must start in any encounter with Shakespeare's works. But that encounter will count for little if the conversation between critic and work is one-sided and the former proves deaf to the voice of the latter. What is needed is a genuine dialogue between the critic in the present and the work from the past, because, as Dominick LaCapra points out,

> a dialogue involves the interpreter's attempt to think further what is at issue in a text or a past 'reality', and in the process the questioner is himself questioned by the 'other'. His own horizon is transformed as he confronts still living (but often submerged or silenced) possibilities solicited by an inquiry into the past.
>
> (LaCapra 1983: 32)

In its justified aversion to the historicist 'rhetoric of contextualization', which cranks out 'documentary readings in which the text becomes little more than a sign of the times', presentist Shakespeare criticism must not commit the historicist's error of evading 'the claims texts make on us as readers' (LaCapra 1983: 14). By respecting the stubborn otherness of Shakespeare's plays, by resisting the urge to make what is strange in them familiar, presentist criticism opens itself to being questioned by them, to having its own horizon transformed by unexpected insights into the present and the past.

Historicist criticism as it stands is unequal to the task of rethinking the present from the viewpoint of a past transfigured by present perception. It would be churlish, of course, not to acknowledge the wealth of archival labour and interpretive ingenuity invested in recent historicist accounts of *Troilus and Cressida*. Eric S. Mallin, for example, has endeavoured to show that 'Shakespeare transforms a de facto Elizabethan policy and its unforeseen consequences into a central plot complication of the Trojan War story' (1995: 29). Having explained how the Troy legend was deployed by the Elizabethan and Jacobean state, Heather James (1997) contends that *Troilus* reflects changing attitudes to the use of that legend, not least in the evolution of the ideology of empire. And Matthew Greenfield, reading the play against early modern chronicles and tracts, concludes that, whereas Shakespeare's histories 'construct genealogies for England, projecting a new social formation backward into the past, *Troilus and Cressida* attacks the very idea of genealogy', and thus 'The play is not a history but a sceptical analysis of history-making' (Greenfield 2000: 181, 187). There is, without doubt, much to be learned from such studies. But, steeped though they are in a rhetoric of contextualization that flaunts its poststructuralist credentials, the play ends up petrified by the Medusan gaze of historicist retrospection. The qualities of *Troilus* that left Heine and Swinburne bewildered are erased by explaining it away as a product of contemporary political and cultural debate. The play becomes transparent and tractable once its meaning and purpose have been pinned down by such rear-view reconstructions.

If it is to avoid its own form of complacency, presentist criticism has to let Shakespeare's plays talk back and listen to them when they do, especially when what they have to say proves disconcerting. A modern account of *Troilus and Cressida* that merely finds its own diagnosis of what ails us confirmed needs to probe further. It can only begin, however, by underscoring the awesome prognostic power of the play. The 'giant mass / Of things to come at large', into which, as Shakespeare predicted, 'The baby figure' of his times would grow, has long loomed over us. *Troilus* constitutes a grim prevision of life under late capitalism at its most predatory, alienating and destructive. Its characters are driven by the ruthless imperatives of egotism, competition and acquisition in love and war alike.

Commerce and consumerism call the tune in a culture infatuated with sex and violence, which feed each other's voracious appetites in the glamorous guise of heroism and romance. Constrained to compete for status and prestige, characters fall prey to the cult of celebrity, which they covet and strive to possess, or possess and strive to preserve. Ironically, however, in a world where personality and repute are at a premium, individuals find themselves divorced from their advertised identities and unable to identify anyone, including themselves, with any certainty. Such a climate breeds gossip, rumour, slander and hype, which drive the wedge between the self and its simulacrum still deeper. Serious philosophical analysis and substantive moral debate are cynical charades, smokescreens for the machinations of the powerful. The success of those machinations is secured by surveillance, which penetrates the covert motives of the subject, aggravating the erosion of agency and intensifying the experience of dispossession. To watch *Troilus and Cressida* today is to watch a savage parody of the real tragedy in which too many people have been cast as travesties of themselves: the tragedy of a culture fatally addicted to self-gratification and aggression, sleepwalking towards the catastrophe it fears has already happened.

The armed Prologue conscripts the present tense to pitch us into the thick of this predicament, seven years into the siege of Troy, 'within whose strong immures / The ravished Helen, Menelaus' queen, / With wanton Paris sleeps; and that's the quarrel' (*Prol.* 8–10). The Prologue's contempt for the indefensible cause of such a 'cruel war' (*Prol.* 5) infects the mood of the play before it has begun. The opening scene confronts us with a Troilus so besotted with Cressida that he has lost his taste for combat, which leaves him emasculated, 'weaker than a woman's tear' (1.1.9), disaffected ('Fools on both sides!' (1.1.86)), and forced to wonder 'What Cressid is, what Pandar, and what we?' (1.1.95). His answer to that question portrays him as a merchant voyaging to India under Pandarus's escort to purchase the pearl of Cressida's love. The metaphor makes Cressida's status as an exotic commodity clear, although the cruder truth of the matter has been betrayed earlier by Pandarus, who makes no bones about her being an object of consumption: 'He that will have a cake out of the wheat must tarry the grinding' (1.1.14–15). Throughout the play, sexual desire is contaminated by the language of trading and tasting. Cressida mocks Troilus as 'a minced man' who should be 'baked with no date in the pie' (1.2.247–48). Troilus argues that Helen must be kept because

> We turn not back the silks upon the merchant
> When we have soiled them; nor the remainder viands

> We do not throw in unrespective sieve
> Because we now are full.
>
> (2.2.69–72)

He savours the prospect of consummating his love for Cressida, the moment when 'the wat'ry palates taste indeed / Love's thrice-repured nectar' (3.2.19–20), like a jaded gourmet. When she deserts him for Diomedes, he consigns to the latter 'The fragments, scraps, the bits and greasy relics / Of her o'ereaten faith' (5.2.166–67). Eating, 'the very image of absorption in the present' (Bayley 1976: 230), eats into the martial discourse twinned with the discourse of desire in Thersites' lament, 'Lechery, lechery, still wars and lechery; nothing else holds fashion' (5.2.201–2), which reveals both war and lechery as commodities at the mercy of market trends. If the Trojans surrender Helen, the Greeks will discount 'honour, loss of time, travail, expense, / Wounds, friends, and what else dear that is consumed / In hot digestion of this cormorant war' (2.2.4–6). The mighty Achilles is seized by 'a woman's longing, / An appetite that I am sick withal, / To see great Hector' (3.3.239–41). And of the embattled 'wenching rogues', Troilus and Diomedes, Thersites says: 'I think they have swallowed one another. I would laugh at that miracle – yet, in a sort, lechery eats itself' (5.4.32–34).

This figurative alliance of commerce, killing, lust and consumption exposes them as concerted expressions of the same collective engrossment in unbridled individualism, which subjects everyone to the tyranny of self-interest. The condition is most conspicuous in Achilles, whose sullen conceit confines him to his tent, where he sulks with his 'masculine whore' (5.1.17), Patroclus, disdaining to fight until the latter's death incites him to butcher the unarmed Hector. The muscle-bound 'lubber Ajax' (3.3.128), equally bloated with self-regard, is as ripe as Achilles for duping by Ulysses, who pits their egos against each other to serve his own turn: 'Two curs shall tame each other; pride alone / Must tar the mastiffs on, as 'twere their bone' (2.1.391–92). By playing Ajax and Achilles off against each other, Ulysses foments precisely that 'envious fever / Of pale and bloodless emulation' (1.3.133–34) he had denounced as the upshot of 'neglection of degree' (1.3.127). Indeed, Ulysses is plainly gripped by the same fever himself, since his whole aim is to take Achilles down a peg or two and tighten his hold on the conduct of the war, and to that end he enlists whatever rhetorical ploy will do the trick. Hector proves the Trojans to be just as eager to illustrate the truth of Agamemnon's adage: 'He that is proud eats up himself' (2.3.152). His cast-iron case for surrendering Helen and ending the war is revealed as cant by his brazen *volte-face* to clinch

the 'rich advantage of a promised glory' (2.2.204). His enslavement to
his renown makes him deaf to the forebodings of Cassandra,
Andromache and Priam, and lures him to an inglorious death, presaged
by his venal pursuit of the 'goodly armour' that masks a 'Most putre-
fied core' (5.9.1–2).

Hector's fate is a paradigm of the fate incurred by the self-absorption
and adhesion to image that govern boudoir and battlefield alike. As the
counterpart in the erotic realm of the political pimp, Ulysses, Pandarus
exploits the same toxic motive of emulation to ignite the lovers' desire
for each other and keep it burning. The constant thrust of his first
scene with Troilus (1.1.) is how well Cressida's beauty compares with
Helen's; in his first exchange with Cressida (1.2.) he harps with equal
tenacity on Troilus's superiority to Hector and Helen's attraction to
Troilus. Like Ulysses, Pandarus understands that rivalry is what makes
people tick in this play; or as Thersites puts it: 'devil Envy say "Amen"'
(2.3.20). Armed with that understanding, he produces, stages, directs
and watches the drama of their doomed love. But what love would not
be doomed in a world where desire is concocted and poisoned at the
source? Pandarus's arresting question, 'Is love a generation of vipers?'
(3.1.127–28) is patently rhetorical. Small wonder that Helen sighs,
'This love will undo us all' (3.1.104). This kind of love will, and it does.
Pandarus and Ulysses personify the involuntary attitudes that dictate
what individuals desire, determine their conduct, and consequently
divorce them from their own intent. Troilus is right to fear that 'something may be done that we will not' (4.4.93).

It is no accident that Pandarus and Ulysses are inveterate voyeurs in
their domains, adepts of the art of surveillance, which 'Keeps place
with thought, and almost, like the gods, / Do thoughts unveil in their
dumb cradles' (3.3.201–2). Deprived of sovereignty over themselves,
the characters become self-divided or detached from their avowed
identities. 'I have a kind of self resides with you,' Cressida tells Troilus,
'But an unkind self that itself will leave / To be another's fool'
(3.2.143–45). Aeneas recognizes neither Agamemnon nor Achilles,
whom Hector is equally unable to identify face to face. Even when
known and there in the flesh, Achilles seems a spectral simulation of
himself, a fetishized abstraction, as Thersites' gibe suggests: 'thou
picture of what thou seemest and idol of idiot-worshippers' (5.1.6–7).
That this plight is not unique to him is established at the start of the
play, when the Trojan idols of idiot-worshippers parade past Cressida
and Pandarus, mere fodder for their idle quibbles, in a far-sighted
burlesque of celebrity culture. Even Thersites, the 'privileged man'
(2.3.55), who sees through everyone else and cuts to the quick of the

matter – 'All the argument is a whore and a cuckold; a good quarrel to draw emulous factions and bleed to death upon' (2.3.69–71) – is not exempt from self-estrangement, as becomes clear when he talks to himself as if he were someone else: 'How now, Thersites? What, lost in the labyrinth of thy fury?' (2.3.1–2).

The moral vanity that feeds Thersites' histrionic rage is merely one more manifestation of the rampant egomania that afflicts both Trojans and Greeks, embroiling them in 'emulous factions'. The apocalyptic outcome of this *bellum omnium contra omnes*, where 'Each thing meets / In mere oppugnancy' (1.3.110–11) is unforgettably foretold by Ulysses:

> Then everything includes itself in power,
> Power into will, will into appetite;
> And appetite, an universal wolf,
> So doubly seconded with will and power,
> Must make perforce an universal prey
> And last eat up himself.
>
> (1.3.119–24)

The reason why 'The enterprise is sick' (1.3.103), however, is not, as Ulysses would have us believe, the *failure* to 'Observe degree, priority and place' (1.3.86), but the universal *observation* of 'degree, priority and place' by everyone condemned to climb 'the ladder to all high designs' (1.3.102). The metaphor Ulysses employs to punch home his point gives the game away:

> The general's disdained
> By him one step below, he by the next,
> That next by him beneath; so every step,
> Exampled by the first pace that is sick
> Of his superior, grows to an envious fever
> Of pale and bloodless emulation.
>
> (1.3.129–34)

The fact of rank, and the unequal distribution of power and status it entails, are the breeding grounds of the 'universal wolf', not the only things that can keep it at bay. Acquisitive individualism, the feverish compulsion to compete and consume that is eating up full-grown consumer societies today, is the spawn of hierarchy, not the deadly cancer that threatens to destroy it.

That compulsion spawns in its turn the mentality Ulysses commends to Achilles two acts later – in flat contradiction of his praise of degree – as the sole way to survive in a world whose watchword is *homo homini lupus*:

> Time hath, my lord, a wallet at his back,
> Wherein he puts alms for oblivion,
> A great-sized monster of ingratitudes.
> Those scraps are good deeds past, which are
> Devoured as fast as they are made, forgot
> As soon as done. Perseverance, dear my lord,
> Keeps honour bright; to have done is to hang
> Quite out of fashion, like a rusty mail
> In monumental mock'ry. Take the instant way,
> For honour travels in a strait so narrow
> Where one but goes abreast. Keep then the path,
> For emulation hath a thousand sons,
> That one by one pursue. If you give way,
> Or hedge aside from the direct forthright,
> Like to an entered tide they all rush by
> And leave you hindmost;
> Or, like a gallant horse fall'n in first rank,
> Lie there for pavement to the abject rear,
> O'er-run and trampled on. Then what they do in present,
> Though less than yours in past, must o'ertop yours;
> For time is like a fashionable host
> That slightly shakes his parting guest by th' hand,
> And, with his arms outstretched as he would fly,
> Grasps in the comer. . . .
> One touch of nature makes the whole world kin,
> That all with one consent praise new-born gauds,
> Though they are made and moulded of things past,
> And give to dust that is a little gilt
> More laud than gilt o'er-dusted.
> The present eye praises the present object.
>
> (3.3.146–69, 176–81)

The mentality that thinks what matters most is now, that privileges 'the present object' over 'things past' and recycles 'things past' as 'new-born gauds', is the accomplice of 'emulation', the brutal competitive ethos bred by capitalism that forces us into 'a strait so narrow / Where one but goes abreast', leaving us little choice but to 'Take the instant way' or end up 'O'er-run and trampled on'. There is no escaping the stark truth that *Troilus and Cressida* presses upon us. The presentist dramatic practice that first produced *Troilus* itself, and the presentist critical practice that makes Shakespeare's *Iliade travestie* speak directly to us today, are symptoms of the very malaise the play lays bare.

## 'What's past and what's to come'

Confronting its complicity in prolonging that malaise might seem plenty for presentism to chew on, but *Troilus and Cressida* is not prepared to leave it at that. The last twist of the tale it has to tell is what has made critics from Heine onwards find the play so enigmatic, implying as it does far more than it is disposed to articulate. Gervinus shrewdly sensed that 'a concealed intention lurks in the background ... We feel throughout the play a wider bearing, a more remote object' (Martin 1976: 49). Swinburne, as we have seen, found it impossible 'to read the riddle of Shakespeare's design' (1880: 199) in *Troilus*. For Mark van Doren, 'something that is not expressed in the play is felt so deeply that conclusions are for the moment impossible' (1939: 203). And sixty years on from van Doren, Harold Bloom professed himself no less perplexed: '*Troilus and Cressida* is a play that defeats any wholly coherent interpretation ... Something we cannot know drives [Shakespeare], in this play, against his greatest strength as a dramatist' (Bloom 1999: 332, 344).

The clearest clue to the play's 'concealed intention' is furnished by the speech in which Agamemnon argues that 'What's past and what's to come is strewed with husks / And formless ruin of oblivion', and therefore all that matters is 'this extant moment' (4.5.167–69). Here the implications of the presentist creed preached to Achilles by Ulysses become fully apparent. It is not only the past that is consigned to oblivion by immersion in 'this extant moment', but also the future. *Troilus and Cressida* reflects the deranged experience of living in a world where, as John Bayley puts it, 'there is neither past nor future: everything takes place in, and ends in, the present' (1976: 222). *Troilus* traps its characters in an eternal present of impending catastrophe from which the disparity of the past and the difference of the future have been drained. The past has no claim on 'The present eye', which is equally oblivious to 'what's to come', because the future means more of the same, an extension of the present so predictable that it feels as though it has already happened – which in this case, as far as author and audience are concerned, it already has. When Troilus and Cressida swear everlasting fidelity to each other before Pandarus, they unwittingly foretell their destinies as bywords for the qualities they epitomize: 'True swains in love shall in the world to come / Approve their truth by Troilus' (3.2168–69); Cressida will still be the touchstone of treachery

'When time is old and hath forgot itself' (3.2.180); and 'all pitiful goers-between' shall be called after Pandarus 'to the world's end' (3.2.195–96). The future is immanent rather than imminent in Shakespeare's Troy, a pre-emptive function of the present that controls it. 'Anticipating time' (4.5.2), wittingly or unwittingly, is the name of the game, and prolepsis the compulsive trope, of everyone engulfed by the Trojan war. The curse of precognition falls most heavily, of course, on Cassandra, whose prevision of 'that mass of moan to come' when 'Troy must not be, nor goodly Ilium stand' (2.2.107, 109) goes as unheeded as her horrifying premonition of Hector's death, which she experiences as an immediate event: 'Look how thou diest! Look how thy eye turns pale! / Look how thy wounds do bleed at many vents!' (5.3.81–82).

'In Troy there lies the scene' (*Prol.*1): as Harry Berger observes, 'the tenses of the Prologue to *Troilus and Cressida* bring the epic there-then of the Trojan war rapidly into the theatrical here-now' (1968: 124). From the first line of the play in performance the audience is induced to regard the action as contemporaneous, as coexisting in their world and time. This impression is enhanced not only by Thersites, who speaks nine of the play's fourteen soliloquies and over half his lines to the audience, but also by Pandarus. Pandarus's direct address to the spectators at the close of the troth-plighting scene – 'And Cupid grant all tongue-tied maidens here / Bed, chamber, pander to provide this gear!' (3.2.206) – locks them into the location and time-frame of *Troilus*; while his insolent, informal epilogue accosts them as syphilitic 'Brethren and sisters of the hold-door trade' (5.11.51) and strands them on the verge of a conclusion postponed anew by each performance:

> Some two months hence my will shall here be made.
> It should be now, but that my fear is this:
> Some galled goose of Winchester would hiss.
> Till then I'll sweat and seek about for eases,
> And at that time bequeath you my diseases.
>
> (5.11.52–56)

The suspended ending is crucial to the final impact of the play. *Troilus and Cressida* invites us to trace in its take on a core myth of Western culture a prefiguration of our time. The Trojan lovers' world and the impending doom of Troy are compressed, foreshortened images of our world and the doom that awaits it as well. Shakespeare's compelling illusion of a continuous, inconclusive present subjects us, too, to the despotism of 'the extant moment' and the prospect of oblivion forged by the lack of an alternative future.

In this respect the audience might well say with Cressida at the close of the play: 'Well, well, 'tis done, 'tis past, and yet it is not' (5.2.104). The story of Troilus and Cressida and Troy may belong to the past, but insofar as it is still our story too, it is not yet over for us. Bayley is wrong, however, to conclude that Shakespeare 'denies and dissolves history' in *Troilus and Cressida* by imprisoning us in 'the nightmare unease of its presentness' (1976: 223, 238). The play does indeed pull off the extraordinary feat of fusing Homer's world, Chaucer's world, Shakespeare's world and ours within the same temporal horizon, and to that extent it does dissolve past and future in an oppressive perpetual present. But *at the same time* it achieves something far more extraordinary. By dramatizing our present in the guise of a tale told long ago whose ending is foreknown, *Troilus* estranges the present, enabling us to perceive our time as history, as the superseded past of a terminal future. The play does not only apprehend the presentness of the past; it also anticipates the pastness of the present. Grasped from this perspective, the whole of *Troilus and Cressida* unfolds in the future perfect: it imagines what *will have been* the fate of our culture from the standpoint of an epoch beyond its conception. The play repeatedly invokes the prospect of oblivion as the point at which the way things are, and thus time as we know it, will have come to an end. Cressida envisages the day

> When time is old and hath forgot itself,
> When waterdrops have worn the stones of Troy,
> And blind oblivion swallowed cities up,
> And mighty states characterless are grated
> To dusty nothing.
>
> (3.2.182)

She looks back upon the present moment of her pledge, like Troilus and Pandarus, from the perspective of 'the world's end' (3.2.196). Hector, too, reaches forward, beyond the fall of Troy Ulysses prophesies, to remind us that 'The end crowns all / And that old common arbitrator, Time, / Will one day end it' (4.5.224–26). In *The Winter's Tale* the personification of 'that old common arbitrator' asks the audience:

> Let me pass
> The same I am ere ancient'st order was
> Or what is now received. I witness to
> The times that brought them in; so shall I do
> To th' freshest things now reigning, and make stale
> The glistering of this present as my tale now seems to it.
>
> (4.1.9–15)

To make 'The glistering of this present' as stale as the tale it retells is exactly what *Troilus and Cressida* seeks to do by envisioning the end of our era and reducing the present to the distant memory of an unknown future.

The play projects a future beyond the one the present is creating for itself. In that future, long after the present age has run its self-consuming course, there can be no place for Shakespeare's theatre or his audience, since both are contaminated by the present and the motives that preserve it. That is why *Troilus* betrays such revulsion from the theatre and such antagonism towards its audience. The play opens with the Prologue's brusque dismissal of our response to it: 'Like or find fault; do as your pleasures are' (*Prol.* 30); and it ends with Pandarus, the epitome of theatricality and *spiritus rector* of the play, conflating theatre and brothel, actors and bawds, and numbering us among the diseased and soon to be dead. *Troilus and Cressida* includes itself and us in its indictment, because its own dramatic art and the pleasure we take in it thrive on the barbarism that produced it. To recognize that the play is as alienated from the present it adumbrates as it is from the past that produced it is to begin at last 'to read the riddle of Shakespeare's design' in *Troilus*.

If *Troilus and Cressida* is indeed 'Shakespeare's most characteristic creation' and powerful proof that Shakespeare is, as Ralph Waldo Emerson noted, 'as unlike his cotemporaries as he is unlike us' (Gross 2002: 44), then presentism has to take on board the fact that Shakespeare's drama at full stretch is not only ahead of his time, but so far ahead of ours that it foresees its own demise. Presentist criticism of Shakespeare will be credible only if it engages in a dialogue with futurity as open and dynamic as the dialogue it must engage in with the past. In a recent symposium on the future of criticism, Fredric Jameson lamented the discipline's chronic neglect of 'the utopian projections works of past and present alike offer onto a future otherwise sealed from us' (2004: 408). For presentist criticism to remain closed to those projections in Shakespeare would be to collude in the perpetuation of the present – to say, in effect, with Paris, 'There is no help. / The bitter disposition of the time / Will have it so' (4.1.49–51) – instead of bringing to bear upon the present, through its accounts of Shakespeare's plays, the prospect of a radically transfigured future.

## Notes

1  All quotations from *Troilus and Cressida* are from this edition.

2  All quotations from Shakespeare's works other than *Troilus* are from Shakespeare 2005.

# References

Adelman, Janet (1985) '"This is and is not Cressid": The Characterization of Cressida' in S. N. Garner, C. Kehane and M. Sprengnether (eds) *The (M)other Tongue: Essays in Feminist Psychoanalytic Interpretation*, Ithaca, NY: Cornell University Press.

Adorno, Theodor (1997) *Aesthetic Theory*, eds. Gretel Adorno and Rolf Tiedemann, trans. Robert Hullot-Kentor, Minneapolis, MN: University of Minnesota Press.

Agamben, Giorgio (1998) *Homo Sacer: Sovereign Power and Bare Life*, Stanford, CA: Stanford University Press.

—— (2005) *State of Exception*, Chicago, IL: Chicago University Press.

Alexander, Peter (1955) *Hamlet Father and Son*, Oxford: Clarendon.

Altman, Joel B. (1987) '"Preposterous Conclusions": Eros, *Enargeia*, and the Composition of *Othello*', *Representations* 18: 129–57.

Althusser, Louis (1977) 'Ideology and Ideological State Apparatuses (Notes Towards an Investigation)', in his *Lenin and Philosophy*, trans. Ben Brewster, London: NLB, 121–73.

Angelou, Maya (1983) *I Know Why the Caged Bird Sings*, reissue ed., New York: Bantam.

Aristotle (1953) *Nichomachean Ethics*, trans. J. A. K. Thomson, Harmondsworth: Penguin.

Atkins, G. Douglas and Bergeron, David M. (eds) (1988) *Shakespeare and Deconstruction: Reclamations of Shakespeare*, New York, Bern, Frankfurt and Paris: Peter Lang.

Austin, J. L. (1962) *How to Do Things with Words*, 2nd edn, ed. J. O. Urmson and Marina Sbisa, Cambridge, MA: Harvard University Press.

Baines, Barbara (1998) 'Effacing Rape in Early Modern Representation', *English Literary History* 65: 69–98.

Bal, Mieke (1994) '*The Rape of Lucrece* and the Story of W', in A. J. Hoenselaars (ed.) *Reclamations of Shakespeare*, Amsterdam: Editions Rodopi.

Bate, Jonathan (ed.) (1995) *Titus Andronicus* by William Shakespeare, the Arden Shakespeare, 3rd series, London and New York: Routledge.

Bayley, John (1976) 'Time and the Trojans', in Priscilla Martin (ed.) '*Troilus and Cressida': A Selection of Critical Essays*, London and Basingstoke: Macmillan.

Becker, Lawrence (1990) *Reciprocity*, Chicago, IL: Chicago University Press.

Belsey, Catherine (1985) *The Subject of Tragedy*, London: Methuen.

—— (1999) *Shakespeare and The Loss of Eden*, Basingstoke: Macmillan.

—— (2006) 'Biology and Imagination: The Role of Culture', in Robin Headlam Wells and Johnjoe McFadden (eds) *Human Nature: Fact and Fiction*, London: Continuum, 111–27.

Benjamin, Walter (1973) "Theses on The Philosophy of History", *Illuminations*, trans. Harry Zohn, Glasgow: Fontana.

—— (1977) *The Origin of German Tragic Drama*, trans. J. Osborne, London: New Left Books.

Bennett, Susan (1996) *Performing Nostalgia: Shifting Shakespeare and the Contemporary Past*, London: Routledge.

Berger, Jr., Harry (1968) '*Troilus and Cressida*: The Observer as Basilisk', *Comparative Drama* 2: 122–36.

—— (1997) *Making Trifles of Terrors: Redistributing Complicities in Shakespeare*, Stanford, CA : Stanford University Press.

*Birmingham Post* (1947) Birmingham, England, 18 August.

Bloch, R. Howard (1991) *Medieval Misogyny and the Invention of Western Romantic Love*, Chicago and London: University of Chicago Press.

Bloom, Harold (1999) *Shakespeare and the Invention of the Human*, London: Fourth Estate.

Boas, F. S. (1896) *Shakespeare and his Predecessors*, London: Murray.

Bowen, Barbara E. (1993) *Gender in the Theatre of War: Shakespeare's 'Troilus and Cressida'*, New York: Garland.

Bowie, Andrew (2003) *Aesthetics and Subjectivity: From Kant to Nietzsche*, 2nd edn, Manchester: Manchester University Press.

Bradley, A. C. (1904) *Shakespearean Tragedy: Lectures on 'Hamlet', 'Othello', 'King Lear' and 'Macbeth'*, London: Macmillan; reprinted London: Penguin, 1991.

—— (1992) *Shakespearean Tragedy. Third Edition*, London: Macmillan. First published 1904.

Bristol, Michael D. (1996) *Big Time Shakespeare*, London: Routledge.

—— (1998) 'How Many Children Did She Have?' in John Joughin (ed.) *Philosophical Shakespeare*, London: Routledge, 1998.

—— (2000) 'Vernacular Criticism and the Scenes Shakespeare Never Wrote', *Shakespeare Survey* 51: 37–51.

—— (2003) 'Humanist Interpretations: *King Lear*', in *Shakespeare: An Oxford Guide*, Oxford: Oxford University Press, 333–51.

Brockbank, Philip (1989) *On Shakespeare: Jesus, Shakespeare and Karl Marx and Other Essays*, Oxford: Blackwell.

Brown, Roger and Gilman, Albert (1989) 'Politeness Theory and Shakespeare's Four Major Tragedies', *Language and Society* 18: 159–212.

Brownmiller, Susan (1975) *Against Our Will: Men, Women, and Rape*, New York: Simon and Schuster.

Bruster, Douglas (2003) *Shakespeare and the Question of Culture: Early Modern Literature and the Cultural Turn*, New York: Palgrave.

Burke, Edmund (1969) *Reflections on the Revolution in France*, Harmondsworth: Penguin.

Butler, Francelia (1966) *The Strange Critical Fortunes of Shakespeare's Timon of Athens*, Ames, IA: Iowa University Press.

Catty, Jocelyn (1999) *Writing Rape, Writing Women in Early Modern England: Unbridled Speech*, New York: St. Martin's Press.

Cavell, Stanley (1987) *Disowning Knowledge in Six Plays of Shakespeare*, Cambridge: Cambridge University Press.

Charlton, H. B. (1948) *Shakespearian Tragedy*, Cambridge: Cambridge University Press.

Charnes, Linda (1993) '"So unsecret to ourselves": Notorious Identity and the Material Subject in Shakespeare's *Troilus and Cressida*' in her *Notorious Identity: Materializing the Subject in Shakespeare*, Cambridge, MA, and London: Harvard University Press.

—— (2006) *Hamlet's Heirs: Shakespeare and the Politics of a New Millennium*, Routledge: London and New York.

Cheal, David J. (1988) *The Gift Economy*, London: Routledge.

Childs, George W. (1890) *Recollections*, Philadelphia, PA: J. P. Lippincot Co.

Cohen, Walter (1985) *Drama of a Nation: Public Theater in Renaissance England and Spain*, Ithaca and London: Cornell University Press.

Coleridge, Samuel Taylor (1969) *Coleridge on Shakespeare*, ed. Terence Hawkes, Harmondsworth: Penguin.

Croce, Benedetto (1941) *History as the Story of Liberty*, London: George Allen and Unwin.

—— (1960) *History: Its Theory and Practice*, New York: Russell and Russell.

Cull, Nicholas John (1995) *Selling War: The British Propaganda Campaign Against American 'Neutrality' in World War II*, New York and Oxford: Oxford University Press.

Dadlez, E. M. (1987) Introduction to his *What's Hecuba to Him? Fictional Events and Actual Emotions*, Philadelphia, PA: Pennsylvania State University Press.

Daiches, David (1971) *A Third World*, Sussex: Sussex University Press.

Dando, John and Hunt, Harry (1595) *Maroccus Extaticus or Bankes Bay Horse in a Trance*, London.

Danson, Lawrence (1974) *Tragic Alphabet: Shakespeare's Drama of Language*, New Haven, CT: Yale University Press.

Davis, L. Clarke (ed.) (1890) *The Story of the Memorial Fountain to Shakespeare at Stratford-upon-Avon*, Cambridge, MA: The Riverside Press (privately printed).

Dawson, Anthony B. (1995) *Hamlet*, Shakespeare in Performance, Manchester: University of Manchester Press.

de Certeau, Michael (1988) *The Writing of History*, trans. Tom Conley, New York: Columbia University Press.

de Grazia, Margreta (1999) 'Ideology, Delay, and the "Old Mole,"' *Shakespeare Quarterly* 50.3: 251–67.

Dekker, Thomas (1979) *The Shoemaker's Holiday*, ed. Robert Smallwood and Stanley Wells, Manchester: Manchester University Press.

Deleuze, Gilles (2005) *Nietzsche and Philosophy*, trans. Hugh Tomlinson, London and New York: Continuum.

Denby, David (1994) 'Queen Lear', *The New Yorker*, 3 October 1994: 88–98.

Derrida, Jacques (1994) *Specters of Marx: The State of the Debt, the Work of Mourning, and the New International*, trans. Peggy Kamuf, New York: Routledge.

—— (1997) *Of Grammatology*, trans. Gayatri C. Spivak, corrected edn., Baltimore and London: Johns Hopkins University Press.

Dinesen, Isak (1957) 'The Blank Page', in her *Last Tales*, New York: Random House, 99–105.

Dobson, Michael (1992) *The Making of the National Poet: Shakespeare, Adaptation and Authorship, 1660–1769*, Oxford: Clarendon.

Dolan, Frances E. (1996) 'Shrews, Taming, and Untamed Shrews', in Frances E. Dolan (ed.) *The Taming of the Shrew: Texts and Contexts*, Boston and New York: Bedford/St. Martin's: 244–326.

Dollimore, Jonathan (2001) *Sex, Literature and Censorship*, Cambridge: Polity.

Dollimore, Jonathan and Sinfield, Alan (eds) (1985) *Political Shakespeare: New Essays in Cultural Materialism*, Manchester: Manchester University Press.

—— (1992) 'History and Ideology, Masculinity and Miscegenation: The Instance of *Henry V*', in Alan Sinfield, *Faultlines: Cultural Materialism and the Politics of Dissident Reading*, Oxford: Oxford University Press, 109–42.

Dover Wilson, J. (ed.) (1926) *The Merchant of Venice*, by William Shakespeare, Cambridge: Cambridge University Press.

Drakakis, John (2000) '*Jew*. Shylock is my name', in Hugh Grady (ed.) *Shakespeare and Modernity: From Early Modern to Millennium*, London and New York: Routledge.

Dromgoole, Dominic (2005) 'Welcome to Bardworld', the *Guardian*, 13 July, G2: 5.

Dryden, John (1984) 'Troilus and Cressida', in *The Works of John Dryden*, vol. 13, ed. M. Novak and G. Guffey, Berkeley and London: University of California Press.

Duncan-Jones, Katherine (ed.) (1997) *Shakespeare's Sonnets*, London: Thomas Nelson.

Edwards, Philip (Summer 1991) 'Shakespeare Yesterday', International Association of University Professors of English *Bulletin*, 1–7.

Eliot, T. S. (1920) 'Hamlet and His Problems', in T. S. Eliot, *The Sacred Wood: Essays on Poetry and Criticism*, London: Methuen; reprinted London: Methuen, 1964.

—— (1929) Preface, *For Lancelot Andrewes: Essays on Style and Order*, Garden City, NY: Doubleday.

Eliot, Valerie (ed.) (1988) *The Letters of T. S. Eliot: Vol. 1, 1898–1922*, London: Faber and Faber.

Ellman, Maude (1996) Introduction, Bram Stoker, *Dracula*, Oxford: Oxford World's Classics.

Elster, Jon (1989) 'Social Norms', in his *The Cement of Society: A Study of Social Order*, Cambridge: Cambridge University Press.

—— (1993) *Political Psychology*, Cambridge: Cambridge University Press.

Erickson, Peter and Kahn, Coppélia (eds) (1985) *Shakespeare's 'Rough Magic': Renaissance Essays in Honor of C. L. Barber*, Newark, DE: University of Delaware Press.

Evett, David (2005) *Discourses of Service in Shakespeare's England*, New York and Basingstoke: Palgrave.

Fawcett, Mary L. (1983) 'Arms/Words/Tears: Language and the Body in *Titus Andronicus*', *English Literary History* 50: 261–77.

Fernie, Ewan (2005a) 'Shakespeare and the Prospect of Presentism', *Shakespeare Survey* 58: 169–84.

—— (2005b) 'The Last Act: Presentism, Spirituality, and the Last Act of *Hamlet*', in Ewan Fernie (ed.) *Spiritual Shakespeares*, London: Routledge, 186–211.

—— (2006) 'Terrible Action: Recent Criticism and Questions of Agency', *Shakespeare: A Journal* 2.1: 95–118.

Fineman, Joel (1989) 'The History of the Anecdote: Fiction and Fiction', in H. Aram Veeser (ed.) *The New Historicism*, New York: Routledge: 49–76.

Foakes, R.A. (1993) *Hamlet verses Lear: Cultural Politics and Shakespeare's Art*, Cambridge: Cambridge University Press.

Forster, E. M. (1936) *Abinger Harvest*; reprinted London: Edward Arnold, 1953.

Foucault, Michel (1977) *Discipline and Punish: The Birth of the Prison*, trans. Alan Sheridan, London: Allen Lane.

—— (1978) *The History of Sexuality, Volume 1: An Introduction*, trans. Robert Hurley, New York: Random House.

—— (1979) *The History of Sexuality, Volume 1, An Introduction*, trans. Robert Hurley, London: Allen Lane.

Fox-Genovese, Elizabeth (1989) 'Literary Criticism and the Politics of the New Historicism', in H. Aram Veeser (ed.) *The New Historicism*, New York: Routledge, 213–24.

*France* (1944) London: Foreign Office.

Frankfurt, Harry (2006) *The Reasons of Love*, Princeton, NJ: Princeton University Press.

Freiligrath, Ferdinand (1844) 'Germany Is Hamlet', trans. A. L. Wister; in Horace Howard Furness (ed.) *A New Variorum Edition of Shakespeare: Vol. 2, Hamlet*, Philadelphia: Lippincott, 1871; 1905, 376–78.

Freud, Sigmund (1900) *The Interpretation of Dreams*; reprinted in James Strachey (ed.) *Standard Edition of the Complete Psychological Works*, vols. 4–5, New York: Avon, 1965.

—— (1985a) *The Complete Letters of Sigmund Freud to Wilhelm Fleiss*, 1887–1904, ed. and trans. J. M. Masson, Cambridge, MA: Harvard University Press.

—— (1985b) 'The Theme of the Three Caskets', *The Pelican Freud Library, vol. 14. Art and Literature*, London: Pelican.

Freund, Elizabeth (1985) 'Ariachne's broken woof: The Rhetoric of Citation in *Troilus and Cressida*', in Patricia Parker and Geoffrey Hartman (eds) *Shakespeare and the Question of Theory*, New York and London: Methuen.

Frey, Charles H. (2004) 'Man's Rage/Woman's Grief: Engaging Death in *Titus Andronicus*', in Evelyn Gajowski (ed.) *Re-Visions of Shakespeare: Essays in Honor of Robert Ornstein*, Newark, DE: University of Delaware Press, 66–88.

Frye, Northrop (1967) *Fools of Time: Studies in Shakespearean Tragedy*, Toronto: University of Toronto Press.

Furness, Horace Howard (ed.) (1877) *A New Variorum of Shakespeare: Hamlet*, vols 1–2, Philadelphia: Lippincott; reprinted Philadelphia: Lippincott, 1905.

Gajowski, Evelyn (1992) *The Art of Loving: Female Subjectivity and Male Discursive Traditions in Shakespeare's Tragedies*, Newark, DE: University of Delaware Press; London and Toronto: Associated University Presses.

Gallagher, Catherine and Greenblatt, Stephen (2000) *Practicing New Historicism*, Chicago, IL: University of Chicago Press.

Garber, Majorie (1987) *Shakespeare's Ghost Writers: Literature as Uncanny Causality*, New York: Methuen.

Garner, Shirley Nelson, Kehane, Claire and Sprengnether, Madelon (eds) *The (M)other Tongue: Essays in Feminist Psychoanalytic Interpretation*, Ithaca, NY: Cornell University Press.

Geertz, Clifford (1993) *The Interpretation of Cultures: Selected Essays*, London: Fontana.

Gergen, David (2001) *Sept. 11 is a New call to Public Service*, Kansas State University. Online. Available: http://www.mediarelations.ksu.edu/WEB/News/Newsreleases/ gergentext.html (accessed 21 November, 2001).

Giddens, Anthony (1979) *Central Problems in Social Theory: Action, Structure, and Contradiction in Social Analysis*, Berkeley, CA: University of California Press.

Girard, René (1972) *Deceit, Desire, and the Novel: Self and Other in Literary Structure*, trans. Yvonne Freccero, Baltimore, MD: Johns Hopkins University Press.

Goethe, Johann Wolfgang von (1905) *Wilhelm Meister's Apprenticeship*, trans. Thomas Carlyle, in his *The Works of Johann Wolfgang von Goethe*, vols 7–8, London: The Anthological Society.

Gossett, Suzanne (1984) ' "Best Men are Molded out of Faults": Marrying the Rapist in Jacobean Drama', *English Literary Renaissance* 14: 305–27.

Grady, Hugh (1991) *The Modernist Shakespeare: Critical Texts in a Material World*, Oxford: Clarendon.

—— (1996) ' "Mad idolatry": Commodification and Reification in *Troilus and Cressida*' in his *Shakespeare's Universal Wolf: Studies in Early Modern Reification*, Oxford: Clarendon.

—— (2002) *Shakespeare, Machiavelli and Montaigne: Power and Subjectivity from Richard II to Hamlet*, Oxford: Oxford University Press.

—— (2005) 'Shakespeare Studies, 2005: A Situated Overview', *Shakespeare: A Journal* 1.1: 102–20.

Graff, Gerald (1989) 'Co-optation', in H. Aram Veeser (ed.) *The New Historicism*, New York: Routledge, 168–81.

Green, Douglas E. (1989) 'Interpreting "her martyr'd signs": Gender and Tragedy in *Titus Andronicus*', *Shakespeare Quarterly* 40: 317–26.

Greenblatt, Stephen (1980) *Renaissance Self-Fashioning from More to Shakespeare*, Chicago, IL: University of Chicago Press.

—— (1988a) *Shakespearean Negotiations: The Circulation of Social Energy in Renaissance England*, Berkeley, CA: University of California Press.

—— (1988b) *Shakespearean Negotiations: The Circulation of Social Energy in Renaissance England*, Oxford: Clarendon.

—— (1989) 'Towards a Poetics of Culture', in H. Aram Veeser (ed.) *The New Historicism*, New York: Routledge, 1–14.

—— (1990) *Learning to Curse: Essays in Early Modern Culture*, New York: Routledge.

—— (1997) 'The Touch of the Real', *Representations* 59: 14–29.

—— (2001) *Hamlet in Purgatory*, Princeton, NJ: Princeton University Press.

—— (2004) *Will in the World: How Shakespeare Became Shakespeare*, London: Cape.

Greene, Gayle (1980) 'Shakespeare's Cressida: "a kind of self"' in Carolyn Lenz, Gayle Greene and Carol Neely (eds) *The Woman's Part*, Urbana, Chicago and London: University of Illinois Press.

Greenfield, Matthew A. (2000) 'Fragments of Nationalism in *Troilus and Cressida*', *Shakespeare Quarterly* 51: 181–200.

Gross, John (ed.) (2002) *After Shakespeare: An Anthology*, Oxford: Oxford University Press.

Gross, Kenneth (2001) *Shakespeare's Noise*, Chicago, IL: University of Chicago Press.

Gubar, Susan (1985) '"The Blank Page" and the Issues of Female Creativity', in Elaine Showalter (ed.) *The New Feminist Criticism: Essays on Women, Literature, and Theory*, New York: Pantheon, 292–313.

Habermas, Jürgen (1991) *Moral Consciousness and Communicative Action*, trans. Christian Lenhardt and Shierry Weber Nicholsen, Cambridge, MA: MIT Press.

Halpern, Richard (1997) *Shakespeare among the Moderns*, Ithaca, NY: Cornell University Press.

Hampshire, Stuart (1983) *Morality and Conflict*, Cambridge, MA: Harvard University Press.

Hardy, Henry (ed.) (2004) Isaiah Berlin, *Letters, 1928–1946*, Cambridge: Cambridge University Press.

Harris, Jonathan Gil (1999) 'Historicizing Greenblatt's "Containment": The Cold War, Functionalism, and the Origins of Social Pathology', in Jürgen Pieters (ed.) *Critical Self-Fashioning: Stephen Greenblatt and the New Historicism*, Frankfurt am Main: Peter Lang, 150–73.

—— (2000) 'The New New Historicism's *Wunderkammer* of Objects', *European Journal of English Studies* 4.3: 111–23.

Hawkes, Terence (1983) 'Telmah', *Encounter* 40.4: 50–60.
—— (1986) *That Shakespeherian Rag*, London: Methuen.
—— (1992) *Meaning by Shakespeare*, London: Routledge.
—— (2002a) *Shakespeare in The Present*, London: Routledge.
—— (2002b) 'The Old Bill', in Arthur F. Kinney (ed.) *Hamlet: New Critical Essays*, London: Routledge: 177–91.
Hazlitt, William (1930) *The Complete Works of William Hazlitt*, vol. 4, ed. P. P. Howe, London and Toronto: Dent.
Hirsch Jr., E. D. (1967) *Validity in Interpretation*, New Haven, CT: Yale University Press.
Hitchens, Christopher (1990) *Blood, Class and Nostalgia*, London: Chatto.
Hodgdon, Barbara (1990) 'He Do Cressida in Different Voices', *English Literary Renaissance* 20: 254–86.
Honigmann, E. A. J. (1976) *Shakespeare: Seven Tragedies: The Dramatist's Manipulation of Response*, London: Macmillan.
—— (ed.) (2003) *Othello*, by William Shakespeare, The Arden Shakespeare, New York and London: Routledge.
hooks, bell (1992) *Black Looks: Race and Representation*, Boston, MA: South End Press.
Howard, Jean E. (1986) 'The New Historicism in Renaissance Studies', *English Literary Renaissance* 16: 13–43.
Howard, Jean E. and Rackin, Phyllis (1997) *Engendering a Nation: A Feminist Account of Shakespeare's English Histories*, London and New York: Routledge.
Howell, Jane (dir.) (1985) *Titus Andronicus*, by William Shakespeare, with Trevor Peacock and Anna Calder-Marshall, BBC-TV Series, dist. Time-Life Videos.
Hughes, William (2000) *Beyond Dracula: Bram Stoker's Fiction and its Cultural Context*, London: Macmillan; New York: St. Martin's Press.
Hulse, Clark S. (1979) 'Wresting the Alphabet: Oratory and Action in *Titus Andronicus*', *Criticism* 21: 106–18.
Ingleby, J. M., *et al.* (eds) (1909) *The Shakspere Allusion-Book: A Collection of Allusions to Shakespeare from 1591 to 1700*, 2 vols, London: Chatto and Windus.
James, Heather (1997) ' "Tricks We Play on the Dead": Making History in *Troilus and Cressida*' in her *Shakespeare's Troy: Drama, Politics and the Translation of Empire*, Cambridge: Cambridge University Press.
Jameson, Fredric (2004) 'Symptoms of Theory or Symptoms for Theory', in 'The Future of Criticism – A *Critical Inquiry* Symposium', *Critical Inquiry* 30: 403–8.
Jardine, Lisa (1983) *Still Harping on Daughters: Women and Drama in the Age of Shakespeare*, Brighton: Harvester.
Jay, Martin (1996) *The Dialectical Imagination*, Berkeley and London: University of California Press.
Johnson, Allen and Malone, Dumas (eds) (1930) *Dictionary of American Biography*, Oxford: Oxford University Press: IV: 70–71.
Johnson, Barbara (1996) 'Muteness Envy', in Diana Fuss (ed.) *Human, All Too Human*, New York and London: Routledge: 132–48.

Johnson, Samuel (ed.) (1765) *The Plays of William Shakespeare*, Vol. 1, London.
—— (1968) *The Yale Edition of the Works of Samuel Johnson*, vols 7–8: *Johnson on Shakespeare*, ed. Arthur Sherbo, New Haven, CT: Yale University Press.
Jones, Ernst (1949) *Hamlet and Oedipus*, New York: Norton.
Jowett, John (ed.) (2004) *The Life of Timon of Athens*, by William Shakespeare and Thomas Middleton, Oxford World's Classics, Oxford University Press.
Kahn, Coppélia (1986) 'The Absent Mother in King Lear', Margaret Ferguson, Maureen Quilligan, and Nancy Vickers (eds) *Rewriting the Renaissance*, Chicago, IL: Chicago University Press.
Kant, Immanuel (1790) *Kritik der Urteilskraft*; trans. Werner S. Pluhar (1987), *Critique of Judgment*, Indianapolis, IN: Hackett.
—— (1988) *Fundamental Principles of the Metaphysics of Morals*, trans. T. K. Abbot. New York: Prometheus Books.
Kastan, David (1999) *Shakespeare After Theory*, New York and London: Routledge.
Kazan, Elias (dir.) (1951) *A Streetcar Named Desire*, by Tennessee Williams, with Vivian Leigh and Marlon Brando, Warner Brothers, dist. Warner Home Video.
Kemp, Thomas C. (1948) *Birmingham Repertory Theatre: the Playhouse and the Man*, Birmingham: Cornish Brothers Ltd.
Kennedy, Richard F. (June 1998) 'Speech-prefixes in Some Shakespearean Quartos', *Publications of the Bibliographical Society of America*, 92.2: 177–209.
Kermode, Frank (2000) *Shakespeare's Language*, London: Allen Lane, Penguin.
Kernan, Alvin (1997) *Shakespeare, The King's Playwright: Theater in the Stuart Court*, New Haven, CT: Yale University Press.
Kingston, Maxine Hong (1975) 'No Name Woman', in *The Woman Warrior: Memoirs of a Girlhood among Ghosts*, New York: Random House, 1–16.
Kingwell, Mark (1993) 'Is it Rational to be Polite?' *The Journal of Philosophy*, 90: 387–404.
Kinney, Arthur F. (2002) Introduction, A. F. Kinney (ed.) *Hamlet: New Critical Essays*, London: Routledge, 1–68.
Klindienst, Patricia (1998) 'The Voice of the Shuttle is Ours', in Julie Rivkin and Michael Ryan (eds) *Literary Theory: An Anthology*, Malden, MA, and Oxford: Blackwell, 612–29.
Knight, G. Wilson (1930) *The Wheel of Fire: Interpretations of Shakespeare's Tragedies*, Oxford: Oxford University Press; reprinted Cleveland: Meridian, 1964.
—— (1940) *This Sceptered Isle: Shakespeare's Message for England at War*, Oxford: Basil Blackwell.
Kopper, John (1988) 'Troilus at Pluto's Gates: Subjectivity and the Duplicity of Discourse in Shakespeare's *Troilus and Cressida*', in G. D. Atkins and D. M. Bergeron (eds) *Shakespeare and Deconstruction*, New York, Bern, Frankfurt and Paris: Peter Lang.
Kott, Jan (1964) *Shakespeare Our Contemporary*, London: Methuen.
Lacan, Jacques (1977) 'Desire and the Interpretation of Desire in *Hamlet*', ed. J. A. Miller, trans. James Hulbert, *Yale French Studies* {55/56}: 11–52.

—— (1999) *The Ethics of Psychoanalysis 1959–60: The Seminar of Jacques Lacan*, ed. Jacques-Alain Miller, trans. Dennis Porter, London: Routledge.

LaCapra, Dominick (1983) *Rethinking Intellectual History: Texts, Contexts, Language*, Ithaca, NY: Cornell University Press.

—— (1989) *Soundings in Critical Theory*, Ithaca, NY: Cornell University Press.

Lentricchia, Frank (1989) 'Foucault's Legacy: A New Historicism?' in H. Aram Veeser (ed.) *The New Historicism*, New York: Routledge, 231–42.

Levin, Harry (1959) *The Question of 'Hamlet'*, Oxford: Oxford University Press; reprinted New York: Viking, 1961.

Lewis, David (1983) 'Truth in Fiction', in his *Philosophical Papers, Vol. I*, Oxford: Oxford University Press.

Loomba, Ania (1992) *Gender, Race, Renaissance Drama*, Oxford: Oxford University Press.

Lowry, Richard (2001) 'Magnificent: This was not a Foggy Bottom Speech', *National Review*, 21 September 2001.

McEachern, Claire (1995) '*Henry V* and the Paradox of the Body Politic', in Ivo Kamps (ed.) *Materialist Shakespeare: A History*, London and New York: Verso: 292–319.

—— ed. (2006) *Much Ado About Nothing*, London: Thomson Learning.

McGann, Jerome (1991) *The Textual Condition*, Princeton, NJ: Princeton University Press.

McIntyre, Alasdair (1990) *Three Rival Versions of Moral Inquiry*, Notre Dame, IN: Notre Dame University Press.

Mack, Maynard (1952) 'The World of Hamlet', *Yale Review* 41.4: 502–23.

Mackenzie, Henry (1780) 'Criticism of the Character and Tragedy of Hamlet', *The Mirror* 99, 18 April 1780; reprinted in Nathan Drake (ed.), *Memorials of Shakespeare*, London, 1828: 371–78; reprinted in Cyrus Hoy (ed.) *Hamlet: An Authoritative Text, Intellectual Backgrounds, Extracts from the Sources, Essays in Criticism*, New York: Norton, 1963, 148–51.

MacKinnon, Catherine (1989) 'Rape: On Coercion and Consent', in her *Toward a Feminist Theory of the State*, Cambridge, MA, and London: Harvard University Press, 171–83.

McLellan, David (1973) *Karl Marx: His Life and Thought*, London, Macmillan.

Mahood, M. M. (ed.) (1987) *The Merchant of Venice*, by William Shakespeare, Cambridge: Cambridge University Press.

Mallin, Eric S. (1995) 'Emulous Factions and the Collapse of Chivalry: *Troilus and Cressida*', in his *Inscribing the Time: Shakespeare and the End of Elizabethan England*, Berkeley, CA: University of California Press.

Manlove, Colin N. (1981) *The Gap in Shakespeare*, London: Vision Press.

Marcus, Jane (1987) 'Still Practice, A/Wrested Alphabet: Toward a Feminist Aesthetic', in Shari Benstock (ed.) *Feminist Issues in Literary Scholarship*, Bloomington and Indianapolis: Indiana University Press: 79–97.

Marcus, Leah (1996) *Unediting The Renaissance: Shakespeare, Marlowe, Milton*, London and New York: Routledge.

Marshall, Norman (1957) *The Producer and the Play*, London: Davis-Poynter.

Marston, John (1939) *Histrio-Mastix*, in *The Plays of John Marston*, vol. 1, ed. H. Harvey Wood, Edinburgh and London: Oliver and Boyd.

Martin, Priscilla (ed.) (1976) '*Troilus and Cressida': A Selection of Critical Essays*, London and Basingstoke: Macmillan.

Marx, Karl (1964) *Economic and Philosophic Manuscripts of 1844*, ed. Dirk J. Struik, trans. Martin Milligan, New York: International.

—— (1967) *Capital: A Critical Analysis of Capitalist Production*, ed. Frederick Engels, trans. Samuel Moore and Edward Aveling, Vol. 1, New York: International.

—— (1973) 'The Eighteenth Brumaire of Louis Bonaparte', *Surveys From Exile: Political Writings*, Vol. 2, ed., David Fernbach, Harmondsworth: Penguin.

Merleau-Ponty, Maurice (1973) *Adventures of the Dialectic*, trans. Joseph Bien, Evanston, IL: Northwestern University Press.

Miller, J. Hillis (1987) 'Presidential Address 1986', *PMLA* 102: 281–91.

Montrose, Louis (1986) 'Renaissance Literary Studies and the Subject of History', *English Literary Renaissance* 16: 5–12.

Moretti, Franco (1983) *Signs Taken for Wonders*, London: Verso.

Moore, Helen (15 August 2003) 'Present and Correct', *TLS*: 22.

Moulton, Richard Green (1903) *The Moral System of Shakespeare: A Popular Illustration of Fiction as the Experimental Side of Philosophy*, New York and London: Macmillan.

Muir, Kenneth (1947) 'Timon of Athens and the Cash Nexus', *Modern Quarterly Miscellany* I; reprinted in his *The Singularity of Shakespeare and Other Essays*, Liverpool: Liverpool University Press, 1977: 56–75.

Mullan, John (2003), 'The appeal of uniform editions', the *Guardian*, 12 April 2003: http://www.books.guardian.co.uk/departments/classics/story/0,6000,934759,00.htm

Murray, Paul (2004) *From the Shadow of Dracula: A Life of Bram Stoker*, London: Cape.

Nairn, Tom (1997) *Faces of Nationalism: Janus Revisited*, New York and London: Verso.

Neill, Michael (1989) 'Unproper Beds: Race, Adultery, and the Hideous in *Othello*', *Shakespeare Quarterly* 40.4: 383–412.

Nicoll, Allardyce (1952) *Shakespeare*, Home Study Books, London: Methuen.

Nietzsche, Friedrich (1956) *The Birth of Tragedy and The Genealogy of Morals*, trans. Francis Golffing, New York: Doubleday.

—— (1996) *On the Genealogy of Morals*, trans. Douglas Smith, Oxford: World's Classics.

Nussbaum, Martha (1993) 'Non-relative Virtues: An Aristotelian Approach', Martha Nussbaum and Amartya Sen (eds) *The Quality of Life*, Oxford: Clarendon.

Oliver, H. J. (ed.) (1959) *Timon of Athens*, by William Shakespeare, Arden edition, London: Methuen.

Orgel, Stephen (2002) 'What is a Text?' in his *The Authentic Shakespeare*, New York and London: Routledge.

—— (2003) 'Imagining Shylock' in his *Imagining Shakespeare*, Basingstoke: Palgrave Macmillan.

Ovid (1960) 'Philomela, Procne, and Tereus', *Metamorphoses*, trans. Horace Gregory, New York: New American Library/Mentor.

Owens, Mackubin (2002) 'Shakespeare Was No Pacifist', Ashland University, November 2002: http://www.ashbrook.org/publicat/oped/owens/02/Shakespeare.html.

Paige, Karen and Paige, Jeffery (1981) *The Politics of Reproductive Ritual*, Berkeley, CA: University of California Press.

Palfrey, Simon (2005) *Doing Shakespeare*, London: The Arden Shakespeare, Walton-on-Thames: Thomas Nelson.

Parker, Patricia (1987) *Literary Fat Ladies: Rhetoric, Gender, Property*, London and New York: Methuen.

Parker, Patricia and Hartman, Geoffrey (eds) (1985) *Shakespeare and the Question of Theory*, New York: Methuen.

Parsons, Talcott (1964) 'The School Class as a Social System: Some of Its Functions in American Society', in his *Social Structure and Personality*, New York: Free Press of Glencoe, 129–54.

—— (1977) *The Evolution of Societies*, ed. Toby Jackson, Englewood Cliffs, NJ: Prentice-Hall.

Phillips, Adam (1994) *On Flirtation: Psychoanalytic Essays on the Uncommitted Life*, Cambridge, MA: Harvard University Press.

Pieters, Jürgen (2001) *Moments of Negotiation: The New Historicism of Stephen Greenblatt*, Amsterdam: Amsterdam University Press.

Raber, Karen (2004) 'Michel Foucault and the Specter of War', in Peter C. Herman (ed.) *Historicizing Theory*, Albany, NY: State University of New York Press, 49–67.

Rabkin, Norman (1967) *Shakespeare and the Common Understanding*, New York: Free Press.

Rackin, Phyllis (2000) 'Misogyny is Everywhere', in Dympna Callaghan (ed.) *A Feminist Companion to Shakespeare*, Alden, MA: Blackwell, 42–56.

—— (2005) *Shakespeare and Women*, Oxford: Oxford University Press.

—— (forthcoming) 'Presentism and Feminist Politics', in Evelyn Gajowski (ed.) *The Presence of Shakespeare, Sexuality, and Gender*.

Robertson, J. M. (1930) *The Genuine in Shakespeare: A Conspectus*, London: Routledge.

Robinson, Peter (2001), in Kathryn Jean Lopez (comp.), 'A. Call to Arms: A Symposium on Bush's Speech to Congress', *National Review*, 21 September 2001: http://www.nationalreview.com/comment/comment-symposium092101.shtml.

Rubin, Gayle (1975) 'The Traffic in Women: Notes on the "Political Economy" of Sex', in Rayna R. Reiter (ed.) *Toward an Anthropology of Women*, New York: Monthly Review, 157–210.

Ruiter, David (2005) 'Harry's (In)human Face', in Ewan Fernie (ed.) *Spiritual Shakespeares*, London and New York: Routledge, 50–79.

Rymer, Thomas (1693) *A Short View of Tragedy: Its Original, Excellency, and Corruption, With Some Reflections on Shakespear, and other Practitioners for the Stage*, London.

Saunders, Frances Stonor (1999) *Who Paid the Piper: the CIA and the Cultural Cold War*, London: Granta Books.

Scott, William O. (1988) 'Self-difference in *Troilus and Cressida*', in G. D. Atkins and D. M. Bergeron (eds) *Shakespeare and Deconstruction*, New York, Bern, Frankfurt and Paris: Peter Lang.

Sedgwick, Eve Kosofsky (1985) 'Gender Asymmetry and Erotic Triangles', in her *Between Men: English Literature and Male Homosocial Desire*, New York: Columbia University Press, 21–27.

Shaftesbury, Anthony, Fourth Earl of (1732) *Characteristics: Advice to an Author*, 5th edn; extracted and reprinted in Horace Howard Furness (ed.) (1877) *The New Variorum Shakespeare: Hamlet*, vols 1–2, 2: 143.

Shakespeare, William (1974) *The Riverside Shakespeare*, ed. G. Blakemore Evans, Boston, MA: Houghton Mifflin.

—— (1995) *Titus Andronicus*, ed. Jonathan Bate, The Arden Shakespeare, Walton-on-Thames: Thomas Nelson.

—— (1998a), *Complete Works*, The Arden Shakespeare, ed. Richard Proudfoot, Ann Thompson and David Scott Kastan, Walton-on-Thames: Thomas Nelson.

—— (1998b) *Troilus and Cressida*, ed. D. Bevington, The Arden Shakespeare, Walton-on-Thames: Thomas Nelson.

—— (1998c), *Henry V*, ed. T. W. Craik, The Arden Shakespeare, Walton-on-Thames: Thomas Nelson.

—— (2003) *Othello*, ed. E. A. J. Honigmann, The Arden Shakespeare, Walton-on-Thames: Thomas Nelson.

—— (2005) *The Complete Works*, ed. J. Jowett, W. Montgomery, G. Taylor and S. Wells, 2nd edn, Oxford: Clarendon Press.

Shapiro, James (2005) *1599: A Year in the Life of William Shakespeare*, London: Faber.

Shaw, George Bernard (1969) *Shaw on Shakespeare*, ed. E. Wilson, Harmondsworth: Penguin.

Shirley, Frances (2005) *Troilus and Cressida*, Shakespeare in Production, Cambridge: Cambridge University Press.

Siegel, Lee (8 May, 2005) 'Freud and His Discontents,' *The New York Times Book Review*, 29–30.

Siemon, James (2002) *Word Against Word: Shakespearean Utterance*, Amherst, MA: University of Massachusetts Press.

Spencer, T. J. B. (1962) '"Greeks" and "Merrygreeks": A Background to *Timon of Athens* and *Troilus and Cressida*', in R. Hosley (ed.) *Essays on Shakespeare and Elizabethan Drama in Honor of Hardin Craig*, Columbia, MS: University of Missouri Press.

Spenser, Edmund (1978) *The Faerie Queene*, ed. Thomas P. Roche, Jr., Harmondsworth: Penguin.

Spivak, Gayatri Chakravorty (1997) 'Translator's Preface', in *Of Grammatology* by Jacques Derrida, corrected ed., trans. Gayatri Chakravorty Spivak, Baltimore and London: Johns Hopkins University Press, ix–lxxxvii.

Stallybrass, Peter (1986) 'Patriarchal Territories: The Body Enclosed', in Margaret W. Ferguson, Maureen Quilligan and Nancy J. Vickers (eds) *Rewriting the Renaissance: The Discourse of Sexual Difference in Early Modern Europe*, Chicago, IL: University of Chicago Press, 123–42.

—— (1991) 'The World Turned Upside Down: Inversion, Gender and the State', in Valerie Wayne (ed.) *The Matter of Difference*, Hemel Hempstead: Harvester Wheatsheaf; Stanford, CA: Stanford University Press, 201–20.

States, Bert O. (1992) *Hamlet and the Concept of Character*, Baltimore, MD: The Johns Hopkins University Press.

Stevenson, William (1978) *A Man Called Intrepid*, London: Sphere Books.

Stimpson, Catherine (1983) 'Shakespeare and the Soil of Rape', in Carolyn Lenz, Gayle Greene, and Carol Thomas Neely (eds) *The Woman's Part: Feminist Criticism of Shakespeare*, Urbana and Chicago: University of Illinois Press, 56–64.

Stoker, Bram (1886) 'A Glimpse of America, a lecture given at the London Institute 28 December, 1885', ed. Richard Dalby, London: Sampson Low, Marston & Co., Westcliff-on-Sea; Essex: Desert Island Books, 2002.

—— (1906) *Personal Reminiscences of Henry Irving* (2 vols.), London: Heinemann.

—— (1996) *Dracula*, Intro. Maude Ellman, Oxford: Oxford World's Classics.

*Stratford-upon-Avon Herald* (1946–47), Stratford, England, 23 August 1946, 27 August 1947.

Styan, J. L. (1977) *The Shakespeare Revolution: Criticism and Performance in the Twentieth Century*, Cambridge: Cambridge University Press.

Swinburne, A. C. (1880) *A Study of Shakespeare*, London: Chatto & Windus.

Taylor, Gary (1990) *Reinventing Shakespeare: A Cultural History from the Restoration to the Present*, London: Hogarth Press.

Taylor, Michael (2001) *Shakespeare Criticism in the Twentieth Century*, Oxford: Oxford University Press.

Taymor, Julie (dir.) (1999) *Titus*, with Anthony Hopkins, Laura Fraser, and Jessica Lange, Clear Blue Sky Productions, dist. Fox Searchlight.

*The Yale Freshman Weekly* (18 January 1940): vol. III, no.14.

*Times Educational Supplement* (1946) London, August 31st.

Trewin, J. C. (1963) *The Birmingham Repertory Theatre 1913–63*, London: Barrie and Rockliffe.

Tyler, Stephen A. (2002) '"Even Steven", or "No Strings Attached"', Edith Wyschogrod, Jean-Joseph Goux and Eric Boynton (eds) *The Enigma of Gift and Sacrifice*, New York: Fordham University Press.

Van Doren, Mark (1939) *Shakespeare*, New York: Holt.

Vickers, Nancy (1985) '"The blazon of sweet beauty's best": Shakespeare's Lucrece', in Patricia Parker and Geoffrey Hartman (eds.), *Shakespeare and the Question of Theory*, New York and London: Methuen: 95–115.

Voltaire, F. M. (1961) *Philosophical Letters*, trans. Ernest Dilworth, New York: Bobbs-Merrill.

Weimann, Robert (1978) *Shakespeare and the Popular Tradition in the Theater: Studies in the Social Dimension of Dramatic Form and Function*, ed. Robert Schwarz, Baltimore and London: Johns Hopkins University Press.

—— (2000) *Author's Pen and Actor's Voice: Playing and Writing in Shakespeare's Theatre*, Cambridge: Cambridge University Press.

Weitz, Morris (1964) *Hamlet and the Philosophy of Literary Criticism*, Chicago, IL: University of Chicago Press; reprinted Cleveland: Meridian, 1966.

Wells, Robin Headlam (2000) 'Historicism and "Presentism" in Early Modern Studies', *Cambridge Quarterly*, 29.1: 37–60.

Wells, Stanley (2002) *Shakespeare For All Time*, London: Macmillan.

Wells, Stanley and Taylor, Gary (eds) (1986) *The Complete Works*, by William Shakespeare, Oxford: Oxford University Press.

White, Hayden (1978) *Tropics of Discourse: Essays in Cultural Criticism*, Baltimore and London: Johns Hopkins University Press.

Williams, Bernard (1985) *Ethics and the Limits of Philosophy*, Cambridge, MA: Harvard University Press.

Williams, Tennessee (1974) *A Streetcar Named Desire*, New York: New American Library.

Wilson, Luke (2000) *Theaters of Intention: Drama and the Law in Early Modern England*, Stanford, CA: Stanford University Press.

Wilson, Richard (1993) *Will Power: Essays on Shakespearean Authority*, London: Harvester.

Wilson, Scott (1995) *Cultural Materialism: Theory and Practice*, Oxford: Blackwell.

Woodbridge, Linda (1987) 'Black and White and Red All Over', *Renaissance Quarterly* 40: 47–97.

Zizek, Slavoj (2000) *The Fragile Absolute*, New York and London: Verso Press.

# Index

*Related titles from Routledge*

# Accents on Shakespeare Series

## General Editor: Terence Hawkes

Books in the *Accents on Shakespeare* series provide short, powerful, 'cutting-edge' accounts of and comments on new developments in the field of Shakespeare studies. In addition to titles aimed at modular undergraduate courses, it also features a number of spirited and committed research-based books.

**The *Accents on Shakespeare* series features contributions from leading figures and the books include:**

*Shakespeare and Appropriation*
Edited by Christy Desmet and
Robert Sawyer

*Shakespeare Without Women*
Dympna Callaghan

*Philosophical Shakespeares*
Edited by John J. Joughin

*Shakespeare and Modernity: Early Modern
to Millennium*
Edited by Hugh Grady

*Marxist Shakespeares*
Edited by Jean E. Howard and
Scott Cutler Shershow

*Shakespeare in Psychoanalysis*
Philip Armstrong

*Shakespeare and Modern Theatre:
The Performance of Modernity*
Edited by Michael Bristol and
Kathleen McLuskie

*Shakespeare and Feminist Performance:
Ideology on Stage*
Sarah Werner

*Shame in Shakespeare*
Ewan Fernie

*The Sound of Shakespeare*
Wes Folkerth

*Shakespeare in the Present*
Terence Hawkes

*Making Shakespeare*
Tiffany Stern

*Spiritual Shakespeares*
Edited by Ewan Fernie

*Green Shakespeare*
Gabriel Egan

*Shakespeare, Authority, Sexuality*
Alan Sinfield

Available at all good bookshops
For a full series listing, ordering details and further information please visit:
www.routledge.com

*Related titles from Routledge*

# Local Shakespeares: Proximations and Power

## Martin Orkin

'*Local Shakespeares* shows just how timid and predictable most comparative criticism is. Timid and predictable, *Local Shakespeares* is not.'

Bruce Smith, *University of Southern California, USA*

This remarkable volume challenges scholars and students to look beyond a dominant European and North American 'metropolitan bank' of Shakespeare knowledge. As well as revealing the potential for a new understanding of Shakespeare's plays, Martin Orkin explores a fresh approach to issues of power, where 'proximations' emerge from a process of dialogue and challenge traditional notions of authority.

Since their first performances, Shakespeare's plays and their audiences or readers have journeyed to one another across time and space, to and from countless and always different historical, geographical and ideological locations. Engagement with a Shakespeare text always entails in part, then, cultural encounter or clash, and readings are shaped by a reader's particular location and knowledge. Part I of this book challenges us to recognise the way in which 'local' or 'non-metropolitan' knowledges and experiences might extend understanding of Shakespeare's texts and their locations. Part II demonstrates the use of local as well as metropolitan knowledges in exploring the presentation of masculinity in Shakespeare's late plays. These plays themselves dramatise encounters with different cultures and, crucially, challenges to established authority.

Challenging the authority of metropolitan scholarship, twenty-first-century global capitalism and the masculinist imperatives that drive it, Orkin's daring, powerful work will have reverberations throughout but also well beyond the field of Shakespeare studies.

ISBN13: 978-0-415-34878-2 (hbk)
ISBN13: 978-0-415-34879-9 (pbk)

Available at all good bookshops
For ordering and further information please visit:
www.routledge.com

*Related titles from Routledge*

# Shakespeare, Authority, Sexuality
## Unfinished Business in Cultural Materialism

### Alan Sinfield

'Alan Sinfield has been one of the most thoughtful and provocative writers on early modern culture for the last two decades and his critical power is evident throughout this book.'

Kate McLuskie, *Director of the Shakespeare Institute,*
*Stratford-upon-Avon, UK*

*Shakespeare, Authority, Sexuality* is a powerful reassessment of cultural materialism as a way of understanding the intersections of textuality, history, culture and politics by one of the founding figures of this critical movement. Alan Sinfield examines cultural materialism both as a body of ongoing argument, and as it informs particular works by Shakespeare and his contemporaries, especially in relation to sexuality in early-modern England and queer theory.

The book has several interlocking preoccupations:

- Theories of textuality and reading
- Authority in Shakespearean plays and in the organisation of literary culture today
- The sex/gender system in that period and the application of queer theory in history

These preoccupations are explored in and around a range of works by Shakespeare and his contemporaries. Throughout the book Sinfield represents cultural materialism, framing it not as a set of propositions, as has often been done, but as a cluster of unresolved problems. His brilliant, lucid and committed readings demonstrate that the 'unfinished business' of cultural materialism – and Sinfield's work in particular – will long continue to produce new questions and challenges for the field of Renaissance Studies.

ISBN13: 978-0-415-40235-4 (hbk)
ISBN13: 978-0-415-40236-1 (pbk)

Available at all good bookshops
For further information on our literature series, please visit:
www.routledge.com/literature/series.asp
For ordering and further information please visit:
www.routledge.com